www.wadsworth.com

wadsworth.com is the World Wide Web site for Wadsworth and is your direct source to dozens of online resources.

At *wadsworth.com* you can find out about supplements, demonstration software, and student resources. You can also send email to many of our authors and preview new publications and exciting new technologies.

wadsworth.com
Changing the way the world learns®

FIRST EDITION

Becoming a 21st Century Agency Counselor:

PERSONAL AND PROFESSIONAL EXPLORATIONS

KATHRYN C. MACCLUSKIE
Cleveland State University

R. ELLIOTT INGERSOLL
Cleveland State University

BROOKS/COLE

THOMSON LEARNING

Australia • Canada • Mexico • Singapore • Spain
United Kingdom • United States

Counseling Editor: Julie Martinez
Assistant Editor: Cat Broz
Marketing Manager: Caroline Concilla
Signing Representative: Shelly Tommasone
Project Editor: Teri Hyde, Matt Stevens
Print Buyer: April Reynolds
Permissions Editor: Joohee Lee

Production Service: Shepherd Incorporated
Copy Editor: Debra DeBord
Cover Designer: Yvo Riezebos
Cover Image: Courtesy of PhotoDisk
Cover Printer: Phoenix Color Corporation
Compositor: Shepherd Incorporated
Printer: Transcontinental Printing

Printed in Canada
2 3 4 5 6 7 04 03 02 01

Library of Congress Cataloging-in-Publication Data

MacCluskie, Kathryn C.
    Becoming a 21st-century agency counselor :
personal and professional explorations /
Kathryn C. MacCluskie, R. Elliott Ingersoll.—2nd ed.
    p.   cm.
    Includes index.
    ISBN 0-534-35605-2
    1. Counseling—Vocational guidance.
2. Psychotherapy—Vocational guidance. I. Title:
Becoming a twenty-first century agency counselor.
II. Ingersoll, R. Elliott. III. Title.

BF637.C6 M255 2001
361'.06—dc21   00-058512

Wadsworth/Thomson Learning
10 Davis Drive
Belmont, CA 94002-3098
USA

For more information about our products,
contact us:
Thomson Learning Academic Resource Center
1-800-423-0563
http://www.wadsworth.com

International Headquarters
Thomson Learning
International Division
290 Harbor Drive, 2nd Floor
Stamford, CT 06902-7477
USA

UK/Europe/Middle East/South Africa
Thomson Learning
Berkshire House
168-173 High Holborn
London WC1V 7AA
United Kingdom

Asia
Thomson Learning
60 Albert Street, #15-01
Albert Complex
Singapore 189969

Canada
Nelson Thomson Learning
1120 Birchmount Road
Toronto, Ontario M1K 5G4
Canada

This book is dedicated to the special men in my life—David, Davey, Alex, Pooh, and Wes. I love you! KM

I would like to dedicate this book to my wife Jennifer for all her love and support and to the mentor/supervisors who guided me in counseling. To Chris Faiver, who taught me the virtues of organization; Ansel Woldt, who taught me the virtues of process; and Warren Hartzell, who taught me the virtue of a good laugh. EI

Contents

Chapter 3

Exploring Ourselves and Our Motives   56

Chapter 4

Ethical Issues in Agency Counseling   75

Chapter 7

Funding and Politics in Agency Counseling   219

Chapter 8

Managed Mental Health Care   243

Preface

We decided to write this book to share with aspiring counselors what we consider to be important information about agency counseling. Certainly, there are many good texts on the topic, but, after teaching an introductory course in agency counseling for several years, we found no texts that compiled all the information our students asked about. There are excellent texts that focus on cultural diversity, theoretical models of service delivery, and areas of counselor specialization. Still other texts may combine several of these features, but relatively few texts contain material on such things as counselor self-care, self-awareness, and the managed care industry.

The topics of self-care and self-awareness were popular in the 1970s but seem to have fallen out of vogue as relevant issues. Certainly, an awareness of one's cultural background is important, but little else is currently emphasized. Despite this lack of attention in other texts, we have met many students in our introductory course on agency counseling who had little awareness of why they want to be counselors or how to take care of themselves when they begin seeing clients. At the beginning of a new millennium, we feel these topics are of critical importance. As we will point out in the pages that follow, counselors must possess self-awareness, self-understanding, and self-acceptance before helping clients toward those ends.

As noted, we also found little material in current textbooks on the managed care revolution taking place in both medical and mental health care in the United States. Understanding managed care is of relevance for any professional hoping to bill for services in the public sector. We know that students with a focus on agency counseling have a wide variety of employment options. They may work for agencies, private practices, or health maintenance organizations, to name just a few. We hope that understanding how the employment settings are changing as a result of managed care will help readers be effective in today's managed care climate.

In addition to employment settings, students constantly ask us about salaries, benefits, and other employment variables related to quality of life. We have tried to offer the most current information available about salaries across the country, and have offered some questions about whether the salaries and working conditions described match students expectations. Although some readers might find this information a bit elementary or unnecessary, we feel it is important to include in an introductory text.

THE INTENDED AUDIENCE

This text is intended for master's-level counseling students across numerous counseling specialties. It can also be useful to students in other mental health tracks, such as psychology or social work, as well as to undergraduates studying community mental health or substance abuse counseling. Since all mental health service providers draw on the same basic knowledge base, we feel the text has cross-professional appeal.

THE GOAL OF THE TEXT

The goal of this textbook is to offer readers a practical, reality-based approach to the world of the agency counselor. The unifying theme and framework are the value and importance of looking at personal and professional aspects of agency counseling—looking inside as well as outside ourselves. We begin in chapter 1 with a review of the history of the field of counseling. In chapters 2 and 3, we ask readers to do some self-exploration, and the remaining chapters, 4 through 8, consider a number of professional, external aspects of agency counseling. Our goal is to integrate several things: first, we provide an understanding of the field as it is evolving. Then, we encourage self-understanding. We want readers to see how self-understanding and the evolving field fit together, fostering a healthy career choice for aspiring counselors. We hope we have achieved this goal while keeping our sense of humor.

From the perspective of emotional health, we have both learned to be sincere without necessarily being too serious. Although seriousness and aspiration toward goals are important, they need to be tempered with a sense of humor and a willingness to see the lighter side of ourselves and our profession. With this end in mind, we have included some cartoons, which came out of long staff meetings and the occasional sleepless night.

THE FEATURES OF THE TEXT

Each chapter has several features. Besides the regular text, there are intermittent segments—explanations of personal experiences we have had in either our work or life experience that offer a practical example of the point being made. At relevant points in chapters, we offer web sites where interested readers can get additional information about the topic. At the end of each chapter, there are discussion items, which can be used in a number of ways. Students can discuss the questions in small groups. Students might also read the questions and consider them without discussing them, or an instructor might assign students to respond to a particular question by writing a reaction paper to it.

ACKNOWLEDGMENTS

We have many people to thank for their assistance and support in the development of this project. A number of our colleagues offered valuable insight—Elizabeth Welfel and Lewis Patterson were particularly instrumental in the early stages of the book. Numerous students suffered through multiple drafts of the manuscript and were gracious enough to offer feedback on important changes in the text. Since they are the primary consumers, their time and effort were especially valuable. We also wish to gratefully acknowledge the faculty at other universities who reviewed the text and offered such excellent suggestions about how to make the book better: William Buffam, Barry University; Lee Ann Eschbach, University of Scranton; Maureen Kenny, Florida International University; Kathleen M. May, University of Virginia; Dennis L. Poole, University of Texas at Austin; David Santoro, Cleveland State University; Nancy Sherman, Bradley University; and Leon Spencer, Georgia Southern University.

Finally, but certainly not least, we would like to thank the editorial staff at Brooks/Cole. Each and every contact with them has been nothing less than great, and it made the writing and completion of the book particularly exhilarating.

Kathryn C. MacCluskie
R. Elliott Ingersoll
Cleveland State University

INTRODUCTION TO THE THERAPEUTIC PROFESSIONS

I say tomato, you say "tomawto." I say potato, you say "potawto."

From the Ira Gerswhin song "Let's Call the Whole Thing Off."

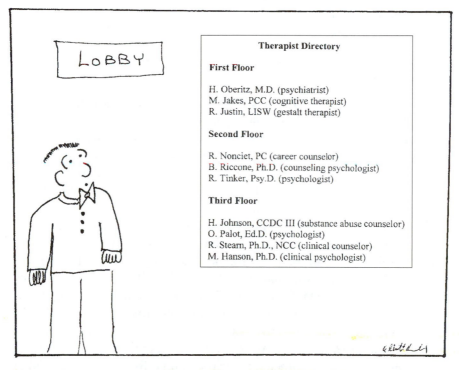

After finally deciding to see a therapist to help him with his indecision, Henry hits an unexpected development.

In this chapter, we will begin personal and professional exploration by discussing the various training models available to those who want to become a mental health professional. Licensure of mental health professionals is done at the state level, with some states offering licensure at the doctoral level only. By understanding various models of graduate training and the history of their development, you may be better able to understand the model that best meets your goals, interests, and temperament.

Imagine you are a therapeutic professional who is asked to treat a client suffering from depression. Chances are that, regardless of your license or credential, you are going to refer to a standard body of literature in selecting a nonmedical treatment (what Bankart [1997] calls "talking cures"). The treatment you choose is drawn from the body of literature that makes up the explicit knowledge of how to treat people suffering from depression. *Explicit* knowledge is cognitive, codified, and transmitted in a formal, systematized language (Yang, 1998). Next, you engage the client in the selected treatment, relying on your *implicit* knowledge, or the subjective knowledge you have gained from practice that guides you in the therapeutic endeavor (Yang, 1998). Finally, you integrate what Yang (1998) calls *emancipatory* knowledge, which is your knowledge of the client's needs, culture, and the values that are related to treating that client. You generally draw on all three types of knowledge, regardless of what program you were trained in and what license you hold. The training model you studied under and the license or title you earned may have focused on one type of knowledge more than another (typically, explicit knowledge), but all three should be present in treating the whole client.

Training models and titles are usually subjugated to therapeutic realities in the manner illustrated in the previous example. In training counselors, social workers, and psychologists (and, to a lesser extent, psychiatrists), the notion of an exclusive professional identity is frequently emphasized, despite its subjugation to the therapeutic reality. As Sturm and Klap (1999) have noted, "there is little evidence that the effectiveness of psychotherapy differs by provider type" (p. 504).

In the treating of the client suffering from depression, the integration of explicit, implicit, and emancipatory knowledge occurs regardless of the specific mental health discipline (that is, counseling, psychology, or social work). Despite the clinical similarities among them, mental health professionals continue to espouse distinct models of professional identity. This confuses students aspiring to be helping professionals (particularly at the master's level) and fuels "turf battles" over third-party reimbursement. This chapter is designed to give an overview of the various therapeutic professions and two specializations. Later in the chapter, we will explore the identities of therapeutic professionals through Ken Wilber's (1995, 1996, 1997) integral paradigm to bring some order to the chaos of professional identity. This chapter was inspired partly by undergraduate students aspiring to be "professional therapists" and asking about paths to that goal. This material is important in providing master's-level trainees a realistic view of the therapeutic marketplace. An important aspect of agency counseling is the diversity of therapeutic professionals who work in agencies. The chances of healthy interprofessional collaboration are increased when professionals understand the training of colleagues who hold different credentials but perform similar therapeutic services.

It is first important to note that "therapeutic professionals" are mental health professionals trained to help people with problems that manifest behaviorally or psychologically and that may have roots in physical, psychological, or spiritual dimensions. A therapeutic professional may help clients with problems that range from difficulties in development to severe mental and emotional disorders. In the past, most therapeutic professions tried to define themselves by the severity of problems in the clients they treated, "identity by client diagnosis."

In the identity by diagnosis model, therapeutic professionals, such as clinical psychologists, were theoretically trained to work more with serious mental/emotional disorders (Barlow & Durand, 1995), whereas counselors were trained to work with developmental problems and difficulties with adjustment. Typically, professionals trained specifically to work with serious mental and emotional disorders (such as psychiatrists and clinical psychologists) had more extensive training, earned more money, and were less likely to work with clients who, because of severe disability, were unable to work, didn't have insurance, and lacked the ability to pay for services themselves.

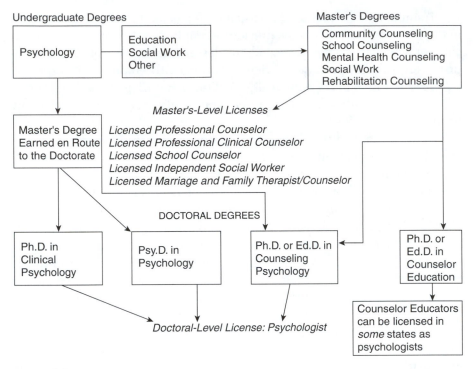

Undergraduate Degrees

| Psychology | Education
Social Work
Other |

Master's Degrees

Community Counseling
School Counseling
Mental Health Counseling
Social Work
Rehabilitation Counseling

Master's-Level Licenses

| Master's Degree
Earned en Route
to the Doctorate | *Licensed Professional Counselor*
Licensed Professional Clinical Counselor
Licensed School Counselor
Licensed Independent Social Worker
Licensed Marriage and Family Therapist/Counselor |

DOCTORAL DEGREES

| Ph.D. in
Clinical
Psychology | Psy.D. in
Psychology | Ph.D. or Ed.D. in
Counseling
Psychology | Ph.D. or
Ed.D. in
Counselor
Education |

Doctoral-Level License: Psychologist

Counselor Educators
can be licensed in
some states as
psychologists

FIGURE **1.1**

Routes for Academic Preparation and Licensure in Mental Health

Master's-level therapists who were lower in agency hierarchies would frequently spend more time with these seriously ill clients.

In addition to the economic factors involved, it seems to be human nature that some people within a profession have broader interests than others and go beyond preset parameters. Identity by client diagnosis failed in establishing exclusive professional identities. Currently, most professions train students to work with the full range of client problems. Although this is true within professions in general, individuals within those professions still may specialize with certain client populations.

The flow chart in figure 1.1 illustrates the academic preparation necessary to be licensed as a counselor, social worker, or psychologist in most states. Undergraduate degrees in psychology are typically required for doctoral-level study in that discipline. Psychology undergraduate degrees, as well as those in education, social work, and a variety of other areas, may be applied to master's-level study in counseling or social work. These master's degrees then may be used to apply to doctoral programs in counseling, counselor education, and sometimes counseling psychology. The criteria for each program vary by state in accordance with each state's licensure laws. As we will discuss, individuals seeking to work as psychiatrists must go through medical school where psychiatry is a specialization.

Figure 1.1 underrepresents the tension among the therapeutic professions by omitting any allusion to the political dimensions of licensure and the ambiguities of professional identity. Hosie (1991) has written that "occupational licensure is viewed as one of the most important characteristics that define an occupation as a profession" (p. 23). As Sweeny (1991) noted, interprofessional rivalry is alive but not well, meaning not healthy for the profession of counseling. Great paradoxes exist regarding professional identities and professional training in general.

The first paradox is that all state regulatory boards that license or certify therapeutic professionals theoretically exist to protect the public. This is fine but begs the question "protect the public from what?" Certainly there are "quacks" in every field, and the therapeutic professions are no exception (there is even a web page called "quackwatch" at www.Quackwatch.com). There are several cases in which people claimed to be therapeutic professionals but had no training and, in some cases, were detrimental to their clients' well-being. In cases such as these, a state regulatory board can call the professional in question to account through formal and informal channels. In this sense, state regulatory boards serve an important function.

Second, with regard to high-quality therapeutic professionals, numerous studies and meta-analyses consistently reflect that there is no discernible difference between high-quality professional therapists and high-quality lay-therapists. Once you rule out the quacks, many effective helpers remain who may have had only minimal formal training. This means that many people who volunteer on hot lines, for example, are as adequate at helping people in pain as those who studied for doctoral degrees in counselor education or psychology. In addition, there is a difference in symptom alleviation between receiving treatment (whether from a professional or a lay-therapist) and not receiving treatment (Berman & Norton, 1985; Christenson & Jacobson, 1994; Durlak, 1979; Nietzel & Fisher, 1981). Clients who seek assistance for their problems report more relief than those who do not. Given these findings, does the small ratio of quacks to competent professionals merit the existence of state licensure boards, if that is their only function? And, yet, licensure boards do allow a certain regulation through the interpretation of the laws passed to govern professions.

Adding to the complexity of licensure is that fact that licensure is determined at the level of state government. As a result, you may be licensed to practice on the population of one state but, because of variations in types of training, not be licensable in a neighboring state. Simply crossing an abstract, geographic demarcation may put you out of business. In this chapter, we will address the topic of professional training, identity, and employment. The first goal of the chapter is to encourage you to embrace the complexity of professional identity. The greatest error in addressing this topic is simplistic thinking. As Peck (1997) wrote, "simplistic thinking is so pandemic in society that it is considered normal and conventional wisdom among some segments of the population" (p. 31). Certainly, it is less comfortable to remain open to complexity, but the reward of a more accurate view of the field is worth it. The chapter's second goal is to help you understand something about the various therapeutic professions and begin cultivating realistic ego-strength regarding your chosen profession. In counseling, realistic ego-strength is best summarized as understanding your strengths and weaknesses and practicing ethically, but not second-guessing yourself based on interprofessional dynamics.

THE ISSUE OF PROFESSIONAL IDENTITY

Professional identity has always been fraught with disagreements and at times has been explosive. Conflicts of territoriality frequently arise as conceptual, political, and economic factors affect various groups of helping professionals (Herr & Cramer, 1987). Early in this century, psychoanalyst Theodore Reik was charged with practicing medicine without a license. He was a psychoanalyst but not a medical doctor, as was the norm at that time. At his trial, Sigmund Freud's manuscript *The Question of Lay Analysis* comprised the primary defense exhibit. Reik was exonerated, and this set a precedent toward recognizing non-medical therapeutic professionals (Vandenbos, Cummings, & Deleon, 1992).

This precedent did not stop established professionals from filing lawsuits to halt the progress of up-and-coming professions. The level of hostility reached in some of these "therapist wars" has been great, indeed. The economic incentive for therapeutic professionals in a capitalist society is to corner the market on services. Although the laws licensing therapeutic professionals are supposed to define the scope of practice, there are huge overlaps between groups of professionals. As a result, some groups engage in a Darwinian struggle for their piece of the perceived economic pie. Ever since medically trained psychiatrists attempted to block the licensure of psychologists in the early 1940s, every new group of professionals seeking licensure has experienced similar efforts. Each new group is targeted by lobbies designed to prevent them from gaining the status of licensed professionals using essentially the same tactics as the psychiatrists did early in this century.

However much we may question the value of licensure, it is important. It is one of the three primary areas of credentialing as described by Bradley (1991). Licensure is established through state legislatures to define scope of practice and arrange for a board of examiners to oversee the granting of licenses and ethical/legal breaches (Herr & Cramer, 1987). By defining the scope of practice, licensing can control who can and cannot offer and charge for certain services. Licensure is usually viewed as a "practice act" because it determines what a licensed person can do and what an unlicensed person cannot do (Hosie, 1991). Although, in theory, licensure's primary purpose is to protect the public, most licensure and occupational regulation are initiated by people within the various professions (Herr & Cramer, 1987; Shimberg & Roederer, 1978). As Hosie (1991) wrote, "the history of attempts at defining a social science profession shows that those attempts do not produce more specificity for practice. Rather, more extensive definitions are created that evolve into attempts to restrict mental health practices to that profession" (p. 30).

> I am currently licensed as a professional clinical counselor and as a psychologist. During my doctoral program, I was working in nursing homes, primarily with clients on Medicare. For nursing home residents with psychological problems, Medicare reimburses psychologists and psychiatrists only as the direct or supervising practitioners. I understood that, if I chose to continue in that field, my counseling license, even at the doctoral level, would not have been enough for me to earn a living, since I could not be reimbursed by Medicare. Thus, I decided to pursue dual licensure, since the state law allowed that. This frustrated some professors in my doctoral program, who advocated a model of professional "purity." I thought long and hard about the question and decided that, since "professional purity" was not going to pay my rent and other bills after graduation, I would have to look after my own interests. After I earned both my licenses, some colleagues across the state jokingly asked me, "So what do you call yourself?"—to which I answer, "Reimbursable."

In this chapter, we will examine four therapeutic professions and the development of their identities, as well as two specialty areas. The four professions are counseling, psychology, psychiatry, and social work, and the specialty areas are substance abuse counseling and marriage and family therapy. Of the first four, each professional group endorses a "professional identity" in its training program. Professional identity is a profession's statement of its philosophy, training model, and scope of practice. In an ideal world, all therapeutic professionals would have clearly defined boundaries delineating which services they can and cannot offer. In the real world of agency counseling, you will work with therapists who have different training backgrounds and hold different licenses but perform duties similar to (if not identical to) your own.

An old joke says that psychiatrists studied medicine but don't practice it and practice psychology but never studied it. Psychologists remain divided on training models (Chiszar & Wertheimer, 1988; George, 1984; Norcross, Gallagher, & Prochaska, 1989; Sprinthall, 1990) and the nature of their practice (for example, is counseling equal to counseling psychology?). Social workers debate using psychology's "Boulder" training model for social work training (Turnbull & Dietz-Uhler, 1995) and criticize peers who leave social advocacy to enter private practice (Specht & Courtney, 1994). Not to be left out of the confusion, counselors provide services that have been traditionally labeled psychotherapy (George & Christiani, 1995). Counseling has been described as "an ambiguous enterprise . . . done by people who can't agree on what to call themselves" (Kottler & Brown, 1996, p. 13). This statement seems accurate for all the therapeutic professions. In addition, these four therapeutic professions squabble among themselves and compete for third-party reimbursement, often for performing the same services.

Despite the interprofessional arguments and debate, all therapeutic professionals, regardless of professional identification, may be found engaging in tasks described as counseling, psychotherapy, or career counseling. We will use the phrase "therapeutic professionals" following the lead of Kottler and Brown (1996), who created the phrase "therapeutic counseling." "Therapeutic professional" seems preferable to the more colloquial "helping professional," which could refer to everything from a counselor to a travel guide.

> At our agency, I was the master's-level counselor. I worked with a psychiatric nurse, a social worker, a cognitive-behavioral therapist with a master's in psychology, a doctoral-level psychologist, and two consulting psychiatrists, one a medical doctor and the other an osteopath. Despite the smorgasbord of credentials, it was pretty clear that the psychiatrists had the last word on treatment, the nurse had her own office for giving injections, and the rest of us shared whatever space we could find to conduct counseling sessions.

HISTORICAL INFLUENCES AND TRAINING MODELS

Psychiatric, social work, counseling, and psychological training use both teaching and supervision approaches. Early training typically includes the classroom portion and later training the supervised experience. These general structures in training therapeutic professionals date from the early twentieth century (Martarazzo & Garner, 1992).

Psychiatry

Psychiatric training and practice are based in schools of medicine (including osteopathic schools) where psychiatry is a specialty. Psychiatrists typically earn a pre-med bachelor's of science degree, go on to a four-year medical school, and then do a two-year residency. Medical training, including psychiatry, is primarily structured through the biomedical model, which focuses on the physical processes thought to underlay mental and emotional disorders (Cohen, 1993; Engel, 1977; Van Hesteren & Ivey, 1990). Kovel (1980) identified the first decade of the twentieth century as the time psychiatry established its biomedical form.

The 1908 publication of Clifford Beers' *A Mind That Found Itself* fueled the Mental Hygiene Movement (Hershenson, Power, & Waldo, 1996). The

Mental Hygiene Movement is identified with activist Dorothea Dix, who advocated reform in how the mentally ill in nineteenth-century American society were treated. The trends that resulted from Beers' memoir of being an abused mental health inpatient and the resulting Mental Hygiene Movement led many psychiatrists and psychologists of the time to label one of their activities "counseling." This early counseling was aimed at therapeutic interaction within a warm relationship (Hansen, Rossberg, & Cramer, 1994). As the Mental Hygiene Movement developed, it merged with psychoanalysis, increasing medical domination in mental health (at that time, only physicians could be psychoanalysts). In addition, Cohen (1993) noted that the impact of the Flexner reports of 1910 established allopathic control in medical training, licensure, and practice and severely limited homeopathic, osteopathic, and other types of competition.

The Flexner reports are one of the most cited publications in medical education. The reports (there are three of them) were authored by Abraham Flexner and published by the Carnegie Foundation in 1910. Ober (1997) notes that the nineteenth century was a time of unregulated medical practice. Allopathic medicine proclaimed itself to be the scientific branch of medicine and led the movement (through the American Medical Association [AMA]) for stricter licensure laws in the late 1800s. The AMA commissioned the Flexner reports to identify inadequate medical schools. The reports describe visits to 163 medical schools across 40 states and recommend the closing of 124 of those schools. The allopathic style of medical training, with its emphasis on what is now called the "medical model," won out in this revised field of medical training (Bender, 1993). As we will see later in this chapter, the victory of the medical model based in allopathic medicine has had a profound impact on all training in mental health counseling through the *DSM-IV*.

Throughout the twentieth century, psychiatry undulated between strict biomedical models and models that consider social and psychological factors in mental illness. Engel (1977) challenged psychiatry to adopt a biopsychosocial model, noting that "in all societies, ancient and modern, preliterate and literate, the major criteria for identification of disease have always been behavioral, psychological, and social" (p. 196). The recent lamentations of psychiatrists such as Cohen (1993), Peck (1993), and Victor (1996) indicate that Engel's call was ignored and that the biomedical paradigm is still dominant in psychiatry. Particularly at mental health agencies, most psychiatrists spend all their time with clients prescribing medications and/or evaluating their effects.

Psychology

Psychology programs are primarily designed to reflect the scientist-practitioner model and are accredited by the American Psychological Association (APA). Despite the dominance of a scientist-practitioner training model (the Boulder model), psychology has a long history of disputes between scientists and practitioners. Psychologists typically earn an undergraduate degree in psychology, a master's en route to a doctorate, and finally a Ph.D. (doctor of philosophy), Ed.D. (doctor of education), or Psy.D. (doctor of psychology). The titles of the doctorate degree have their own history. The oldest title, doctor of philosophy, originally referred to moral philosophy (humanities, social sciences, and so on) or natural philosophy (natural sciences). Current holders of Ph.D.s have a particular emphasis, such as a Ph.D. in clinical psychology or Ph.D. in counseling psychology. More recently, doctorates in education and psychology (Ed.D. and Psy.D.) were implemented to reflect the area of emphasis, as well as slightly different criteria to earn the degree.

Like programs in counselor training, psychology programs began with close ties to schools of education where programs in counseling psychology still reside (Chiszar & Wertheimer, 1988; Schmidt & Chock, 1990). The late nineteenth and early twentieth centuries saw psychology aim to be recognized as a science in its own right, and this led to experimental and clinical psychology programs residing in colleges of arts and sciences (Ash, 1983; Cushman, 1992).

Since the 1940s, psychologists have been seen as specialists in psychological assessment (Exner, 1995). Pressure to develop an academic model for training led to the establishment of the Boulder model at the Boulder, Colorado, conference of the American Psychological Association (APA) in 1949. This model, still dominant today, emphasizes both research skills and clinical skills. The model itself has been debated for years, with several studies implying that it is ineffective in its goal to have graduates be both researchers and clinicians (George, 1984; Norcross, Gallagher, & Prochaska, 1989). Research has indicated that most students tend to be clinicians or researchers, but rarely both (Adams, 1982; Frank, 1984; Garfield & Kurtz, 1974; Levy, 1962; Thorndike, 1955). In 1976, detractors of the Boulder model proposed an alternative, the Vail model, named for the APA conference of 1976 that endorsed a scholar-professional model over the scientist-practitioner model. The professional degree of doctor of psychology (Psy.D.) is an outgrowth of the Vail model.

To make matters more complex, in 1955 the APA Division of Counseling and Guidance was renamed the Division of Counseling Psychology (Perry, 1955). Although counseling psychology still uses the Boulder training model, it reflects Lanning's (1990) "educator/practitioner" model, which is discussed in more detail on p. 20 in connection with counselor training. Despite the goal to make counseling psychology a separate field working with human development (Super, 1955), or what Pallone (1977) called "hygiology," the result was identity diffusion across the spectrum of applied psychology from normalcy to pathology (Pallone, 1977; Sprinthall, 1990). Delworth (1977) noted that neither psychological professionals nor the public can readily identify counseling psychologists, and counseling psychologists cannot succinctly and exclusively describe what they do. Krauskopf, Thoreson, and McAleer (1973) wrote that being housed in schools of education further preclude counseling psychologists from being readily identifiable as psychologists. Sprinthall (1990) concluded that counseling psychology has forsaken its roots in human development and normalcy-oriented work to compete for increasingly scarce third-party reimbursement usually requiring a *DSM* diagnosis.

Counseling

Descriptions of counseling and counselor preparation are often in conflict with one another. In some states, counselors earn a 48-semester-hour master's degree with little focus on psychopathology. In other states, counselors earn a 60-semester-hour master's degree, including a mental health counseling focus on personality, psychopathology, diagnosis, testing, and treatment of mental/emotional disorders. The diversity of programs is reflected in the written statements of counseling theorists. Whereas one theorist may say that counseling helps "normal" individuals with problems in daily living (Gladding, 1996), another may use the terms *counseling* and *psychotherapy* synonymously (Corey, 1996). Counselor education programs are accredited by the Council for Accreditation of Counseling and Related Educational Programs (CACREP).

Tracing the history of counseling and counselor preparation seems to follow two themes (Tyler, 1969). The first starts with the notion of professionalization, using Caplow's (1966) and Greenwood's (1962) characteristics of a profession. These include (a) a specialized body of knowledge, (b) research that is theory-driven, (c) the overseeing of training programs, (d) a code of ethics, and (e) standards for admission and the policing of members/practitioners. The primary problem with identifying any therapeutic profession through these criteria is the specialized body of knowledge, since there is great overlap in the body of therapeutic knowledge. A second method for tracing the evolution of counseling considers the functions of therapeutic "healers" throughout history. This method, used by Kottler and Brown (1996) and Hershenson, Power, and Waldo (1996), includes religious figures such as the Buddha or Christ, philosophical figures such as Socrates, and influential artists such as Shakespeare and da Vinci. Although this is a much broader method, it holds no hope of defining the boundaries of each therapeutic profession.

If one traces the historical development of counseling through figures in vocational counseling (Frank Parsons) or school guidance (Jesse Davis), one sees substantial overlap with historical accounts of counseling psychology (Schmidt & Chock, 1990; Pallone, 1977; Sprinthall, 1990). Similarly, if one wishes to trace the history of counseling through the various mental health movements, the similarities only increase. Despite the striking similarities between descriptions of the practice of both counseling and counseling psychology, legal battles stemming from the nature of competition in a free-market economy seemed to guarantee their separation as identified fields. Hosie (1991) and Sweeney (1991) described two cases in which the American Psychological Association tried to criminalize the use of educational and career assessment instruments by professionals not fitting its definition of a psychologist. One case (*Weldon v. Virginia State Board of Psychological Examiners,* 1972) led to a law in Virginia certifying personnel and guidance counselors for private practice. Another case (*Ohio v. Cook,* 1975) was decided in favor of a counselor in Cleveland, Ohio, where the Municipal Court judge ruled that many professions may use instruments that are psychological. Interestingly, the Ohio attorney general more recently issued a similar opinion on the use of the term *psychological* by professional counselors (Montgomery, 1996).

One way to differentiate counselor training is to describe it as the only training in a therapeutic profession that has two levels of preparation (master's and doctoral), which lead to an equal level of licensure (Hosie, 1991). Another reality separating counseling from psychology, in particular, has been the training model it uses. Although Lanning (1990) noted that a major difference between a counseling psychologist and a counselor is more in the identity of the person rather than the quality of training, he further stated that perhaps a clearer differentiation could be developed through emphasizing an educator/practitioner model for doctoral-level counselor trainees. This model would emphasize the teaching of graduate classes, supervision of master's-level trainees, advanced practice, and systematic inquiry into the field of counseling. Ivey and Rigazio-Digilio (1991) discussed a variation of this for master's-level training called the educational-developmental view, which is holistic and includes the physical, psychological, and interactional dimensions. As in the case of counseling psychology, this training model requires modification in the states, such as Ohio, that license counselors to diagnose and treat mental and emotional disorders (Ohio Counselor and Social Work Board, 1997).

Social Work

According to the Standards for Social Service Manpower (1973), social work includes helping individuals, groups, and communities enhance or restore social functioning and create societal conditions favorable to their goals. Its activities consist of providing counseling and psychotherapy for individuals, groups, and families. Social work training is done at the associate, undergraduate, master's, and doctorate levels (Bernard, 1995), and social work programs are accredited by the Council on Social Work Education (CSWE). A large number of people practice social work with undergraduate degrees, but we will focus more on the master's-level training in this chapter, since the master's-level social work licenses typically are those that allow for the independent practice of mental health counseling.

Independently licensed social workers earn a master's degree that is 56 to 66 semester hours in length, depending on whether they have an undergraduate degree in social work. The knowledge bases used in social work training include human development; human behavior; and social, economic, and cultural institutions. Social work differentiates itself from counseling, psychology, and psychiatry in that its mission includes mandates to negotiate social systems and advocate for change, to understand clients' habitats (physical and social settings within cultural contexts) and niches (statuses and roles in community), and to provide social services (Hepworth, Rooney, & Larson, 1997; Zastrow, 1997). Also, the National Association of Social Work insists that social work programs be located in schools of social work, as opposed to education and arts and sciences (Altekruse & Wittmer, 1991).

In addition, since the 1960s, social work training has emphasized a systems approach, as opposed to the medical model approach (Zastrow, 1997). One variation of the systems approach is the "ecological model" of human behavior. The ecological model integrates individual treatment into social reform through a focus on unhealthy transactions between people and their social/physical environments (Zastrow, 1992). In addition to the ecological model, some theorists (Turnbull & Dietz-Uhler, 1995) have explored integrating psychology's Boulder model to enhance the relationship between research and practice. It should be noted, that despite variations in title, all states have some license for master's-level social workers to diagnose and treat mental and emotional disorders. This is under social work's philosophy of direct service, which also requires an understanding of client cultures and their social context (Hepworth et al, 1997).

Summary of Historical Influences and Training Models

It appears that the clearest way to differentiate among the therapeutic professions is through their respective training models. Due to overlaps in history, practice, and definition, further differentiation muddies the waters of interprofessional communication and complicates goal setting for students seeking training programs. Toward the goal of increasing clarity about professional training models and demonstrating the complementarity of the various professions, next we will view the professions through what is called "the integral model" (Wilber, 1995, 1996, 1997). The model provides one example of the big picture of the various therapeutic professions.

INSIDES, OUTSIDES, GROUPS, AND INDIVIDUALS

Ken Wilber is a contemporary philosopher and writer in the areas of human development, transpersonal psychology, and integrative philosophy. His works are wide-ranging in topic, and they endeavor to integrate findings from numerous fields into a cohesive entity that he calls "the integral model." He created this model while studying philosophies from various cultures across time. Each philosophy he studied was like a map of reality, and his goal was to find one unifying map. He noted that he had literally hundreds of these maps from multiple disciplines (religion, psychology, human development, anthropology, sociology, and so on). Wilber realized that, rather than sharing a basic structure, these maps reflected one of four complementary perspectives, which, when brought together, formed a sort of big picture. Figure 1.2 shows the basic outline of Wilber's integral model.

The four quadrants in the model in figure 1.2 represent various perspectives on whatever subject the model is being used to understand. "Outsides" are things that can be measured objectively, whereas "insides" are subjective experiences that require dialogue and interpretation. Wilber calls the two columns the left- and right-hand paths (Wilber, 1995, 1996). The right-hand path (the column under "Outsides") is the stereotype of the Western approach to things, which focuses on measurement and the data you can collect. The left-hand path (the column under "Insides) represents an Eastern approach to things, which focuses on consciousness. These are then complemented by the individual and group perspectives (the rows). The consideration of all the quadrants, or perspectives, results in an integral vision of the subject under consideration.

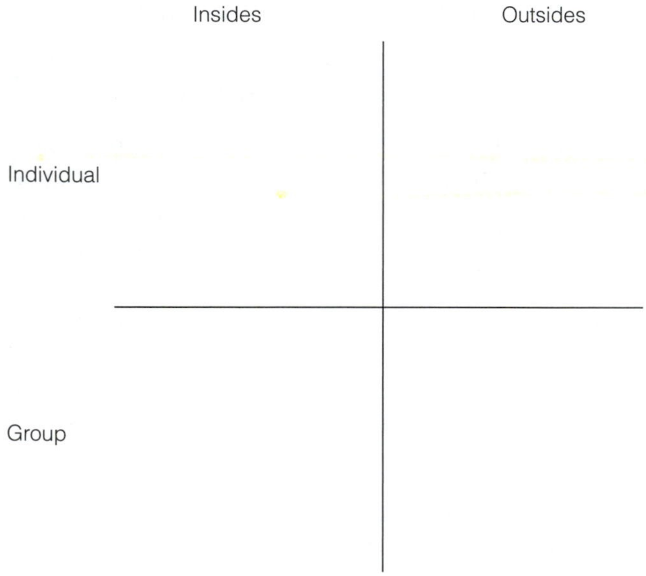

FIGURE **1.2**

Wilber's Integral Model

Wilber (1996) offers the example of going to the grocery store to illustrate the integral model. He notes that first he experiences the thought "I am going to the grocery store." The symbols, images, and ideas in this thought all appear in the upper left quadrant, individual insides. Moving to another quadrant, the thought corresponds to physiological changes that can be measured—changes in neurotransmitters, in the release of acetylcholine to execute the motor behavior of walking to the car to drive to the store, and so on. These elements belong in the upper right quadrant, individual outsides, representing the elements of going to the grocery store that can be empirically observed and measured. The lower left quadrant, group insides, reflects the cultural community Wilber lives in, which provides the context for understanding the images, symbols, and meanings of going to the grocery store. Wilber notes that thoughts do not just pop into our heads but arise from this cultural background. In a different culture or at a different time in history, "go to the grocery store" might mean "time to kill the bear" or "time to churn butter." The fourth quadrant, group outsides, comes into play because cultures all have measurable social components, including types of technology, institutions, forces of agricultural production, and economic systems. These are all measurable to some degree and constitute the lower right quadrant. Figure 1.3 summarizes this example of going to the grocery store through the integral model.

	Insides	Outsides
Individual	The images of the store and symbols relevant to the trip	The corresponding physical changes and behaviors associated with going to the store
Group	The cultural context that makes the thought relevant to getting food	The social institutions that support the phenomenon of grocery stores

FIGURE 1.3

The Integral Model Applied to Going to the Grocery Store

Certainly, there are many more elements related to going to the grocery store that could be explored through the model, but this is a brief example to give a basic explanation of the quadrants. Again, the main idea is that, the more perspectives that are represented in a particular exploration, the more complete is our knowledge of whatever is being explored. Next, we will use the integral model to examine the foci of the four therapeutic professions discussed thus far in this chapter.

Wilber (1997) notes that mental health is commonly defined as being "in touch with reality." However, the models that are supposed to reflect reality are often incomplete, overemphasizing one perspective (insides, outsides, individual, or group) rather than considering all four. As noted, the upper right quadrant of the integral model deals with the outsides of individuals. Those in the helping professions are quite familiar with this quadrant. Consider the following excerpts from case notes on four clients:

- *Client A:* The client appeared lethargic and apathetic.
- *Client B:* The client was inappropriately dressed for the weather and wrung her hands throughout the interview.
- *Client C:* The client spoke of his mother in glowing terms, all the while clenching his fists.
- *Client D:* The client's EEG pattern showed an abnormal frequency of delta waves throughout her night's sleep.

These are all observations of the outsides of individuals. These outsides can be measured to some degree and can be observed without understanding the client's internal state of mind. All good therapists learn the value of an individual's outsides in their first lesson on nonverbal behavior. It is through observing and/or measuring the outsides of individuals that therapeutic professionals pick up inconsistencies in a client's presentation, like that of previously mentioned Client C, speaking positively about his mother but showing a sign of tension or aggression with his clenched fists. These inconsistencies can then be fed back to the client in the form of a confrontation: "On the one hand, you were telling me you have very positive feelings toward your mother, but, on the other hand, you clenched your fists the entire time you were talking about her. How do those go together for you?" As such, individual outsides are very important to all therapeutic professionals.

The upper left quadrant deals with the insides of individuals. All therapeutic professionals work with this aspect of clients as well. Consider the following case note excerpts:

- *Client A:* Regarding her lethargy, the client stated that she really didn't see that it mattered if she lived or died.
- *Client B:* The client said she believed she received a special message about the apocalypse coming today (July 3) in the form of a nuclear winter. She said her inappropriate dress was in preparation for this event.

- *Client C:* The client stated what a horrible person he was because he was angry with his mother for relying on him so often.
- *Client D:* The client stated she almost never feels rested when she awakens, that she is always exhausted, and that she feels as if she is being punished by God or someone.

Each of these excerpts about the clients relays something in addition to the excerpts about their outsides. This second set of notes, corresponding to the insides of these clients, are not elements that can be directly measured—they must be disclosed and interpreted in the context of dialogue. Each of these excerpts reveals some meaning the individual holds that can be obtained only through dialogue. Honest dialogue requires a degree of working alliance between client and therapist. Consider Client A, who is demonstrating lethargy. Although lethargy is a sign of depression, we cannot be certain until the client reveals more. Until we enter into dialogue, we can't know if the client is depressed or suffering from sleep deprivation. And, even if the client has a sleep disorder, we do not know what her sleeping difficulty means to her until we engage in a dialogue. Whereas the individual outsides can be gathered through somewhat detached observation, information about the individual's insides must be acquired through a working alliance, honest dialogue, and sometimes interpretation.

The lower left quadrant deals with the insides of groups of which the client may be a part—particularly, the client's culture. Culture permeates our thoughts, and even the manner in which our thoughts arise. Like the individual insides, the experience of culture can be understood only through dialogue with people in that culture. By way of example, consider some more case note excerpts:

- *Client A:* The client lived in poverty and for years suffered hypertension. She stated that she felt "beat down" by the racism she experienced at the hands of dominant members of the society.
- *Client B:* The client, who attended a fundamentalist, Protestant church, said she first heard of the apocalypse in a sermon at church. It turns out that the pastor of the client's congregation placed a great deal of emphasis on the "end times," even having authored a book on the topic.
- *Client C:* The client, a first-generation Italian American, recalled how many messages he got from his culture about loving and taking care of his mother.
- *Client D:* It turns out that the client was trying to offset considerable financial debt by volunteering for double shifts to the degree that she had severely disrupted her sleep cycle.

In each of these excerpts, a cultural variable, including race/ethnicity, age, gender, spiritual path, sexual orientation, socioeconomic status, and ability/disability is figured into the total client picture. Again, although we may observe many aspects about cultures, other things we cannot really learn about until we talk with members of that culture about what it means. The client who was angry with his mother talked about the emphasis on harsh judgment he experienced, both in church and at home, around the issue of anger at his mother. The client with the sleep disturbance felt so compelled by the stress of her financial debt that she was ruining her health to pay it off. In these examples, the cultural perspective increases the richness of the client profile and increases the chance of an effective intervention.

The lower right quadrant deals with the outsides of groups or collectives. This is basically what we can observe and learn about groups without necessarily understanding what the observed variables mean to members of that group. As before, consider the following set of case note excerpts:

- *Client A:* The client, an African American, lived near a predominantly Korean inner-city neighborhood, where frequent disputes between African Americans and Koreans had been documented.
- *Client B:* The client's church congregation had been the subject of a local news story detailing several of its questionable home-schooling practices.
- *Client C:* Being a member of this client's Roman Catholic parish, you had heard many of the priest's exhortations about the virtues of mother-child love.
- *Client D:* Twice the IRS has audited this client, and you know that more lower-class tax filers are audited than taxpayers in any other income bracket.

Again, each of these excerpts points to something we know or observe in groups of which the client is part or by which she or he is affected. As before, knowledge in this quadrant enhances our understanding of the client's situation.

Returning to our discussion of how the training models of therapeutic professionals fit Wilber's integral model, we can start by observing that the various training models of the therapeutic professions place different emphases on particular quadrants. Because there is so much confusion and overlap in professional identity among the therapeutic professions, perhaps one way to bring some order to the situation is to describe the degree to which the training in each profession relies on particular quadrants in the integral model. This may assist individuals aspiring to be professional therapists in choosing training that is suited to their temperaments. The four therapeutic professions discussed in this chapter can be arranged initially to illustrate the primary quadrant each emphasizes in its training. The overlap in the functions of the various professions can be illustrated as well. The application of Wilber's model corrects misunderstandings about areas of overlap and supports interprofessional collaboration, rather than interprofessional squabbling over professional identity.

	Insides	Outsides
Individual	**Counseling Psychology**	**Psychiatry Psychology**
Group	**Social Work**	**Social Work**

FIGURE **1.4**

Therapeutic Profession Training Models in the Integral Model

Figure 1.4 shows each therapeutic profession in the quadrant emphasized in its training model. Assuming the biomedical paradigm as dominant,
psychiatric training places primary emphasis on the upper right quadrant,
where the focus is on the outsides of the individual organism. The focus on
individuals is reinforced by the format of the *DSM-IV*, which allows the diagnosis only of individuals. In agency settings, psychiatrists are frequently over-
whelmed by the sheer number of clients needing to be assessed for
medications, side effects, and efficacy of psychotropic interventions. Psychiatrists with the sincerest intentions to offer therapeutic as well as
diagnostic/prescriptive contact are often thwarted by the enormity of their
caseloads. In these situations, the psychiatrists are limited to focusing on the
upper right quadrant, the outsides of the client. Under these difficult conditions, psychiatrists often rely on other therapeutic professionals who have
more contact with the client to supply information from the other quadrants.
Although this situation is not what most psychiatrists hope for, it is consistent
with their training's medical model emphasis.

The Boulder model of psychology also has a primary emphasis on the
upper right quadrant to the extent that it focuses on the concept of science informing practice more than practice informing science. Science informing
practice is based in finding generalities about human beings that can be
applied to particular clients. Practice informing science takes the form of

interventions that are successful with particular clients (efficacy studies), which are then tested for their generalizability to larger populations (effectiveness studies) (George, 1984). In particular, psychologists' use of diagnostic tests and inventories represents science informing practice and provides a good example of how psychology practice via the Boulder model fits into this quadrant. Consider a client who is referred for a Minnesota Multiphasic Personality Inventory (MMPI). The client will answer more than 500 questions designed to assess various domains of pathology. Although the inventory is a self-report, more emphasis is placed on the client's endorsing or not endorsing certain items, rather than what particular items mean to the client. If the client's response profile is valid, it will describe the level (if any) and general types of pathology likely to plague the client. Again, this merely helps the clinician categorize the client's symptoms on the basis of their client's MMPI responses. The category, if accurate, then helps the clinician move in the direction of particular interventions shown to be useful with people who are similarly categorized. All this can be done without dialogue with the client (although, ethically, it should not be). This is why it is included in the upper right quadrant of Wilber's model. Psychology's Boulder model is also represented in the upper left quadrant because practice is still emphasized in the scientist-practitioner model.

Counselor training, to the extent that it follows Lanning's (1990) educator-practitioner model, is rooted in the upper left quadrant in that it focuses more on skill-training in clinical dialogue for the purpose of understanding the insides of individuals. The accreditation board for counselor education programs is the Council for Accreditation of Counseling and Related Educational Programs (CACREP). The CACREP program areas identify core areas, many of which require the interpersonal skills that make for a good clinician. Core areas such as Social and Cultural Foundations, Helping Relationships, Group Work, and Career Lifestyle and Development are typically presented with an eye to application in the counseling session. Of particular importance in counseling is the counseling of clients from diverse backgrounds. This specialty area has been a strong focus of the American Counseling Association (ACA), which has organized several international conferences around diversity issues.

Finally, social work training is placed primarily in both the lower left and right quadrants to illustrate the focus of its training model on understanding client culture and the culture's social context. The mission statement of the National Association of Social Workers (NASW) specifically states that the primary mission of social work is "to enhance human well-being and help meet the basic human needs of all people, with particular attention to the needs and empowerment of people who are vulnerable, oppressed, and living in poverty. An historic feature of social work is the profession's focus on individual well-being in a social context and the well-being of society" (NASW, 1996).

	Insides	Outsides
Individual	**Counseling** **Psychiatry** **Psychology** **Social Work**	**Psychiatry** **Psychology** **Counseling**
Group	**Social Work** **Counseling** **Psychology**	**Social Work** **Psychology** **Counseling**

FIGURE **1.5**

Relative Emphases of the Therapeutic Professions' Training Models

The mission statement reflects the systems theory and ecological model described earlier in this chapter.

We have seen that professional identity is a complex issue. One use of Wilber's model is to represent that complexity. No one training model discussed in this chapter falls exclusively in its dominant quadrant. The training models may all have a place in each quadrant. Figure 1.5 illustrates each training model's degree of emphasis in each quadrant, relative to the others. In figure 1.5, the degree of emphasis each profession's training places on each quadrant is denoted by the size of the font labeling each professional group. The largest font denotes the strongest emphasis; the smallest font denotes the least. The primary focus of psychiatry is in the upper right quadrant (individual outsides). This reflects the medical model focus on biological variables and observable symptoms. The secondary focus is in the upper left, since many psychiatrists engage in dialogue to work further with clients therapeutically. Increasingly, psychiatrists, like other therapeutic professionals, are including the knowledge of human diversity in their work (Lu, 1996). This is represented as the third focus in the lower left quadrant.

Due to psychology training's emphasis on the "scientist" aspect of the Boulder model, psychology training remains most strongly represented in the upper right quadrant. The secondary emphasis in the upper left follows the secondary emphasis on clinical practice, and the tertiary emphasis in the lower left and right quadrants reflects psychology's growing concern with issues of diversity and community psychology. Counselor training shows its strongest emphasis in the upper left quadrant to the degree that it focuses on the educator-practitioner model. For counseling, the secondary emphasis is in the lower left quadrant, since the literature seems to focus more on understanding diversity than testing and diagnosis. With more states including testing and diagnosis in their counselor practice laws, the tertiary focus for counseling is in the upper right quadrant. Finally, there is a fourth emphasis in the lower right quadrant for counseling, as client advocacy is becoming increasingly mentioned in the literature. Social work begins with a primary emphasis in both the lower left and right quadrants, reflecting the concerns of its ecological systems training model and its direct service philosophy. The secondary emphasis is in the upper left, since a great number of social workers do counseling and psychotherapy, and the least emphasis is in the upper right. To the degree that figure 1.5 accurately represents the emphases of training in the therapeutic professions, a person seeking to work in those professions could begin to consider the best fit for their skills and temperament.

To develop further this application of Wilber's model, we will review the notions of holon and holarchy. Holon, coined by Koestler (1967), refers to an element that is simultaneously a whole and a part. Just as the word *bark* is a whole, it is also a part in the phrase "the bark of a tree." Just as psychiatry is a whole profession, it is also a part of the web of mental health research and treatment provided by numerous therapeutic professions. The therapeutic professions too often view themselves as discreet professions battling each other for clients, prestige, and reimbursement. As a holon, each therapeutic profession retains its wholeness and is equally a part of the larger pattern of mental health research and treatment. In this sense, the professions can function in a complementary manner, as well as a competitive one. The notion of holons is also useful in viewing the specialties of a therapeutic profession within that profession. Each professional specialty is a holon; equally a part and a whole within its respective therapeutic profession such as career counseling is a whole specialty and simultaneously a part of both counseling and counseling psychology. In the same manner, mental health counseling is one part of or specialty within the broader counseling profession, while maintaining its integrity as a whole.

An interesting aspect of holons is that they form holarchies. A holarchy is really a hierarchy of holons. The difference is that, in a hierarchy, a given level can be eliminated without necessarily disturbing the rest of the hierarchy. In a holarchy, however, each level transcends and includes lower levels, so that to eliminate one level is to eliminate all the levels above it. For example, in the holarchy of mental health treatment, consider the relationship among interviewing skills, empathy, and counseling in general. Interviewing skills are viewed as the basis of the counseling interaction (Ivey, 1994). Empathy, or the ability to feel what it is like to be in the client's position, transcends and includes interviewing skills. Finally, the counseling process transcends and includes both interviewing skills and empathy. If you take away empathy or interviewing skills, you also take away the counseling process.

The proponents of exclusive professional identities (Gladding, 1996; Super, 1955) encourage emphasizing differences as a means of maintaining a foothold in service delivery. However, if our examination of professional identity is accurate, most therapeutic professions have ambiguity in their professional identities. The alternative integral model of a holarchy of therapeutic professions illustrates the complementarity of the professions and highlights some differences.

One benefit of an integral approach to understanding the therapeutic professions could be a more unified front as therapeutic professionals stop their in-fighting to challenge managed care companies. Managed care companies view therapeutic professionals hierarchically, and professionals may fuel this dynamic through incessant squabbling. Since in a hierarchy one level can be removed without affecting the function or structure of the other levels, therapeutic professionals are at each other's throats, and this works to the advantage of the third-party payers who effectively split the large community of therapeutic professionals. The integral model poses the possibility of a unified front. Similar to a treatment team approach in which a psychiatrist, counselor, psychologist, and social worker may all be necessary for effective treatment, the integral view sees each as important to the overall systems of mental health treatment. Also, the integral model clarifies the training approaches and emphases of each therapeutic profession. This understanding is advantageous to those seeking to become professional therapists but are unsure of what paths are available and what they require.

Although proponents of discreet professional identities emphasize knowledge of one's roots and uniqueness, to ignore the similarities of the therapeutic professions is to wear psychological blinders in denial of their reality. It increases adversarial interactions among professionals and creates an atmosphere of antagonism. The consequences of an atmosphere of antagonism are far worse than those of embracing the similarities among the various professions.

As noted, one consequence of an atmosphere of antagonism has been an increase in the power of managed care companies. Although managed care has initiated some positive changes, such as accountability, all therapeutic professions, acting with a unified front, may have more leverage to negotiate the treatment dictated by clients' conditions and the therapeutic reality. There is more agreement than disagreement regarding the problematic aspects of managed care in the face of this reality. The time has come to spend energy and resources considering how counseling, social work, psychology, and psychiatry can collaborate instead of compete.

OTHER THERAPEUTIC PROFESSIONALS

In this section, we will discuss two specializations in the therapeutic professions. A therapeutic professional either may be licensed and then pursue this area of specialization or may be licensed/certified (depending on the state) in the particular area. Many specialists question whether a practitioner with a generalist license (counselor, psychologist) is qualified to do therapeutic interventions in these specialty areas. As for the licensed, generalist practitioners, they are ethically bound not to practice outside their areas of competence, but many feel that, with proper continuing education (as opposed to a certification process), they may practice in the specialty areas of substance abuse counseling and marriage and family counseling.

Substance Abuse Counselors

Substance abuse counseling is an area in which the debate between professionals and paraprofessionals is very lively. For the purposes of this section, *paraprofessional* is defined as a person with either a high school or a baccalaureate education, whereas *professional* is one with an advanced degree at the master's or doctoral level. In substance abuse counseling, the paraprofessionals are usually in recovery themselves, whereas the professionals may or may not have been substance dependent at some point. The reliance on helpers who themselves have been substance abusers or substance dependent is based on the belief that they are more effective with substance abusing clients than are those who have never had a substance use problem (Wright, 1980). In addition, paraprofessionals note that the characteristic trait of their interventions is a personal relationship with the client, whereas professionals rely (sometimes too much, in the opinions of the paraprofessionals) on theories and treatment procedures. From the other side of the debate, many professionals view paraprofessionals as lacking in basic therapeutic skills and being less effective in helping the client move from maintenance to treatment (Stude, 1990).

Currently, most states have a credential to recognize chemical dependency counselors. Since the 1970s, there has been a nationwide recognition of the need to check the quality of service provision for substance abuse counseling (Judd, 1987). One problem is that the requirements vary drastically from state to state. In all states that license counselors, those seeking licenses must hold at least a master's degree from an accredited institution. For substance abuse counseling, one state may offer a blanket licensure (such as New Hampshire's Alcohol and Drug Abuse Counselor), whereas other states may offer levels of certification (such as Ohio's three levels of Certified Chemical Dependency Counselors). One state may require only a high-school-level education, whereas another may require an undergraduate degree. The primary difference between licensure and certification in most states is that certified professionals can not engage in unsupervised practice.

The multitiered certification system stems from the National Association of Alcoholism and Drug Abuse Counselors (NAADAC), which is the largest national organization for substance abuse professionals in the United States. In addition to education and legislative lobbying, NAADAC provides training leading to three levels of certification of National Certified Addictions Counselors (NCACs). The first level requires state licensure or certification as a substance abuse counselor, three years of full-time experience as a substance abuse counselor, 270 contact hours of related education, and a passing score on an exam given by NAADAC. The next level requires a bachelor's degree, current licensure or certification, five years of full-time related work experience, 450 contact hours of education, and a passing score on the exam for this level. The highest level is called Master Addictions Counselor (MAC) and requires a master's degree in a related field, 500 contact hours of specific training, three years of supervised experience (two of which must be postmaster's), and a passing score on the MAC exam. There is a broad range of employment settings for substance abuse counselors, including traditional community agencies, residential programs, managed care companies, private practice, partial hospitalization, and employee assistance programs (EAP). In Wilber's integral model, substance abuse counseling could easily fit into any of the quadrants, depending on the approach used. There are interventions that look at systems (lower right, group outsides), family interventions (lower left, group insides), physiological factors and behavioral interventions (upper right, individual outsides), and approaches that rely on intrapsychic factors such as insight and even spiritual transformation (upper left, individual insides).

Marriage and Family Therapy

Currently, 40 states regulate marriage and family therapy, with roughly two-thirds offering a license and the remaining one-third offering a certificate. The training experiences can be obtained through training programs in psychology, social work, and counseling as an area of specialization. Paradoxically, training in marriage and family therapy is offered in a diversity of programs, but, if there is any therapeutic profession/specialization with a strong case for an exclusive professional identity, it is marriage and family therapy. We will examine this case for a separate identity by referring back to the criteria summarized earlier in this chapter from Caplow (1966) and Greenwood (1962).

As previously noted, Caplow's and Greenwood's first two criteria posed the greatest problems in trying to separate fields such as counseling, social work, and psychology. Marriage and family therapy does not have the same problems laying claim to an exclusive professional identity through these criteria. Recall that the first criterion is possession of a specialized body of knowledge. Marriage and family therapy certainly has that. Although its knowledge base arguably draws from systems theory and family studies, these are uniquely applied in the clinical setting. Probably the only overlap in this area is John Bell's (1961) family group therapy, in which he treated families as groups. The second criterion is research that is theory-driven. The generation of research techniques specific to marriage and family therapy began in the early 1980s with *The Journal of Marriage and the Family* and *The Journal of Family Issues,* both devoting entire issues to such specific research techniques.

The history of family therapy in the United States is a brief one, if by *history* we are referring to an organized professional orientation to therapeutic interventions. Systematized work with families did not occur until about the 1940s (Gladding, 1995). Among the obstacles to family therapy were the established therapeutic professionals (particularly psychiatrists) and the dominant therapeutic theories of psychoanalysis and behaviorism. Despite the opposition, in the 1950s numerous practitioners/theorists advocated the treatment of the entire family, a modality antithetical to the emphasis on individual treatment up to that time. We saw earlier that it was paradoxical that marriage and family therapists, of all the therapeutic professionals we have discussed, seem to have the best case for an exclusive professional identity. This paradox increases when we consider that the pioneers in the field come from a vast number of other disciplines. Carl Whitaker and Salvador Minuchin were trained as psychiatrists; Virginia Satir and Michelle Weiner-Davis were trained as social workers; Rachel Hare-Mustin was trained in psychology; and more recent authors in the field, such as Sam Gladding, John West, and Don Bubenzer, were trained as counselors. If we were to place marriage and family therapy training in the integral model such training would clearly emphasize both lower quadrants (the insides and outsides of groups).

Interestingly, one of the more powerful blocks to the treatment of entire families is the *DSM-IV.* As noted in the section on psychiatry's biomedical model, the *DSM* can be used to diagnose and treat only individuals. This has led to marriage and family practitioners being in the position of having to name an "identified client"—one family member who ethically can be given a diagnosis. Once this member has been diagnosed, work can then proceed with the entire family. There has been a great deal of work in trying to establish a system for diagnosing family problems, and there is even an appendix in the *DSM-IV* suggesting a scale called the Global Assessment of Relational Functioning (the GARF scale). This is an axis that requires further study but can be used to indicate an overall judgment of family functioning. Only time will tell whether or not this scale will be officially recognized in the next version of the *DSM.*

THE IMPACT OF THE *DSM* ON PROFESSIONAL IDENTITY

Before ending this discussion of professional identity, we should touch on the impact of the *DSM-IV* on training in the therapeutic professions we have discussed. We will examine the *DSM* more thoroughly in chapter 6. The *DSM* pulled psychiatry away from psychoanalysis and, according to Wylie (1995), saved it from professional oblivion. The *DSM* remedicalized the diagnosis of mental and emotional disorders and became the standard of diagnostic conceptualization in all the therapeutic professions. It seems that, despite the differences that exist in training models for the various therapeutic professions, the degree to which a profession has power in the therapeutic marketplace rests on the degree to which its practitioners are licensed to use the *DSM* for diagnosis. The obvious ethical imperative is that, if a professional is going to use the *DSM*, that person must be adequately trained in its use both in school and as part of a practicum or an internship. The catch-22 is that, although such training increases the chance of producing competent, ethical practitioners, it also increases the homogeneity of training programs. As the history of training therapeutic professionals illustrates, it is difficult for a training program to maintain a wellness orientation, or any other nonmedical orientation to mental health, when it is overshadowed by such a universal tool as the *DSM*.

PROFESSIONAL ORGANIZATIONS

A chapter on professional identity would be incomplete without a section on professional organizations. Perhaps you already belong to one or several. Professional organizations can provide opportunities for developing and maintaining professional attitudes and ideals (Scott, 1980), important opportunities for networking, and opportunities for remaining updated on recent trends.

One way to conceptualize professional organizations is by constituency—professional groups exist at the national, state, and regional levels. Probably the most widely known national organization among counseling professionals is the American Counseling Association (ACA). The ACA has subdivisions based on specialization areas, such as school counseling; multicultural counseling; spiritual, religious, ethical, and value issues; mental health counseling; counselor education and supervision; and group work; to name a few. A complete description of the subdivisions and other information can be found at the ACA web site, *www.counseling.org/* Other national organizations include the American School Counselors Association (ASCA), the National Association of Social Workers (NASW), the American Psychiatric Association (APA), and the American Psychological Association (also APA). The web site addresses for these and other professional associations are listed at the end of this chapter. You will usually find that each state has its own state-level organization (many of whom also have web sites), with regional affiliates.

The Functions of Professional Organizations

In a paper viewing long-term goals in the ACA, Nejedlo, Hansen, and Myers (1994) reported the results of a national survey of ACA members and leaders as to the goals and priorities for the organization. The members and leaders agreed that the top two priorities should be (1) the maintenance of professional standards and (2) personal and professional development. The most important example of standards in counseling is the ACA Code of Ethics, which stipulates the parameters of ethical behavior for all counselors (the entire code can be found at the end of chapter 4). Although the Code of Ethics is not law, it represents the moral and ethical ideals to which counselors are expected to aspire, and the code is referred to in most laws regulating counselors—state licensing boards can call licensed counselors to account for breaches of the ethical code. The second top priority of ACA members, professional development, includes keeping abreast of changes and advancements in one's field. Most state licensing boards require continuing education after granting a license, and professional organizations play a role in providing such education. If you've ever attended a state or national conference, you may have noticed a notation about the number of continuing education units (CEUs) available for attending sessions.

Professional organizations can provide a sense of cohesion within a community of professionals who share concerns and goals. As noted, such a community can be an important source of networking. Professional organizations provide the opportunity to meet others beyond your classmates or co-workers in the field. Many of the colleagues you meet at a professional conference will have encountered some of the same professional challenges as you and may have generated solutions you have not. It can be exciting to exchange ideas and experiences with such people.

The Pros and Cons of Membership in Professional Organizations

National Membership   Belonging to a national organization offers some advantages. It gets you on mailing lists for professional publications, which are one of the main vehicles for disseminating new knowledge in the field. You have the opportunity to belong to specialty divisions, such as those noted earlier in the chapter, each of which has its own journal. Your membership dollars go in part to support leaders working to advocate for federal legislation to benefit clients and counselors. A recent example is The Health Professions Education Partnerships Act of 1998, which was signed into law in October 1998 (PL 105-392). This law allows counselor education programs and graduates to participate in seven federal health professional training programs previously available only to clinical psychology, social work, and some marriage and family therapy education programs (American Counseling Association, 1998; Barstow & Goetz, 1998). Another advantage of membership in national organizations is that they typically offer reasonable rates for malpractice insurance, a necessity for any therapeutic professional in a litigious society.

Two disadvantages of national organization membership are the tendency of members to form a biased view of the profession and the cost of membership. National organizations are like any other large group of people—they are political animals. The political climate changes, depending on individuals who are in leadership positions at any given point in time. A national organization may adopt a set of strategic goals, for example, that are not consistent with what you believe. In addition, professionals with dissenting views or values may not spend the money or time to belong to a group with whom they strongly disagree. In this sense, you may develop a biased view of the profession through its national organization. Another issue is cost. If you peruse membership applications, you may note that there is a substantial difference in membership fees between students and professionals. You always want to think carefully about spending your membership dollars in a manner that will net you the largest return on your investment. Although you may have interests in many specialty areas, you probably cannot afford to belong to them all and must choose the areas most relevant to your work.

State/Regional Membership   There are several advantages to belonging to state-level professional organizations. First, in terms of legal involvement and advocates for legislative change, the laws at the state level are likely to affect how you conduct your work as a counselor or another therapeutic professional. Professional organizations at the state level are usually involved in legislative efforts relevant to the profession and can keep you informed, as well as get you involved. A second advantage of state organizations is that you get to network on a more local level with other professionals. You can meet with counselors practicing in similar specialties, network for referral sources, and reconnect with former classmates from your training program. A final advantage of membership in state professional organizations is that the member fees are usually less expensive than those at the national level.

You should get involved with at least one national or state organization while still in training. Spruill and Benshoff (1996) made the point that organizations need to recruit newly emerging professionals to maintain the vitality of the organizations. Often, the tasks that can be accomplished by a collective group exceed those that can be accomplished by an individual. When you find a professional organization whose mission statement is consistent with your ideals and aspirations, membership will be beneficial to both you and the organization.

SUMMARY

This chapter has attempted to acquaint you with some of the therapeutic professions you will come across in the field of agency counseling. Certainly, it has not exhausted the varieties and permutations of professionals or their duties, offering only an overview of key professions, the emphases of their training, and the relationship of their training to their professional duties, which may overlap a great deal. In the following discussion items, reflect on this material and how it relates to your choice of counseling as a profession.

DISCUSSION ITEMS

- Reflect on a time you may have been helped by a professional therapist. If you have had such an experience, what was the therapist's professional identity? Do you feel that this identity had an impact on the services you were offered? If you have never been to a professional therapist, imagine a situation in which you might go to one. Is there one type of professional you would seek out and, if so, why?
- If someone in your family with little knowledge of the various therapeutic professions needed to seek therapy, what type of professional do you think they would seek and why?
- Based on the various emphases in the integral model proposed in this chapter, which therapeutic profession do you think fits your temperament and why?
- Based on the chapter material, what do you think are the pros and cons of exclusive professional identities?
- What do you think is the best approach to collaboration across the professions discussed in this chapter?

REFERENCES

Adams, H. E. (1982). Alleged incompatibility of research and clinical training. *The Clinical Psychologist, 36*(1), 8–9.

Altekruse, M. K., & Wittmer, J. (1991). Accreditation in counselor education. In F. O. Bradley (Ed.), *Credentialing in counseling.* Alexandria, VA: Association for Counselor Supervision and Education.

American Counseling Association. (1998). Congress passes bill recognizing counselors under health professional training programs. *Counseling Today, 41,* 1, 11, 17, 19.

Ash, M. (1983). The self-presentation of a discipline: History of psychology in the United States between pedagogy and scholarship. In L. Graham, W. Lepinies, & P. Weingart (Eds.), *Functions and uses of disciplinary histories* (pp. 143–189). Boston: D. Reidel.

Bankart, P.C. (1996). *Talking cures: A history of Western and Eastern Psychotherapies.* Pacific Grove, CA: Brooks/Cole.

Barlow, D. H., & Durand, V. M. (1995). *Abnormal psychology: An integrative approach.* Pacific Grove, CA: Brooks/Cole.

Barstow, S., & Goetz, B. (1998). Senate bill makes counselors full partners in federal health professional training programs. *Counseling Today, 40*(10), 1.

Beers, C. (1908). *A mind that found itself.* New York: Doubleday.

Bell, J. E. (1961). *Family group therapy* (Public Health Monograph No. 64). Washington, DC: U.S. Government Printing Office.

Bender, W. (1993). Abraham Flexner: A crusader against medical maleducation. *Journal of Cancer Education, 8*(3), 83–189.

Berman, J. S., & Norton, N. C. (1985). Does professional training make a therapist more effective? *Psychological Bulletin, 98,* 401–406.

Bernard, L. D. (1995). North America and South America. In T. D. Watts, D. Elliott, & N. S. Mayadas (Eds.), *International handbook on social work education.* Westport, CT: Greenport Press.

Bradley, F. O. (Ed.). (1991). *Credentialing in counseling.* Alexandria, VA: Association for Counselor Supervision and Education.

Caplow, T. (1966). The sequence of professionalization. In H. M. Vollmer & D. L. Mills (Eds.), *Professionalization.* Englewood Cliffs, NJ: Prentice Hall.

Chiszar, D., & Wertheimer, M. (1988). The Boulder model: A history of psychology at the University of Colorado. *Journal of the History of the Behavioral Sciences, 24,* 81–86.

Christensen, A., & Jacobson, N. S. (1994). Who (or what) can do psychotherapy? The status and challenge of nonprofessional therapies. *Psychological Science, 5*(1), 8–14.

Cohen, C. I. (1993). The biomedicalization of psychiatry: A critical overview. *Community Mental Health Journal, 29*(6), 509–521.

Corey, G. (1996). *Theory and practice of counseling and psychotherapy* (5th ed.). Pacific Grove, CA: Brooks/Cole.

Cushman, P. (1992). Psychotherapy to 1992: A historically situated interpretation. In D. K. Freedheim (Ed.), *History of psychotherapy: A century of change* (pp. 21–65). Washington, DC: American Psychological Association.

Delworth, U. (1977). Counseling psychology: A distinct practice specialty. *The Counseling Psychologist, 7*(2), 43–45.

Durlak, J. (1979). Comparative effectiveness of paraprofessional and professional helpers. *Psychological Bulletin, 86,* 80–92.

Engel, G. L. (1977). The need for a new medical model: A challenge for biomedicine. *Science, 196*(4286), 129–136.

Exner, J. E. (1995). Why use personality tests? A brief historical view. In J. N. Butcher (Ed.), *Clinical personality assessment: Practical approaches* (pp. 10–18). New York: Oxford University Press.

Frank, G. (1984). The Boulder model: History, rationale, and critique. *Psychology: Research and Practice, 15*(3), 417–435.

Freedheim, D. K. (Ed.). (1992). *History of psychotherapy: A century of change.* Washington, DC: American Psychological Association.

Garfield, S. L., & Kurtz, R. (1974). A survey of clinical psychologists: Characteristics, activities, and orientation. *The Clinical Psychologist, 28*(1), 7–10.

George, R. L., & Christiani, T. S. (1995). *Counseling: Theory and practice* (4th ed.). Boston: Allyn & Bacon.

Gladding, S. T. (1995). *Family therapy: History, theory, and practice.* Englewood Cliffs, NJ: Merill.

Gladding, S. T. (1996). *Community and agency counseling.* Upper Saddle River, NJ: Prentice Hall.

Greenwood, E. (1962). Attributes of a profession. In S. Nosov & W. H. Form (Eds.), *Man, work, and society* (pp. 206–218). New York: Basic Books.

Hansen, J. C., Rossberg, R. H., & Cramer, S. H. (1994). *Counseling: Theory and process.* (5th ed.). Boston: Allyn & Bacon.

Hepworth, D. H., Rooney, R. H., & Larsen, J. A. (1997). *Direct social work practice: Theory and skills.* (5th ed.). Pacific Grove, CA: Brooks/Cole.

Herr, E. L., & Cramer, S. H. (1987). *Controversies in the mental health professions.* Muncie, IN: Accelerated Press.

Hershenson, D. B., Power, P. W., & Waldo, M. (1996). *Community counseling: Contemporary theory and practice.* Boston: Allyn & Bacon.

Hosie, T. W. (1991). Historical antecedents and current status of counselor licensure. In F. Bradley (Ed.), *Credentialing in counseling* (pp. 23–52). Alexandria, VA: American Counseling Association.

Ivey, A. E. (1994). *Intentional interviewing and counseling: Facilitating client development in a multicultural society* (3rd ed.). Pacific Grove, CA: Brooks/Cole.

Ivey, A. E. & Rigazio-Digilio, S. A. (1991). Toward a developmental practice of mental health counseling: Strategies for training, practice, and political unity. *Journal of Mental Health Counseling, 13*(1), 21–36.

Judd, P. (1987). Certifying substance abuse counselors: A unique training experiment pays off. *Journal of Alcohol and Drug Education, 32*(3), 49–52.

Koestler, A. (1967). *The ghost in the machine.* New York: Macmillan.

Kottler, J. A., & Brown, R. W. (1996). *Introduction to therapeutic counseling.* (3rd ed.). Pacific Grove, CA: Brooks/Cole.

Kovel, J. (1980). The American mental health industry. In D. Ingleby (Ed.), *Critical psychiatry.* New York: Pantheon.

Krauskopf, C. J., Thoresojn, R. W., & McAleer, C. A. (1973). Counseling psychology: The who, what, and where of our profession. *Journal of Counseling Psychology, 20,* 370–374.

Lanning, W. (1990). An educator/practitioner model for counselor education doctoral programs. *Counselor Education and Supervision, 30,* 163–168.

Levy, L. H. (1962). The skew in clinical psychology. *American Psychologist, 17,* 244–249.

Lu, F. G. (1996). Transpersonal psychiatry in psychiatric residency and training. In B. W. Scotton, A. B. Chinen, & J. R. Battista (Eds.), *Textbook of transpersonal psychiatry and psychology.* New York: Basic Books.

Martarazzo, R. T., & Garner, A. M. (1992). Research on training for psychotherapy. In D. K. Freedheim (Ed.), *History of psychotherapy: A century of change.* Washington, DC: American Psychological Association.

Montgomery, B. D. (1996). Opinion number 96–029. Official communication to The Ohio Counselor and Social Worker Board.

National Association of Social Workers. (1973). *Standards for Social Service Manpower.* Washington, DC.

National Association of Social Workers. (1996). *NASW Code of Ethics.* Washington, DC: Author.

Nejedlo, R. J., Hansen, L. S., & Myers, J. E. (1994). A strategic plan for AACD's future: The precursors of ACA. *Journal of Counseling and Development, 72,* 276–280.

Nietzel, M. T., & Fisher, S. G. (1981). Effectiveness of professional and paraprofessional helpers: A comment on Durlak. *Psychological Bulletin, 89,* 555–565.

Norcross, J. C., Gallagher, K. M., & Prochaska, J. O. (1989). The Boulder and/or Vail model: Training preferences of clinical psychologists. *Journal of Clinical Psychology, 45*(5), 822–828.

Ober, K. P. (1997). The pre-Flecnerian reports: Mark Twain's criticism of medicine in the United States. *Annals of Internal Medicine, 126*(2), 157–163.

Ohio Counselor and Social Work Board. (1997). *Laws and regulations governing the practice of counseling and social work.* Columbus, OH: Author.

Pallone, N. J. (1977). Counseling psychology: Toward an empirical definition. *The Counseling Psychologist, 7*(2), 29–32.

Peck, M. S. (1993). *Further along the road less traveled: The unending journey toward spiritual growth.* New York: Simon & Schuster.

Peck, M. S. (1997). *The road less traveled and beyond: Spiritual growth in an age of anxiety.* New York: Simon & Schuster.

Perry, W. G. (1955). The findings of the commission in counseling and guidance. *Annals: New York Academy of Science, 63,* 396–407.

Schmidt, L., & Chock, S. (1990). Counseling psychology at Ohio State University: The first fifty years. *Journal of Counseling and Development, 68,* 276–281.

Scott, R. A. (1980). Professional associations: The off-campus organizations of collegiate middle-managers. *College and University, 55,* 125–128.

Shimberg, B. & Roederer, D. (1978). *Occupational licensing: Questions a legislator should ask.* Lexington, KY: The Council of State Governments.

Specht, H., & Courtney, M. E. (1994). *Unfaithful angels: How social work has abandoned its mission.* New York: Free Press.

Sprinthall, N. A. (1990). Counseling psychology from Greyston to Atlanta: On the road to Armageddon? *The Counseling Psychologist, 18*(3), 455–463.

Spruill, D. A., & Benshoff, J. M. (1996). The future is now: Promoting professionalism among counselors-in-training. *Journal of Counseling and Development, 74,* 468–471.

Stude, E. W. (1990). Professionalization of substance abuse counseling. *Journal of Applied Rehabilitation Counseling, 21*(3), 11–15.

Sturm, R., & Klap, R. (1999). Use of psychiatrists, psychologists, and master's-level therapists in managed behavioral health care carve-out plans. *Psychiatric Services, 50,* 504–508.

Super, D. E. (1955). Transition: From vocational guidance to counseling psychology. *Journal of Counseling Psychology, 2,* 3–9.

Sweeney, T. J. (1991). Counselor credentialing: Purpose and origin. In F. Bradley (Ed.), *Credentialing in counseling* (pp. 23–52). Alexandria, VA: American Counseling Association.

Thorndike, R. L. (1955). The structure of preferences for psychological activities among psychologists. *American Psychologist, 10,* 205–207.

Turnbull, J. E., & Dietz-Uhler, B. (1995). The Boulder model: Lessons from clinical psychology for social work training. *Research on Social Work Practice, 5*(4), 411–429.

Tyler, L. E. (1969). *The work of the counselor.* (3rd ed.). New York: Appleton-Century-Crofts.

Vandenbos, G. R., Cummings, N. A., & Deleon, P.H. (1992). A century of influences. In Freedham, D. K. (Ed.), *History of psychotherapy: A century of change.* Washington, DC: American Psychological Assn.

Van Hesteren, F., & Ivey, A. E. (1990). Counseling and development: Toward a new identity for a profession in transition. *Journal of Counseling and Development, 68,* 534–536.

Victor, B. S. (1996). Transpersonal psychopharmacology and psychiatry. In B. W. Scotton, A. B. Chinen, & J. R. Battista (Eds.), *Textbook of transpersonal psychiatry and psychology.* New York: Basic Books.

Wilber, K. (1995). *Sex, ecology, spirituality: The spirit of evolution.* Boston: Shambhala.

Wilber, K. (1996). *A brief history of everything.* Boston: Shambhala.

Wilber, K. (1997). *The eye of spirit: An integral vision for a world gone slightly mad.* Boston: Shambhala.

Wright, G. N. (1980). *Total rehabilitation.* Boston, MA: Little, Brown.

Wylie, M. S. (1995, May/June). Diagnosing for dollars? *The Family Therapy Networker,* 22–33.

Yang, B. (1998). *Examining the relationship among three facets of knowledge: A holistic view.* Paper presented at the 1998 Adult Education Research Conference (AERC), San Antonio, TX.

Zastrow, C. (1992). *The practice of social work* (4th ed.). Belmont, CA: Wadsworth.

Zastrow, C. (1997). *Introduction to social work and social welfare* (6th ed.). Pacific Grove, CA: Brooks/Cole.

WEB SITES FOR NATIONAL ORGANIZATIONS

American Counseling Association	*www.counseling.org*
American Psychiatric Association	*www.psych.org*
American Psychological Association	*www.apa.org/*
American Mental Health Counselors Association	*www.amhco.org/home2.html*
National Association of Social Work	*www.naswdc.org/*
Council on Social Work Education	*www.cswe.org*

LIFE AS A COMMUNITY AGENCY COUNSELOR

CHAPTER

2

"You already have the precious mixture that will make you well. Use it."

Rumi

In the parking lot, waiting for the college reunion to begin, Edna wonders again about switching from Business to Human Services.

Our exploration of internal, personal qualities, beliefs, and preferences continues in this chapter, beginning with a discussion about the types of agencies in which you might find yourself employed. We will look at the types of duties and hours expected of you in those agencies. We will also describe the chain of command most commonly found in agency work and the types of credentials and qualifications held by people at each level in the chain. Later in the chapter, we will look at some harder to find information about other elements of the lives of agency counselors, including salaries, working conditions, paths for career advancement, and the importance of caring not only for your clients but for yourself.

The purpose of this chapter is to provide a realistic view of the life of an agency counselor and to clarify your expectations regarding the field. The field is changing; although your academic training may identify you as being a community agency counselor or mental health counselor, there are many places of employment outside of the typical agencies in which you might compete for a position.

The concluding sections of this chapter focus on self-care strategies and burnout. Burnout is a phenomenon that occurs in many professions, and it seems to take on added importance when an impaired employee is responsible for providing care to others. Burnout and self-care/wellness are paramount issues, regardless of one's position or profession. There is a high probability that, at some point in your career, you will have close contact with a professional who is experiencing burnout—if not yourself, then one of your co-workers. If you have not yet begun to use self-care strategies regularly, this chapter may help you do so. If you have, this chapter should reinforce that good choice.

EMPLOYMENT SETTINGS

We will begin first with a look at the kinds of settings you might find yourself working in after receiving your hard-earned university degree. Traditionally, federally funded mental health facilities typically offer services in at least the five categories of inpatient, partial hospitalization (alternatively referred to as intensive outpa-tient), outpatient, emergency care, and education/prevention/consultation (Thompson & Bass, 1984). The type of service they provide or the populations to whom they provide services can categorize human service agencies. Obviously, the level of functioning of the clients you are dealing with will depend somewhat on the nature of the agency for which you are working. You may work with clients who range from those who suffer from chronic mental illness and function mar-ginally to those who are highly successful in many areas of their lives.

Many clients with milder emotional disturbances are employed and may have some health benefits that cover mental health services. As the severity of a person's psychological impairment increases, it becomes increasingly un-likely that she or he will be able to maintain employment. Without employ-ment, most people could never afford their own health insurance; as a result, Medicaid is the only type of coverage these people may have. The type of cov-erage a client has (or doesn't have) dictates the types of services available to him or her. Changes in funding policy can have harmful effects on those suf-fering from severe mental/emotional disorders (see chapter 7, "Funding and Politics in Agency Counseling").

The primary distinction used in describing service delivery has been be-tween inpatient and outpatient. Since the 1960s, the norm has been to serve as many clients as possible in the least restrictive setting. Inpatient is the most restrictive setting and can include locked wards and restraints, if necessary. The next most restrictive setting is a residential treatment program—which may include locked areas, depending on the situation—but where clients are usually not assumed to be a threat to themselves or others. In most residential treatment settings, the clients live, do some work, and receive treatment. Staff are frequently "on-call," meaning that they wear a beeper and are available "24/7"—24 hours a day, 7 days a week.

Clients may also live in group homes that vary in the degree to which the clients are supervised. Often, clients who live in group homes attend a partial hospitalization or intensive outpatient program. Partial programs consist of structured programming that lasts several hours a day, with clients receiving group and individual counseling, participating in social-recreational groups, and perhaps receiving treatment in interpersonal/social and daily living skills. Partial programs may service clients suffering from more severe forms of mental/emotional disorders to clients who are suffering from a single episode disorder with only moderate impairment. Partial programs are typically day-treatment programs and rarely include on-call duty. For the person who en-joys a "9-to-5" day, the hours of partial programs may be attractive. There are also more and more day-treatment programs for elderly people that are run similar to partial programs.

Finally, there are outpatient counseling centers where the more tradi-tional one-to-one, group, and family therapy are done. Although you might imagine the stereotypical "50-minute-hour" in these settings, innovations, such as time-limited therapy (Budman & Gurman, 1988) and solution-focused therapy, are becoming the norm. The hours at outpatient centers need to be more flexible to accommodate clients who work a 9-to-5 day and may desire therapeutic services after work. Currently, there are many variations of outpatient treatment in which an agency counselor may be employed. Outpatient work includes private practice and participation in a managed care network. Also common in outpatient centers is the provision of consultation services, in which the counselors consult with ministers, teachers, and employers—individuals who are not themselves the identified patient.

The categories of service described may be uniquely tailored for specialization purposes. Some examples of service specialization, are agencies that specialize in delivering services to children or that focus on chemical dependency. You will also find residential agencies that deliver alcohol and substance abuse treatment only to adolescents. Although most internships and jobs for agency counselors are at out-patient facilities (including residential facilities), counselors are also employed in inpatient treatment centers. Funding policy plays an important role. In Cleveland, Ohio, one of the hospitals that provides mental health services will train interns only at its inpatient facility because Medicare/Medicaid funding will not reimburse for outpatient treatment done by unlicensed workers. Each service setting and client population has its own unique challenges, advantages, and disadvantages. The degree of comfort you experience working with specific clients depends on your temperament, preferences, and strengths and the place where you feel you have the most to offer those in need. In particular, your degree of comfort with certain types of clients is related to "blind spots"—areas in which you have disproportionately strong feelings—a topic we will discuss in chapter 3. Again, the clearer your understanding of yourself, the wiser your choice will be regarding the type of client with whom you work.

PRODUCTIVITY

The term *productivity* is one that has historically been associated with manufacturing and business. For reasons that will become clearer as you progress through this text, productivity now plays a significant role in many jobs in the mental health field. Productivity is an aspect of agency management that greatly affects working conditions.

In the context of mental health agency work, *productivity* refers to the number of billable hours a clinician generates in the course of a day, week, or other specified period of time. The billable hours generate money for the agency and your paycheck. If you are working in an agency, productivity will be very important to the administration. If you work in private practice, it will be very important to you.

We will discuss funding structures for agencies in greater detail in chapter 7. Presently we do need to note that an agency's financial solvency comes down to the collective staff's generating enough money through billing, grant writing, and state and federal funds to cover the overhead costs of salaries and operating expenses. This statement is no surprise in a capitalist society, but it is amazing how many of us fail to understand the need for financial solvency in human services. In years past, most agency funding came from the state and federal governments, and staff did not need to concern themselves very much with income sources. Now, most agencies have a specified number of client contact hours, which must be averaged over a period of time. The staff's ability to fulfill these expectations becomes their productivity rating. Usually, the expectations are reasonable, but there are exceptions.

> I was working in an agency where the client caseload was close to 100 clients per therapist. This went on for almost a year, with the therapists expected to see each client at least twice monthly. Staff requests were consistently denied a fair hearing by the administrators, and finally a therapists' union was formed (the first ever in that town). Within a month of the union's moving in, a strike ensued and staff demands were finally negotiated. The process was quite adversarial and, even though working conditions improved dramatically, staff morale and the relationships between therapists and administrators never recovered.

Productivity expectations will have a direct impact on your experience of your work. The productivity standards will dictate how many clients per week you are responsible for treating to meet your minimum billing requirement. Some agencies now offer profit-sharing incentives, in which a clinician can earn a bonus on her or his base salary if production exceeds a certain number of billable hours within a given period. For example, an agency may set productivity at 25 contact hours per week and offer clinicians a salary increment of 2.5 percent of their base if they meet 95 percent of the production standard or a 3.3 percent increment if they meet 100 percent of the production standard over a six-month period of time. An agency that tried the latter incentive found staff to be quite pleased with the arrangement; the agency increased its revenues as well (Buckner & Larcen, 1985).

One recent job posting stipulated a minimum of one hour of billable time for every hour of nonbillable time. This would mean an average of 20 billable hours in a 40-hour week. To further break it down, getting 20 contact hours in a 5-day week would mean seeing four clients per day. This is a reasonable production standard. In a 40-hour workweek, a common production rate is between 22 and 25 hours per week. Remember that, in those 40 hours, you have additional responsibilities besides counseling. You will be expected to complete paperwork (such as authorizations for treatment, treatment plans, progress notes, and releases of information), to provide possible emergency coverage, to provide crisis intervention, and to attend staff meetings and supervision sessions.

When your schedule moves smoothly, and clients keep their scheduled appointments, the productivity standards do not add significantly to the job pressures. However, things often do not run according to plan and schedules are frequently rearranged. One major source of rearranged schedules is clients who habitually reschedule and/or miss appointments. The degree to which this will be a problem is linked directly to the client population with whom you will work.

Clients who are court-ordered or not strongly committed to treatment tend to miss more sessions, but even clients with whom you have a good therapeutic alliance will occasionally miss an appointment. Some clinicians whose clients miss a lot of appointments handle this problem by scheduling clients in every available hour of the day, "overbooking" as an airline does. The problem with this strategy is that a couple of days in which every client comes to her or his appointment can exhaust you and decrease the quality of services you offer. Other clinicians manage the problem by setting firm limits and response-cost punishments with clients who miss appointments.

A common response-cost punishment is requiring clients to pay for appointments not canceled 24 hours in advance. The disadvantage of this strategy is that it is not easy to enforce and many clients receive sliding-fees or do not pay for their sessions at all because of their insurance benefits. With most clients who are motivated to be in counseling, this arrangement seems to work. If the client cancels the appointment ahead of time, then the hour can be rescheduled to maintain productivity. For clients who consistently miss appointments, some agencies have a policy that after a specified number of "no shows" services to that client will be terminated. When you are interviewing for an agency job, it is important to inquire about productivity rates and the no show policy. A bad combination of high productivity rates and a lax no show policy can easily feed counselor burnout.

One way recent graduates of master's programs get their foot in the door of potential full-time employment is through p.r.n. counseling. The borrowed medical abbreviation simply means "as needed." Many agencies will contract with therapists on a p.r.n. basis. Although this is a good way to begin working with clients and show an agency what skills you have, there are important elements you should consider before taking such a position.

First, you will usually get paid only for time spent with the client; thus, time spent on ever present paper work is essentially unpaid unless you can negotiate a high enough wage to make up for that time. Second, if a client cancels an appointment, you will not usually get paid for the session unless there is an agreement between the agency and the client about uncancelled appointments and the agency is able to collect the fee. Last, there are substantial federal tax penalties when your status is self-employed, not the least of which is the Federal Insurance Contributions Act (FICA), tax which covers Social Security, workers' compensation, and Medicare. The total FICA tax equals approximately 15 percent of your wages. When others employ you, your employer deducts 7.65 percent from your pay and then matches it, so your employer pays 50 percent of the FICA and files the appropriate forms. When you are self-employed, you pay the total FICA (15.3 percent of your wage) and must frequently file quarterly returns.

One other agency job worth mentioning is case management. Many therapists enter the workforce by taking jobs as case managers. Case management has traditionally been differentiated from the therapeutic professions in that it is typically a position requiring only an undergraduate degree and it is less involved with the provision of therapeutic services. State mental health authorities have recently begun to prioritize case management as an area for both development and funding (Ellison, Rogers, Sciarappa, Cohen, & Forbess, 1995). It is important to understand that there are a number of case-management models in use. Your particular duties and job description would be based on the model used by your place of employment. Ellison et. al (1995) conducted a national survey of case-management programs to get descriptive information about the types of case-management services available to people with severe mental/emotional disorders. The average case managers were age 20–39, female, with a bachelor's degree in social work. The typical case-management caseload ranged from 1 to 300, depending on the client's needs. The case manager supervisors were more likely to hold master's degrees, were less likely to identify themselves as social workers, and had an average of 11 years' work with people suffering from mental/emotional disorders. The typical case manager annual salary was $20,559, whereas the case manager supervisor salaries averaged $29,873. The most common case-management activities were linking clients to services, performing crisis intervention, planning services, and performing assessment. By far the most common purpose of the case-management programs was the prevention of hospitalization, followed by the improvement of quality of life, the improvement of clients' levels of functioning, the empowerment of clients to determine their own goals, and the maximization of client's independence.

TYPICAL CAREER PATHS IN COMMUNITY AGENCY WORK

In career planning, it can be helpful to know what paths of advancement are typically available within an agency structure. There are usually four or five levels in the chain of command of a service agency. The lowest level in terms of salary and responsibility is usually the support staff. These people provide clerical and other support services, such as processing billing, submitting insurance claims, and functioning as receptionists. The next level of salary and responsibility are the staff who provide direct services to the clients. These positions are the typical entry-level positions for people trained as therapeutic professionals at the master's level. There can also be staff in direct care positions who have advanced degrees in psychology or who are psychiatrists.

The next level in the agency organization is midlevel management. Most often, people in mid-level management positions have several years of experience providing direct care to the client population. Common titles of staff in agency mid-management include clinical supervisor, clinical director, and medical director. They usually have a variety of responsibilities, often a combination of direct service and administrative tasks. For example, a clinical supervisor might be expected to carry a caseload of clients that is approximately half of what the direct care staff carries. The rest of the time, the clinical supervisor provides supervision to direct service staff, arranges for emergency coverage, troubleshoots problems, and interviews prospective interns and new employees. The larger the agency, the higher the number of midlevel supervisor positions that are necessary for the agency to run smoothly. Some large agencies that have residential and outpatient components may have 10 to 12 midlevel supervisors, whereas a small community mental health agency in a rural area might have only 1 or no midlevel supervisors.

Further up the chain of command is upper management. This is the highest agency position to which you might aspire if your ultimate career goals are set on administration. Typical job titles include assistant director, executive director, chief of services, and chief executive officer. People in these positions usually have totally administrative duties with no client contact (although it probably helps if they have some prior experience as a therapeutic professional). A large responsibility of upper management is securing funding, especially in the form of grants. At this level of employment, grant writing is a critical skill and public relations is an important duty. Even though an agency may begin with grant monies, those monies are typically time limited, and it is the administrators' responsibility to secure ongoing funding at the local, state, and federal levels. Knowledge of research design is critical because, to convince funding sources to give money, you must be able to demonstrate that your agency is effective in addressing its clients' mental health problems. Other administrative duties include negotiating contracts with managed mental health care organizations, reporting to the agency's board of directors, and making sure that the agency is running efficiently.

People who serve as agency directors might have a graduate degree in a therapeutic profession but may just as likely hold a degree in business. Some graduate programs that train therapeutic professionals offer academic tracks in administration.

A number of agency administrators began their careers providing direct clinical services. Having an employment background as a counselor, and becoming an administrator, can have advantages and disadvantages. Sometimes people who are stellar therapists are ineffective managers or administrators because the interpersonal and clinical skills that lend themselves to providing good therapy are not necessarily conducive to running an agency. Being able to empathize and structure relationships in an egalitarian manner are important to many types of therapeutic encounters, but to run an agency difficult decisions must often be made without consultation, and structure must sometimes be imposed on people who would rather not deal with it. If you find administration attractive, you may consider some coursework in administration or management or, at the very least, do some reading in these areas. Take a minute to think about a good supervisor under whom you worked. What were the characteristics related to that person's success? Would your own strengths and abilities be a good fit for that type of work?

STANDARD OF LIVING

Money can't buy you love, but it sure comes close!

Anonymous

As our personal, inner exploration continues, we will cover typical salaries, typical work schedules, and other aspects of life as an agency counselor that will affect how you live. Many students express curiosity about typical starting and median salaries for agency counselors. Salaries vary depending on the geographic region and the source of funding for the agency. In the United States, human services are among the lower-paid occupations. This seems to result from a conflict of the myth of the "rugged individualism" underlying our capitalist system and questions about how responsible a democratic government is for providing for those who are unable to be "rugged," and "individualistic." Regardless of the reasons underlying the amount human services workers earn, you must keep in mind that, to land an attractive position, human services work is like any other profession.

You must hone your skills, understand what the strongest markets are, and then adequately market yourself when you are competing for positions. For example, a booming area in counseling is working with elderly clients, particularly those living in nursing home facilities. With the exponential growth in the number of elderly people in this country, there has been a subsequent growth in the number of facilities for those who cannot care for themselves. All nursing home clients are required to have some psychological screening done to check their well-being and, if necessary, to receive the option of counseling services. Although no master's-level therapist can currently bill for Medicare reimbursement, one *can* work under the supervision of psychologists and psychiatrists. Since the increase in the elderly segment of the population, many private companies have been created whose sole function is to provide contracted counseling services in as many nursing homes as possible.

One general rule to keep in mind is that there tends to be a connection between the status of a counselor's license or certification and the counselor's employability and earning potential. Although some states do not have licensure laws, in the states that do, having a license clearly improves your attractiveness to employers and increases the amount of money you can expect to make. Sometimes, unfortunately, the difference between licensed and unlicensed counselors' salaries is not huge. Nevertheless, in a state that has a counselor licensure law, the likelihood of employment and competitive salary is increased for counselors who have their license.

In chapter 3, we will focus on the importance of clarifying your motives for pursuing a career in counseling. For most students, there is probably some element of wanting or needing to give to other people. A conflict can result when the performance of that service means the sacrifice of things that are important to you—such as income and time. It is much easier to serve others, whether vocationally or personally, when your own basic needs are met. If the salary you are earning is not enough for you to make rent payments, or buy the type of clothing you are expected to wear at work, you will probably find it hard to focus on your clients' needs.

It is important to have a clear vision of what sort of lifestyle you desire and an understanding of how much money you need to earn to support that lifestyle. For example, are you married, partnered, or single? Will your income be primary or secondary? Do you have to pay for medical costs or do you have insurance? To help you identify an acceptable salary range to meet your expenses, see the budget worksheet at the end of this chapter. Financial considerations are of vital importance if you are to experience satisfaction in your career.

Each of us must determine for ourselves what elements of our lives are most important for our own happiness. For some people, those important elements are materially based, whereas for others they are more spiritually or relationally based. Some people find great enjoyment engaging in activities that cost little money, such as walking in the woods, whereas others enjoy activities that can be costly, such as fine dining or skydiving. The important point is that you must be honest with yourself about the aspects of your life that need to be fulfilled to feel satisfied and what conditions are required to incorporate those elements. If your income is not sufficient to support your lifestyle, you can opt to make more money, adjust your priorities, or find other activities that are as satisfying without costing as much money. If proximity to family is of utmost importance, you need to consider the job market for counselors in the immediate geographic area to where your family members reside.

Regardless of the particulars, without considering life fulfillment issues, you may enter the field and find yourself feeling disillusioned or misled. This

TABLE 2.1 **A COMPARISON OF EDUCATIONAL REQUIREMENTS AND NATIONALLY AVERAGED SALARIES OF MENTAL HEALTH PROFESSIONALS**

	Degree	Salary
Case manager	B.A.	$ 22,000
Licensed independent social worker	M.S.W. (2–3 years post-B.A.)	$ 37,000
Licensed clinical/ professional counselor	M.Ed., M.S. (2–3 years post-B.A.)	$ 35,800
Psychologist	Ph.D., Psy.D. (3–5 years post-master's)	$ 55,000
Psychiatrist	M.D., D.O. (B.S., 4 years medical school, 2 years residency)	$124,000

Source: U.S. Department of Labor (1998).

is an issue best dealt with at the beginning of your graduate training, before you have invested great amounts of time, energy, and money. For some students, the issue of income and salary is a big part of this picture. If you honestly consider your own needs for financial stability, leisure activities, liquid assets, and so on and ascertain that the salary ranges in counseling will not meet those needs, you might need to do some further career exploration of options that will allow you to meet them. You may supplement your income with a second job, or you might aspire to the higher-paying positions in the human services. In table 2.1 is information about several occupations in the mental health field, the amount of time it takes to obtain the minimum degree, and typical salary range (U.S. Department of Labor, 1998). Again, keep in mind that these are *national* averages, combining figures from the rural, sparsely populated regions with figures from the more urban areas and heavily populated regions. There will be variations in these numbers either higher or lower, depending on the region of the country.

Salary ranges vary, depending on the cost of living in the area where you reside and the type of fee that pays your salary. For example, professional counselors in private practice across the country earn a median fee of approximately $60 per hour from managed care contracts. Counselors in southern and eastern states earn more per hour from third-party reimbursement and direct-pay clients than do counselors in western and midwestern states. Although managed care is becoming the norm in terms of mental health benefits, more and more clients are paying out-of-pocket to see therapists because of the lack of confidentiality in managed care settings (Ridgewood Financial Institute, 1997). According to the Ridgewood Institute, 1997 was the first year since 1979 in which all therapeutic professionals' fees showed a decrease.

Among the various types of therapeutic professionals, psychiatrists and psychologists are generally paid the most, with masters'-level practitioners (counselors, social workers, and marriage and family therapists) being paid less. In chapter 1, we discussed the duties of various therapeutic professionals. In summary, there is a great deal of overlap between the professionals, despite sometimes significant differences in salary levels.

A Typical Work Schedule

The societal norm in the United States for defining full-time employment is 40 hours per week. This is usually understood as an 8-hour workday with either a half-hour or hour-long lunch. The specific times you work will depend on the type of agency, the client population, and the position you hold. For example, programs dealing with troubled youth have hours after school, whereas partial hospitalization programs run through the day. Other programs, such as those for chemical dependency, have evening hours, so clients can receive treatment after work. A mental health center offering a range of services typically has normal business hours, 8:30 A.M. to 5:00 P.M., perhaps with selected weeknights when evening appointments are available. Some residential facilities have staff that may actually live in the facility with clients for specified periods (three days on, three days off). Residential staff are typically bachelor's-level employees who are not doing counseling per se with clients. Even in residential facilities, most of the therapeutic staff have graduate degrees and leave the facility at the end of the day.

> At one mental health center where I worked, it was left to the therapists' discretion how they wanted to accumulate their 40 hours, so the therapists were permitted to work more hours per day to have a four-day workweek with a three-day weekend. Many therapists found working from 8:30 A.M. to about 7:00 P.M. to be a lengthy day but worth it to have Fridays off. Another common arrangement was for the therapists to work a regular day plus 4 additional hours until 9:00 P.M. on one day so they could leave at noon on Friday. My half-day off I spent doing an outdoor activity, such as hiking or biking.

A planned schedule from a typical workday in a community counseling center might be as follows:

8:30–9:00	Arrive at work, return phone calls from previous day if necessary, review charts for clients scheduled that day
9:00–10:30	Staff meeting
10:30–11:00	Return phone calls, handle emergencies
11:00–12:00	Client A
12:00–1:00	Lunch, check messages
1:00–2:00	Client B

2:00–3:00	Client C
3:00–4:00	Client D
4:00–5:30	Call insurance companies, return phone calls, write progress notes

In reviewing this schedule, you might note that there are no scheduled times for intervening in crisis situations with current clients.

EFFECTIVE COUNSELING AND COUNSELOR WELLNESS

In chapter 3, we discussed the value of knowing yourself and understanding your motivations for becoming a professional counselor. Also within the realm of providing competent services to your clients is the issue of taking care of yourself. The adage *do as I say, not as I do* has always been a horrific failure when applied to childrearing and is equally useless as a motto for counselors. The concept of modeling self-care if you want your clients to be healthy is based on the principle that you cannot expect others to do what you yourself are unwilling to do. As Jeff Kottler has written, this is one of the positives of being a therapeutic professional. If you are not doing what you need to do to take care of yourself, you will have difficulty helping clients engage in their own self-care plans.

> At one point, I was teaching part-time at three universities, working evenings as a musician, studying for my licensure exam, and finishing my postdoctoral internship. For the internship, I was seeing nursing home clients, for the most part suffered from depression related to their many losses. One woman in particular, when she saw me come into the home, would make a point to ask me to stop in to see her. This I would do weekly. After about a month, it seemed clear that, unlike most of her peers, she had adjusted quite well to the nursing home, had family visits, and was relatively active in attending the social-recreational functions. Realizing this, I asked her why she wanted to meet with me weekly. Smiling, she said, "You just seem so exhausted all the time I thought you could use some 'easy' conversation."

Sleep

One thing most of us learn in graduate school is that sleep and recreation are luxuries for the independently wealthy. Although this lesson probably gets many of us through higher education, it needs to be unlearned when we leave that environment. When you arrive at work in the morning with six or seven clients scheduled that day, you need to be well rested and enthused spiritually and emotionally. The desired effect of being well rested and centered is that you can then put your own issues and concerns aside to focus fully on your clients. This is essential for an effective therapeutic relationship to develop and be maintained. If you have ever cared for a newborn or an infant you are probably aware of the depression and disorganization that can accompany sleep deprivation.

One student revealed that she was seeing a counselor who actually fell asleep during two sessions. Far from executing an effective paradoxical technique, the counselor was simply exhausted. The student did not return to that counselor. Perhaps the therapist was having personal difficulties that were disrupting her sleep, or perhaps she had a medical problem. Whatever the case, the client was short-changed in several ways—paying for sessions that were not beneficial and, even more harmful, receiving nonverbal messages that her concerns were unimportant.

Burnout

Feeling rested and reasonably energetic during your workday is clearly the optimal condition. Even under the best of circumstances, a full day of seeing clients can be very draining. Working with clients who are in emotional pain, have traumatic histories, and may be resistant and noncompliant takes a toll. A relatively new phenomenon, this "secondary trauma" has become a focus of professional attention. Secondary trauma can occur among mental health professionals who work with clients who have been exposed to severe trauma, such as child abuse, rape, family violence, or war.

Other work pressures, such as productivity, paperwork deadlines, and hassles with insurance reimbursement can all contribute to therapist stress and burnout. The term *burnout* comes from the psychiatric concept of patients who are "wasted" physically, emotionally, spiritually, interpersonally, and behaviorally (Paine, 1982). It was first coined by Herbert Fredenberger, who used it to describe young, idealistic volunteers who were working with him in alternate health-care settings and who started looking and acting worse than the clients they were treating. Burnout is when all your psychic energy is consumed in trying to fuel the fires of existence. All your energy is going into basic survival. Because of this, your ability to cope is severely compromised. Gladding (1997) defined burnout as being so emotionally or physically drained that you cannot perform your job functions meaningfully. Skorupa and Agresti (1993) found that some psychologists actually conceptualize burnout as a form of therapist impairment, making it unethical for such therapists to continue seeing clients until the situation is rectified.

Some authors have observed that, in addition to emotional exhaustion, burnout is typified by a cynical and dehumanizing perception of clients, and sometimes the labeling of clients in a derogatory manner. Other symptoms of burnout include absenteeism, substance abuse, marital conflict, and the exacerbation of other mental/emotional disorders. Gilliland and James (1993) summarized the cornerstones of the burnout experience as (a) the loss of a sense of clarity about your roles (role ambiguity), (b) work demands that are in conflict with your ethics and values (role conflict), (c) work demands that are too great to be met by one person (role overload), and (d) a sense that, no matter how hard you work, nothing changes (inconsequentiality). Edelwich and Brodsky (1982) observed that burnout seems to progress through recognizable stages. In the first stage of "enthusiasm," a person enters the helping professions with high hopes and few reality-testing skills. In the second stage, labeled "stagnation," the worker begins to feel that her or his needs are not being met. These needs are value-oriented, financial, or another type. If a change or reinforcement does not occur here, the person will likely move on to the "frustration" stage, where she or he starts questioning her or his effectiveness, value, and general worth. If no intervention occurs, the person will likely move to the "apathy" stage, where she or he will suffer from chronic indifference, excessive "gallows humor," and general cynicism.

Certainly, most people who enter human service professions are highly motivated and expect their work to add meaning to their lives. What happens along the way that causes burnout? Burnout is "overdetermined'," meaning there are multiple causes. The causes can be characterized as coming from internal (intrapersonal), external, or cultural sources. Internal factors that contribute to burnout include idealism, perfectionism, difficulty drawing boundaries, and poor ego-strength. Difficulty drawing boundaries with clients can profoundly affect your perception of the counseling process when your clients are in a great deal of pain. External factors that play into the burnout process include long, erratic work hours; low pay; low-functioning clients; highly resistant clients; lack of control over agency bureaucracy; paperwork; hassles with managed care companies or other insurance carriers; and strings of crises. The cultural contributions to burnout include the conservative climate in terms of spending on mental health and the conflict between the "wellness" and "illness" paradigms in mental health. This conflict was alluded to earlier in chapter 1 when we examined the power of the medical model in mental health. Although many therapeutic professions (such as counseling psychology and counseling) begin with an emphasis on wellness, they eventually end up focused on pathology because of the medical domination in the realms of diagnosis and research. Knowing this (as well as the other factors that can lead to burnout) can help you establish a proactive strategy to preclude it.

The Prevention of Burnout   Preventing burnout and developing an effective stress-management lifestyle for yourself are two sides of the same coin. It doesn't take a Ph.D. to realize that the pace of American society is unnatural and produces harmful levels of stress. In this section, we will explore some practices that can help you maintain your mental health and wellness. Be aware that some of these suggestions do not derive from data-based studies. As noted in chapter 6, most outcome studies of what makes therapy effective, for example, hinge on the uncontrolled variable of the therapeutic relationship. This teaches us that often, what is effective is not always easily measured in the traditional ways. Most therapists accept this, and some use rituals as a nontangible practice to maintain wellness at work. One example is a clinician who has been in the field 12 years and says the serenity prayer at the beginning of each workday. This prayer states, "God grant me the ability to change what I can, the ability to let go of what I cannot, and the wisdom to know the difference." The prayer reminds the clinician of what he can offer his clients to help them improve and that, ultimately, each client must make the decision to get better. An intended message of the serenity prayer is to encourage people to distinguish between stressors over which they have no control versus those over which they have control. This understanding of the prayer transforms its use into a cognitive strategy.

A more detailed cognitive strategy was presented by Fetsch (1992), wherein you identify stressors, prioritize the top three or four, and then assign a number that represents how much control you have over the prioritized stressors. In subsequent steps, you assess your beliefs about the stressors, as well as the resources you have for dealing with stressors over which you have little control. This can be a very helpful technique as you begin your work as an agency counselor. You must understand the degree of responsibility you have for your clients' improvement and not foster irrational beliefs about being primarily responsible for their meeting their goals.

One other technique for preventing burnout, which transcends many other variables, is appropriate assertiveness. Some people may habitually assume more responsibilities than they can reasonably meet, because they fear declining the responsibilities or believe that others expect more of them. You need to be aware of what responsibilities you can handle and when the load of responsibility becomes to heavy to bear. Setting appropriate limits at work means not volunteering to help with extra projects, such as fund raisers and peer reviews, if those activities are not considered part of the paid 40-hour week. Setting appropriate limits elsewhere means keeping enough free time in your schedule to do the activities that are important to you for your own mental health.

Gilliland and James (1993) noted several interventions for burnout. The first is preventive intervention through training. Knowing the signs and symptoms, being able to recognize them in yourself, knowing how to set limits, and deciding how you are going to deal with bureaucracy can all help you preclude having a burnout experience. In addition, learning how to correct attitudes that lead to overinvolvement and that facilitate therapeutic detachment will keep your boundaries strong and your work life healthy.

Counseling Interventions for Burnout   Since much burnout is situational, an organizational intervention can prove effective if the organization is open to it. The paradox is that, the more an organization needs the burnout intervention, the less receptive it is to that intervention. Lack of reinforcement in human service institutions is quite common. One advantage of managed care is that, if you see more clients, the odds are you will earn more money. This type of built-in reinforcer can help prevent burnout. Organizations can also move to enhance the functioning of the organization through support systems, support in supervision, therapeutic services, and workshops. Interventions with the individual typically include engaging in counseling, prioritizing needs, and learning relaxation. This is most effective at the frustration stage.

One strategy that seems to help some therapists recharge their batteries is to allow 10 to 15 minutes between clients, rather than saying goodbye to one client while ushering the next one through your office door. It can also be helpful, if you know you have a difficult client coming in, to schedule that person at the time of day you feel most energized. Being aware of what you need in terms of your work schedule accomplishes the dual tasks of maximizing your effectiveness and modeling healthy time (and energy) management.

Physical Health

The cost of neglecting yourself can manifest in areas other than work performance and interpersonal relationships. Some studies have found a significant relationship between physical disorders and one's degree of stress. For example, it has been estimated that there are approximately 7 million people who suffer back pain that is most likely stress-related (Veninga & Spradley, 1981). Hypertension can also be stress-related, and cancer patients whose symptoms were in remission sometimes suffer reactivation of the cancer after periods of extreme stress (Yates, 1979). Although you probably hear about the following practices in the media and from the medical profession, they are sufficiently important to discuss them here in the context of healthy lifestyle. One is adequate nutrition—eating a balanced diet not too high in fat or processed foods. At the very least, this means using your lunch hour to eat lunch or relax rather than working through it.

There is substantial evidence that points to exercise as a way to maintain both physical and psychological health. Particularly, exercise seems to alleviate some symptoms of depression (which is one of the most common mental/emotional disorders in industrialized countries). The specific physiological mechanism appears to be related to endorphins (opiates produced in the brain), which are released with prolonged, strenuous activity (Lobstein, Rasmussen, Dunphy, & Dunphy, 1989; Thoren, Floras, Hoffman, & Seals, 1990;

Williams & Getty, 1986). Schafer (1987) cited some very specific emotional benefits in subjects who exercised for a minimum of 20 minutes per day, three or more times per week. Those who exercised five times per week reported significantly more internal control, energy, self-esteem, and playfulness than those who exercised only three times per week. The more frequent exercisers also reported significantly fewer symptoms of distress, irritability, emotional tension, depression, and loneliness.

The type of work you will be doing as a therapist is usually quite sedentary: sitting with clients, talking on the phone, doing paperwork. Exercise is also beneficial from the standpoint of both physical and mental health; regular exercise should be part of your weekly schedule. With regular exercise, moods are more stable and bodies feel better.

Substance Abuse

Good, Thoreson, and Shaughnessy (1995) identified substance abuse as a potentially serious problem among counseling psychologists. In a survey of psychologists in a midwestern state psychological association, 9 percent of the respondents self-identified as having an alcohol problem (Thoreson, Miller, & Krauskopf, 1989). Maslach and Ayala (1977) made a similar statement about day-care workers being at higher risk for substance abuse when they are burned out. Despite the national hysteria surrounding substance use, moderate drinking is actually correlated with longer life expectancy than are both abstinence and chronic consumption (Turner, Bennett, & Hernandez, 1981). Although it can be very reinforcing to unwind with alcohol at the end of a long day, as a habit this can lead to other health problems and, in some people, dependence. Along with moderation, being able to recognize your reasons for drinking can help you identify when it is better to abstain. Although there are fierce debates on this issue, there is alcohol "use" and alcohol "abuse." The category your consumption fits is directly related to your reasons for drinking. Each person must honestly discern relevant situations and make her or his own choices.

Obviously, alcohol is not the only substance therapeutic professionals use or abuse. Therapists (like many Americans) may use illicit substances. There are numerous illicit drugs of abuse, with some far more dependence-inducing than others. Across cultures, human beings seek ways to alter their consciousness chemically, and our society is no different. Great debate still wages on such issues as marijuana legalization and whether marijuana is even as potentially dangerous as legal drugs, such as alcohol. For some drugs, such as marijuana, the legal risks may outweigh the health risks. Many states' licensure laws include the use of illicit substances under the impaired practitioner guidelines. This means that an arrest related to the use of illegal substances could cost you your license and your career. Perhaps in the future, drugs such as marijuana will be legal options for those who desire them, but presently the climate in our society is unforgiving on this issue.

It is best to keep the use of alcohol to a minimum, and other psychoactive substances should simply be avoided. Relying on alcohol or drugs for stress reduction puts the user at risk for emotional or physical dependence. It is healthier both physically and emotionally to seek other strategies to obtain relaxation and well-being.

SUMMARY

We have covered a number of issues related to how your daily life will be after you have completed your graduate training. You should be aware of variables that will contribute to your level of satisfaction with your career choice, standard of living, and general lifestyle. We have explored those issues in a context that is respectfully aware of the multitude of belief systems and worldviews.

The strategies we have discussed in this chapter will help you maintain a fresh outlook and positive feeling about the work you are doing. It is critical that you work out a schedule for yourself that allows ample time to recharge the battery. This means developing and maintaining stability in your personal schedule and meeting your physical, spiritual, emotional, and social needs in healthy ways.

DISCUSSION ITEMS

1. Think of someone you have known who was burned out at work. What were the main things she or he did that exemplified burnout?
2. What warning signs would tell you that you were experiencing an unhealthy stress level?
3. Rank the following items in order from most to least important. Discuss your ranking in your discussion group.

Salary	Working conditions
Co-workers	Schedule flexibility
Clientele	Adequate supervision

BUDGET WORKSHEET

CATEGORY	MONTHLY EXPENDITURE
Housing	_____
Food	_____
Clothing	_____
Automobile/transportation	_____
Insurance (home, car, health)	_____
Medical expenses	_____
Support for other family members or dependents	_____
School	_____
Payment for debts incurred	_____
Taxes	_____
Other	_____

Once you get a total, add $150–$200. This is for those expenses that come up unexpectedly or those that you may not be thinking about as you fill out this sheet.

REFERENCES

Buckner, M., & Larcen, S. W. (1985). Strategies for increasing productivity and revenues in community mental health centers. *Community Mental Health Journal, 21,* 237–251.

Budman, S., & Gurman, A. S. (1988). *Theory and practice of brief psychotherapy.* New York: Guilford Press.

Edelwich, J., & Brodsky, A. (1982). Training guidelines: Linking the workshop experience to needs on and off the job. In W. S. Paine (Ed.), *Job stress and burnout.* Beverly Hills, CA: Sage.

Ellison, M. L., Rogers, E. S., Sciarappa, K., Cohen, M. F., & Forbess, R. (1995). Characteristics of mental health case management: Results of a national survey. *The Journal of Mental Health Administration, 22,* 101–112.

Fetsch, R. J. (1992) The predicament-problem continuum: Dealing with stressors outside our control. *Journal of Counseling and Development, 71,* 192–193.

Gilliland, B. E., & James, R. K. (1993). *Crisis intervention strategies* (2nd ed.). Pacific Grove, CA: Brooks/Cole.

Gladding, S. T. (1997). *Community agency counseling.* Upper Saddle River, NJ: Merrill–Prentice Hall.

Good, G. E., Thoreson, R. W., & Shaughnessy, O. (1995). Substance use, confrontation of impaired colleagues, and psychological functioning among counseling psychologists: A national survey. *The Counseling Psychologist, 23,* 703–721.

Lobstein, D. D., Rasmussen, C. L., Dunphy, G. E., & Dunphy, M. J. (1989). Beta-endorphin and components of depression as powerful discriminators between joggers and sedentary middle-aged men. *Journal of Psychosomatic Research, 33,* 293–305.

Maslach, C., & Ayala, P. (1977). The burn-out syndrome in the day care setting. *Child Care Quarterly, 6*(2), 100–113.

Paine, W. S. (1982). *Job stress and burnout.* Beverly Hills, CA: Sage.

Ridgewood Financial Institute. (1997). Therapists' fees and incomes are under growing pressure. *Psychotherapy Finances, 23*(5), 1–12.

Schafer, W. (1987). *Stress management for wellness.* New York: Holt, Rinehart, & Winston.

Skorupa, J., & Agresti, A. A. (1993). Ethical beliefs about burnout and continued professional practice. *Professional Psychology: Research and Practice, 24,* 281–285.

Thompson, J. W., & Bass, R. D. (1984). Changing staffing patterns in community mental health centers. *Hospital and Community Psychiatry, 35,* 1107–1114.

Thoren, P., Floras, J. S., Hoffman, P., & Seals, D. R. (1990). Endorphins and exercise: Physiological mechanisms and clinical implications. *Medicine and Science in Sports and Exercise, 22,* 417–428.

Thoreson, R. W., Miller, M., & Krauskopf, C. J. (1989). The distressed psychologist: Prevalence and treatment considerations. *Professional Psychology: Research and Practice, 20,* 153–158.

Turner, T. B., Bennett, V. L., & Hernandez, H. (1981). The beneficial side of moderate alcohol use. *Johns Hopkins Medical Journal, 148,* 53–63.

U.S. Department of Labor. (1998). *Occupational outlook handbook (1998–99 ed.).* Lincolnwood, IL: VGM Horizons.

Veninga, R. K., & Spradley, J. P. (1981). *Work-stress connection.* Boston: Little, Brown.

Williams, J. M., & Getty, D. (1986). Effects of levels of exercise on psychological mood states, physical fitness, and plasma beta-endorphin. *Perceptual and Motor Skills, 63,* 1099–1105.

Yates, J. E. (1979). *Managing stress: A businessperson's guide.* New York: AMA-COM: Division of American Management Association.

EXPLORING OURSELVES AND OUR MOTIVES

We say seeing is believing but actually, as Santayana pointed out,
we are all much better at believing than seeing.

Robert Anton Wilson

Frustrated with agriculture, a young Carl Rogers experiments with "cow"nseling.

As explained in the preface, this text focuses on agency counseling in two realms—the internal, personal realm of yourself and the external, professional realm of the field of counseling and the larger social and political contexts in which counseling is embedded. This chapter focuses on the internal realm by directing your attention inward—by encouraging you to engage in self-exploration. Cultivating the practice of knowing yourself provides a firm foundation from which you can then apply knowledge about the field.

Self-exploration is the process of becoming aware of what you *really* believe that enables you to consolidate and find a good fit for your life experiences. You have doubtless had a great deal of experience finding good fits in different areas of your life, and that has guided you to study agency counseling. The better you know yourself, the better chance you have of a good fit with the profession of counseling. Though we all believe certain things about ourselves, we constantly test those beliefs in experience, checking what we know or assume about ourselves against experiences we have.

This chapter attempts to help you clarify and articulate your own beliefs and life experiences and to help you understand the critical importance, in the context of agency counseling, of knowing yourself. Another intended outcome of this chapter is for you to gain an awareness of the advantages and disadvantages of personal counseling during your counselor training, to understand the concept of *personal meaning* and how it has an impact on your educational process, and to engage in some introspection and discussion about your views on these topics. Finally, this chapter will help you become more aware of your personal needs related to your interest in becoming a counselor.

> When I took my first agency job, I was searching for spiritual meaning in my life experiences. I took a job working with difficult, court-ordered clients in an inner-city area. The pay (in 1986) was only $13,500 a year, so I lived in a run-down part of the city where I worked (rent plus utilities totaled $185 a month). I believed that, since I was on a "spiritual" journey, I should be able to make the experience beautiful. After two years of unfulfilling work, break-ins at my home, and attempted muggings, I was burnt-out and believed I must have failed in both my career and my spiritual journey. It was only later that I understood how erroneous my beliefs were about spirituality and counseling.

"WOUNDED HEALERS" AND NEED FULFILLMENT

We cannot change anything unless we accept it. Condemnation does not liberate, it oppresses. I am the oppressor of the person I condemn, not his friend and fellow-sufferer.

Carl Jung

Swiss psychiatrist Carl Jung believed deeply in mapping one's own mind through therapy before attempting to guide another through the same terrain. In this sense, Jung believed the therapist to be a "fellow-sufferer." Additionally, this creates a degree of empathy that builds the therapeutic alliance. The concept of the "wounded healer" is at least as old as Shamanism (25,000 years). The wounded healer has faced woundedness, engaged in healing practice, and shared the boon of wisdom that came from the journey (Eliade, 1964). Like Jung's concept of fellow-sufferers, the wounded healers have *been there,* and this helps them relate to those who *are there.* The success of Alcoholics Anonymous is often described in terms of the wounded healer concept. For one suffering from a drinking problem, a good guide is another who suffers similarly but has traveled the road of recovery. The counterargument is that one does not need to have suffered every malady one's clients suffer to be helpful to them. To paraphrase the Buddha, anyone who lives also suffers. This is not a pessimistic statement on life but one aspect of being a mortal, self-aware creature. By engaging in the human experience and practicing the art of being human, we all can touch our wounds and travel paths to recovery.

Many effective therapists have recovered from their own traumas and have integrated the experience into their counseling approach. Such therapists are highly empathic with clients suffering similar problems. Common examples include integrating the experience of having an alcoholic parent, suffering sexual abuse, caring for a mentally or physically ill loved one, and having problems with substance abuse. When counselors recover from their wounds, the wounds can be integrated into who the counselor is as a person. On the other hand, a counselor who does not embark on the path to heal her or his wounds will be limited in the extent to which she or he can help a client. Since life always involves suffering, learning how to engage and recover from it is a developmental process. When we refine the art of being human to the level where we can recognize, accept, engage in, and transcend suffering, this milestone services ourselves and our clients.

One way to conceptualize the interaction of life experiences and growth is to imagine a rope that increases in thickness as it spirals upward, as we grow toward greater knowledge and enlightenment. Every experience, both pleasant and unpleasant, is represented by a strand. As each experience we have becomes integrated with other life experiences in our memory, more strands are added to the rope. Thus, as we grow, the rope is made up of an increasing number of strands twisted together, so that each strand is virtually indistinguishable from the whole of the rope. Strands are added as life experiences are encountered. This is why the rope thickens as it ascends; as it thickens, it becomes stronger. As the rope ascends, both pleasant and unpleasant experiences become more integrated into it. The addition of new strands aids in the process of integration, just as in life, later experiences may help us reframe, adjust to, or even heal certain traumas. Each spiral on the rope may represent a developmental period.

Imagine a point on the rope where a painful experience has been assimilated into your self-concept, the "you" that you present to others in the world. Currently, the emotional residue in question is part of who you are. In many situations you encounter, that residue has only peripheral influence on your thoughts and perceptions. When you encounter situations that resemble the original trauma, though, you reexperience some of the feelings that accompanied the original painful experience. If you have not worked to understand or integrate the original experience, subsequent similar experiences may only evoke pain similar to that which you originally experienced. However, if you have gained spiritual and emotional insight through soul searching, counseling, or other significant learning experiences, the meaning and significance you attach to the original experience may change drastically. Perhaps this is what Anne Wilson Schaef (1992) meant when she wrote of the ability to change the past through therapy. At the end of this chapter, we have provided a visualization exercise to assist you in gaining awareness of the creation and evolution of your own "rope" of life experiences.

Human growth is cyclical. At each new stage of development, we are challenged to transcend and include existing structures. Wilber (1996) wrote that, at any given level of development, we can "die to" exclusive identification with that level to ascend to a more complex level, or we can cling to existence at that level. Recall a point in your life at which you knew a much beloved time was coming to an end (perhaps a graduation or the dissolution of a group). At that point, you were being called to transcend *and* include the experience as part of your learning history. For example, consider one client who had been in a spiritual seekers group for three years. The group was designed to engage the members in seminars and experiences led by people from many spiritual traditions. The group was very powerful for this man and toward the end of the three years he began to dread its dissolution. For a period, he became more aloof with the members and in his counseling sessions. In subsequent sessions, he discovered he was dissociating from the experience to avoid saying goodbye to the group. His aloofness was an attempt to transcend without integrating the full experience, which, like all of life, included an ending. In struggling with how to say goodbye, the client laid the groundwork for including the experience and transcending it.

On our analogy of the rope, movement can stop or occur upward or downward. Extreme situational stress, such as financial hardship, the dissolution of a long-term relationship, or serious physical illness, might cause us to stop or

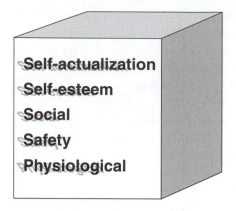

Self-actualization
Self-esteem
Social
Safety
Physiological

FIGURE **3.1**

Maslow's Hierarchy of Human Needs

move down the spiral to a previous level or developmental structure. Stopping or reverse temporarily to gain the strength to go on is what Freud called regression in service of the ego. Once movement begins again, we might reach a level at which we experience new perceptions about the original trauma.

Maslow's (1954) hierarchy can also be a useful framework for understanding our motivations to enter the therapeutic professions. His need levels correspond to the levels in our spiral analogy. The needs ascend from physiological (air, water, food, and so on), to safety (shelter, relative freedom from threat), to social (companionship and acceptance), to self-esteem (appropriate recognition) and peak in self-actualization (self-fulfillment). (See figure 3.1.) The theory claims that the lowest unfulfilled need is usually the strongest motivator. The biological and physiological needs can be thought of as the base—the level at which we begin to become aware of our own existence. As our personal growth unfolds, we move up the hierarchy to meet other needs and levels of development. Keep in mind that this model, to the extent that it reflects reality, is ever-changing. A shift in life circumstances can refocus us on lower or higher needs, and the extent of the shift in focus can vary. A common example is sitting in a class when hungry and waiting to go home to a favorite meal. The hungrier you are, the more difficult it is to focus on the lecture. To a small degree, you have become focused on a lower level for a brief period.

Maslow's model has been elaborated on by Wilber (1980), who noted that having a lower need unmet can distort the process of development and the meeting of higher needs. He also noted that meeting higher needs can help a person resolve traumas at lower levels. At the end of this chapter, there is an exercise using the rope model to help you consider the origin of your motivation for being a counselor.

> I chose to enter the counseling profession because I felt that the best contribution I could make to society was to help other people. I liked the feeling I experienced when people I was helping made gains as a result of my contact with them. The definition of success I used for myself was based on achievement and mas-

tery in serving other people; the need to establish this competence probably arose from esteem needs. As I progressed in my own personal counseling, I discovered that my desire to care for other people seemed to be related to the original trauma of not having my own safety needs met as a child. My mother's mental illness rendered her emotionally unavailable to me. As a result, I was attempting to reparent myself through parenting and caring for my clients.

ENGAGEMENT IN THE COUNSELING PROCESS

Know thyself.

Delphic motto

Philosopher Alan Watts (1966) said that the most interesting question a person can explore is "Who am I?" The question has been at the center of the human drama since the beginning of recorded time. Shamans, mystics, therapists, and other pioneers of the mind have left monuments to mark the breakthroughs they experienced on the inner journey of self-exploration. The writing of therapeutic professionals who have explored themselves and their clients is of particular relevance to this discussion. Regarding work as a therapeutic professional, author, therapist, and teacher Jeff Kottler (1993) wrote, "The practice of psychotherapy permits a unique life-style in which one's personal and professional roles complement each other. There are few other careers in which the boundaries between work and play are so permeable" (p. 39). Self-exploration encompasses work and play, and professional counseling at agencies can feel like both. Therapists and counselors experience everything from peak moments of meaning to agonizing self-confrontation as they embark with their clients on the journey of self-exploration and recovery.

Because work with clients can be emotionally intense for the client, some counselor educators believe that counselor trainees should participate in counseling themselves as part of their counselor training. The question of counseling for counselor trainees received focus and research a number of years ago. In this chapter, we will examine this question because it continues to have relevance, despite the lack of recent research efforts on the topic. Further, in studying counseling theories, you will find that most theorists recommend that therapeutic professionals have experience as clients receiving counseling. Who the counselor is as a person makes a major contribution to the counseling process (Corey, 1996; Kottler, 1993; Kottler & Brown, 1996), and one way of understanding and strengthening who you are is through receiving your own counseling. Authors from a diversity of theoretical orientations have endorsed this practice (Frankl, 1967; May, 1953; Ramsey, 1980; Yalom, 1975).

Self-exploration as a client is never an easy process. As Peck (1978) wrote, entering into any type of counseling relationship is an act of courage. It is important to consider how your own life experiences and values have contributed to your interest in becoming a counselor and how personal counseling could enhance your self-knowledge. The self-exploration/discussion questions at the end of this chapter are intended to help you reflect on experiences and events that have shaped who you are.

Several schools of counseling and psychotherapy assert that you need not be "sick" to benefit from counseling (Corey, 1996). Most people can benefit from efforts at personal exploration and growth. The caveat is that the degree of growth attained from personal exploration parallels the degree of discomfort experienced during that exploration. In a sense, it is a "no pain, no gain" experience. Psychological distress occurs on a continuum, and even people who are not aware of pressing distress can increase their insight, self-understanding, and effectiveness in their daily lives. When they are aware of mental and emotional distress, there usually are additional elements of which they are unaware. These elements may be thinking processes, emotions, aspects of the past, life situations, or perspectives of life situations. They remain unaware of these elements because to have awareness would cause or increase distress. Despite this, when clients go to a counselor, they are usually at a point at which *remaining* unaware of these elements is causing equal or greater distress.

The counseling process helps a person become aware of whatever emotions, or thought processes, need to be integrated (Wilber, 1980). Just because it is time for someone to integrate these elements into awareness does not mean the process is easy. Most people can relate to the analogy of leaving a relationship they are unhappy with but that has not been *too* bad. To stay in the relationship may offer certain securities but will impede fulfillment. To leave the relationship will open the frontier to fulfillment but bring with it a degree of insecurity. It is a difficult choice. Such is the case with the counseling process once engaged in by client and therapist.

Counselors who are self-aware and have insight into how their life path led to the counseling profession are better equipped in counseling clients through the same process of insight. Kottler and Brown (1996) noted that the richness of the counselor's life and the strength of her or his personality are enhanced in counseling, and these, in turn, are helpful to clients she or he will see. Self-knowledge includes understanding what motivates us to want to help others and being willing to engage in self-exploration. This is part of being an effective therapeutic professional.

> In my master's program, we had several assignments geared toward self-exploration. In one course, we were asked to share our experience of self-exploration with the class. The professor said that he hoped as second-year cohorts we felt safe enough to share our self-exploration experiences with each other. I remember walking down the hall after class and overhearing one of my classmates exclaim, "I'm not telling anyone anything about myself!" Why was I having trouble imagining her as my counselor?

By knowing what motivates us to want to help others, we lessen the chances that we will inappropriately use our clients to meet our own needs or to heal our own wounds. This is called countertransference. Unfortunately, some therapeutic professionals use therapeutic relationships to work through their own issues.

> I worked in a community where a person claiming to specialize in pastoral coun-
> seling had a practice. This person diagnosed all his clients as having been ritualis-
> tically abused in satanic cults and having dissociative identity disorder. The sheer
> number of clients given the diagnosis made its accuracy highly suspect. It is likely
> that the man had his own issues with evil, spirituality, or possibly sexual abuse. It
> is also likely that, by making these diagnoses and focusing on these "symptoms,"
> he was attempting to resolve his own concerns rather than his clients'. Many of
> his clients had negative experiences with him, and many more would probably
> never seek counseling again based on this experience. Perhaps if the person in
> question had participated in personal counseling himself, some of his issues could
> have been resolved and the adverse impact on his clients lessened.

Encouraging counseling students to engage in their own counseling while in training has long been a controversy within the profession (Visokey, 1987). Some of the controversy has centered on who should provide the therapy for counselor trainees. Hess (1980) stated that therapy in the context of supervision—that is, the supervisor counseling the supervisee—is appropriate as long as it is limited to the problems that interfere with the trainee's development as a counselor. Others (Altucher, 1969; Banikiotes, 1975; Blocher, 1983) have maintained that a supervisor who attempts to do therapy with a supervisee is initiating a dual relationship that is unethical. There is often therapeutic value in certain types of supervision that deal with the supervisee's countertransference reactions. Is it counseling per se? No. Is it therapeutic? Yes. So how best should the interaction be labeled? This is a topic we will discuss in the next section.

Rationales for Personal Therapy Among Counselors in Training

> How is the poor wretch [the analyst] to acquire the ideal qualifications which he will
> need in his profession? The answer is in an analysis of himself.
>
> Sigmund Freud

With Freud's position on psychoanalysts receiving their own analysis, the debate began about therapeutic professionals receiving therapy as part of their training. Multiple authors (Fouad, Hains, & Davis, 1990; Peebles, 1980; Post-Kammer & Davis, 1986; Rubinfine, 1971) strongly agree that counselors' personal issues, of which he or she may or may not be aware, limit their effectiveness counseling clients. Numerous rationales are offered for this position, including the following:

1. Counselors can block the progress of a client because they are uncomfortable. Personal counseling decreases the probability that that will happen.
2. Counselors can benefit from working as clients to scrutinize themselves and introspect.

3. Counselors can become sensitized to the power differential between therapist and client and how to act responsibly within this.
4. The process of self-disclosure and increased self-understanding can increase self-acceptance and the subsequent acceptance of others.

In contemporary settings, it has been observed that students' unresolved problems, anxieties, and conflicts often emerge during their training as counselors (Post-Kammer & Davis, 1986). It only stands to reason that if your job, in self-exploration, is to engage your mind to shed light on itself, you will have blind spots. You can understand your own mind only *with* your own mind to a certain point. It is like the town barber trying to cut his own hair—he may do all right with top and side burns, but it is best to go to another barber to cut the back. As a counselor, you want to be mirrors, not sponges. Just as a mirror reflects back elements the client is blind to or avoiding, a sponge absorbs the things the client needs to see to relieve symptoms. If these things are absorbed, the client never sees them and progress is impeded. As an example, a counselor trainee was on internship, working with a client who went to each session with a new presenting problem. The trainee was so concerned about excelling in her internship that she was unable to confront the client about his lack of focus, yet the trainee was unaware that her overriding concern to be a good counselor actually created a barrier to her making an effective intervention with the client. Clearly, then, the fewer the blind spots, the richer the reflection for the client. When the counselor's blind spots block the client's progress, the counselor must seek assistance in supervision; otherwise, this becomes an ethical breach.

Research Findings on Trainees in Counseling

In this section, we will examine the debate about whether counseling for counselor trainees should be required, supported, or discouraged. We will first look at some research that supports the idea and then follow with thoughts offered by authors that contraindicate trainee counseling. You will need to consider the pros and cons and then make your own decision to undergo counseling.

Post-Kammer and Davis (1986) hypothesized that counselor trainees need to use counseling to develop insight into conflicts that are blocking their growth in order to be helpful to clients in the therapeutic encounter. They sampled 210 students, 70 percent of whom were enrolled in graduate programs and had taken at least one counseling class. Forty-eight percent of the sample had been in counseling prior to entering the counseling program. Of the total sample, 61 percent thought personal counseling should be a requirement for graduation from a counselor education program. Obviously, requiring therapy would breach the ethic of not coercing clients into therapy, but the point remains that the most of these students thought counseling important in their training as professionals.

Another study, by Fouad, Hains, and Davis (1990), investigated whether students believed counseling should be required for graduation from a counselor education program. The authors evaluated whether the students' endorsement of counseling as a requirement was related to their previous experience with counseling. They also investigated whether the students who supported required counseling were more likely to have issues to explore than those who did not endorse required counseling. Of the 106 counseling students in their sample, 66 percent endorsed counseling as a requirement. The students who endorsed counseling as a requirement were also more likely to have had good experiences in counseling. Interestingly, the students who endorsed counseling as a requirement were not any more likely than other students to seek counseling help with their issues. The authors noted that their results indicate an awareness on the part of students of how their personal concerns might interfere with their clients' therapeutic progress.

Another notable study was done by Peebles (1980), who investigated the relationship between personal therapy and the ability to display empathy, warmth, and genuineness in the therapy session. Counselors who had been clients were compared with those who had never been clients. The sample was made up of students in a counseling psychology program, and they were rated in therapy sessions on warmth, empathy, and genuineness by a panel reviewing tapes of their sessions. Peebles found a significant relationship between the number of hours the therapists had spent in therapy and their ability to display empathy and genuiness.

There also are compelling arguments against required counseling for counselor trainees. One of the more obvious is that, when counseling is not entirely voluntary, the client is less motivated to look honestly at personal issues and to try to work through and resolve them. This is actually quite logical—"requiring" counseling mandates those actions that have the most impact if chosen of one's own free will. Mandating counseling is akin to telling children that they are "supposed" to love their parents but that their love is valued only if it is spontaneous (Watts, 1966). Because engaging in the counseling process as a client causes distress, one needs to be motivated to form what is called the therapeutic alliance.

The therapeutic alliance is the bond between counselor and client that reinforces and increases the probability of working together to reach agreed-on goals (Bordin, 1979). This alliance is completely dependent on mutual trust, respect, and confidence between counselor and client (Kleinke, 1994). With these in place, counselor and client are most likely to engage in the counseling process. Another way to think of it is that the client and counselor both have a job to do in therapy. The counselor's job is to use her skills, training, and self to foster a healthy environment and assist the client in clinically appropriate ways. The client's job is to talk honestly about his problems, state what he hopes to get from counseling, and respond honestly to the counselor. Although the client's job may sound simple, it is not.

> I remember getting counseling the second year into my Ph.D. I was already a master's-level counselor and had been a client twice before. Despite my experience and previously successful counseling relationships, I could not seem to tell my therapist what was really bothering me for the first three sessions. I guess it took me that long to trust her, to believe that she was interested in me as a client and capable of helping me with a very painful set of symptoms.

Working with clients who have been court-ordered for counseling illustrates the problems that occur when client motivation is lacking. Frequently, the sessions do not progress, and the counselor tries to do more and more of the client's job, resulting in a tired counselor, an unchanged client, and wasted time. The same dynamics may hold true if counselor trainees are routinely required to get their own counseling, whether they want it or not. There may be more tired counselors, more unchanged clients, and more wasted time. Furthermore, if a counselor education program were to require that students demonstrate "progress" in the sessions, the contingency could be even more detrimental.

Baumgold (1983) wrote about his experiences enrolled in two academic programs, which both required personal counseling as a condition for completion. In both cases, the students were strongly encouraged to seek out, as therapists, faculty members in the programs he was attending. For Baumgold, the dual relationships inhibited his openness in the sessions. To express yourself openly, you must experience the trust that develops in the therapeutic alliance. If you are graded by the same person you are supposed to be sharing openly with, how can you know that what is shared will not be inappropriately reflected in a course grade? This type of arrangement only exacerbates the power differential that already exists between therapist and client. It is unethical and inappropriate because it creates a dual relationship. Dual relationships are explained and defined in the ACA Code of Ethics, found at the end of Chapter 4.

Leader (1971), in debate with Rubinfine (1971), stated that a sound, rigorous training program is a good alternative to requiring students to participate in therapy. Two disadvantages of requiring therapy are (1) the use of therapists' time and expertise on nonessential problems when there are not enough therapists to meet the needs of the community at large and (2) the costs the students would be required to incur (as if graduate school were not expensive enough!).

Garfield and Bergin (1971) concluded that personal therapy is negatively correlated with client outcome in therapy. More specifically, researchers (Bandura, Lipsher, & Miller, 1960; Bergin, 1966; Garfield & Bergin, 1971; Vandenbos & Karon, 1971) have found that, with evidence of disturbance in the therapist, the client (not surprisingly) shows less progress. Outcome differences between counselors who had been clients and those who had not was unrelated to the magnitude of their problems.

THE POWER DIFFERENTIAL

Continuing in the realm of discussion about human need, we will now look at needs and the means each of us choose to fulfill them. The question we must ask ourselves is not whether we have needs but, rather, what they are and how we can go about meeting them.

As the "professional," a counselor is in a position to exert some influence over the client in the counseling process. Clients assume that counselors' motivations are honorable. The closest parallel is when you visit a physician with the assumption that she or he has your optimal health as the goal and that the doctor will do her or his best to help you recover from your illness. When clients come to you for counseling, they will assume (as they have every right to) that you are there to help them, with no hidden agenda of your own. They will look to you as an expert, someone who can offer guidance as they struggle with painful issues. It is a breach of trust to give a client anything less than this. By coming to you as an expert, clients covertly assume that you will strive to understand their worldview and help them arrive at solutions compatible with their values. You can do this only by being aware of your own worldview and values. If you are unaware of your own views and assumptions, you increase the chance of unknowingly imposing your value system on your clients. In the example about the pastoral counselor on page 63, clients often came away from their work with him confused, fearful, and perhaps in worse shape than before they started seeing him.

This is not to say that counseling is value-free. All therapeutic professionals *do* possess values as part of their belief system, and their clients have a right to know what those values are. A value of life over death and the valuing of the potential to grow within given parameters, are general values most therapeutic professionals possess as part of their belief system and values. Obviously, within these broader values, the counselor must explore the client's individual and cultural worldviews so as to support these larger values in what is a healthy context for each client.

It is also imperative that you be sensitive to the power clients give you simply by coming to the session. What you say and do in counseling clients can have a lasting impact on them. This does not mean you should fear confronting clients and asking them difficult questions. It does mean that, when you confront a client, you should do it with the client's best interests as your motivation and in a manner that is respectful of the trust the client has placed in you. One way to keep alert to these issues is by asking yourself what you want your clients to remember about you and your work together after they have left.

DIVERSITY

Human diversity and cultural diversity are currently prominent topics in the therapeutic professions. Awareness of the diversity among people is a necessity in the field. Knowledge of how cultural variables affect the counseling process is also absolutely necessary. Knowing and understanding your own culturally based biases and values is as important as understanding your clients' culturally based world views.

An example of how culturally based values have an impact on counseling might help clarify the importance of self-awareness. Sally, a counselor trainee, was raised in a family of origin in which conflict resolution was encouraged in a straightforward manner. If Sally was angry about something her mother had done, for example, both her parents encouraged her to tell her mother directly about the anger she was feeling. Sally's client, Qia Ling, comes from a family of origin in which direct communication about conflict is expressly prohibited. If Sally is unaware that other cultures prohibit direct confrontation in conflict, she might encourage Qia Ling to confront directly someone with whom Qia Ling is in conflict. This could pose great difficulty for Qia Ling, and Sally's encouragement could actually increase Qia Ling's emotional distress. It is Sally's responsibility to understand the nature of cultural differences and to be respectful of clients' values and beliefs. Moreover, Sally needs to be aware of her own beliefs, so that she knows when they are affecting her choice of counseling strategies and techniques with her clients. Figure 3.2 illustrates these cultural considerations and membership in cultural subgroups. Speight, Myers, Cox, and Highlen (1991) proposed that every person has at least three types of characteristics. Figure 3.2 provides a diagram of this concept. Universal characteristics, such as the human nervous system, are characteristics that unite humans us as a species. Cultural characteristics are those that describe aspects of ourselves, such as gender, age, race, ethnicity, ability/disability, spiritual tradition, sexual orientation, and socioeconomic status. In figure 3.2 each cultural group is depicted by its own medium-sized circle. However, most people are simultaneous members of multiple groups. It is the simultaneous membership in multiple groups that contributes to the uniqueness of each individual. Finally, individual characteristics are those unique to each person. The individual characteristics are those derived from a multitude of sources—on a macro level, by membership in particular cultural groups and, on a micro level, by membership in a particular family of origin, by birth order within that family, and by key life experiences unique to each of us.

Membership in each of these groups carries with it elements and features with which we define ourselves. Membership in these groups additionally increases the likelihood that a person will have certain significant life experiences. Such experiences include discrimination and oppression. Although a

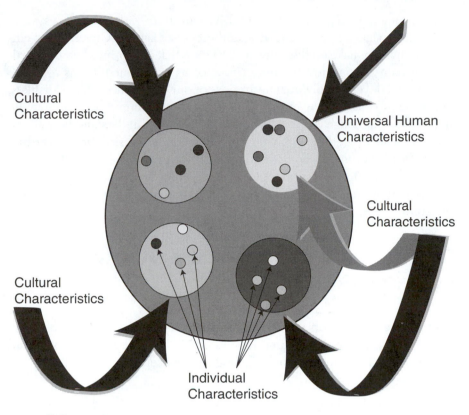

FIGURE **3.2**

A Model of the Origin of Human Diversity

complete discussion of the detrimental or devastating psychological effects of discrimination is beyond the scope of this chapter, it is critical to recognize how pervasively such life experiences affect one's self-concept and perception of the world. This statement is made in the context of both self-understanding, and the understanding of the life experiences of clients. The accumulation of life experiences creates a filter—a tint on the window through which we see the world and other people. Despite our best efforts not to let that filter affect how we perceive and interact with other people, it is an inescapable and integral part of who we are. It is the unique filters of each individual and the ways in which individuals interact and perceive one another that create the basis of the contemporary focus and concern about diversity and multicultural counseling.

Another analogy of this concept is to consider computers. We might think of universal characteristics as akin to computer hardware, cultural characteristics as akin to software, and individual characteristics as the personalized touches on a personal computer, (PC). We are born with a nervous system (hardware), which receives, encodes, and processes signals. Genetics and culture combine to make up the software program that is imprinted on the hardware. Finally, in our development, most of us experience life as separate entities and develop individual awareness of our experiences, likes, dislikes, and so on, just as we may customize our personal computers. You may be thinking that, although you use a PC, you really do not understand how all the components fit together. Many people are in the same situation regarding themselves—they usually do not think about how their universal, cultural, and individual characteristics interact to form who they are. Having some awareness of all three sets of characteristics is an important part of self-exploration for aspiring counselors.

THE INTEGRATION OF SELF-AWARENESS IN COUNSELOR TRAINING: PERSONAL MEANING

Most counselor educators view Carl Rogers as one of the most influential figures in contemporary counseling. Rogers (1957) identified six necessary and sufficient conditions for personality change in counseling:

1. Psychological contact between the client and counselor
2. The counselor's being congruent or integrated
3. The client's being in a state of incongruence (which results in vulnerability and anxiety)
4. The counselor's experiencing unconditional positive regard for the client
5. The counselor's empathizing with the client
6. The counselor's communicating this empathy to the client

What Rogers really offers is insight into the counselor's *attitude* and the *quality* of the relationship. Both of these refer to the subjective experiences of the counselor and client—to the *insides* of the counselor and client. Many theorists and counselor educators have offered behavioral descriptions of the therapy process as defined by Rogers. Ivey and Authier (1971) and Ivey (1994) created a system of microskills that educators can use to train counselors. Very briefly, the microskills break down counseling skills into small, discrete behaviors, each of which can be described in detail, modeled, and practiced. Behavioral descriptions are useful but tell us only about the *outsides:* the externally observable aspects of the client and counselor.

As Wilber (1995) has written, all outsides have insides, and both need to be considered because they interact. To evaluate the quality or accuracy of an observation based solely on an observation of external characteristics is to neglect important information about internal characteristics. As an example, consider that you can have EEG electrodes attached to your head to measure the electrical activity of your brain. If you think of the equation $2 + 2 = 4$ or the equation $2 + 2 = 1,176$, the EEG may record similar levels of brain activity, the first equation reflects a meaning accepted as truthful, whereas the second does not. The meaning and accuracy of the equations in the example can be explained only through dialogue that explores *insides*. The *outside* EEG measurement gives no indication of the exact nature of the brain activity—that is, accurate versus inaccurate—and thus is only of value in identifying that brain activity has occurred (Wilber, 1996).

Near the end of his life, Rogers (1980) was disturbed that his work had been simplified in a behavioral manner (a summary of *outsides*) that neglects the larger aspects of the counselor-client relationship (the experience, or attitude, or *insides*). This example dealing with the works of Rogers applies to all of your graduate training. You will receive plenty of training and evaluation on *outsides*, but you must not neglect the equally important *insides*. Mahon and Altman (1977) and Combs (1982) noted that students must associate the skills they learn with personal experience. Behavioral skills are only one important aspect of the counseling process. They accurately describe outsides but neglect the insides. Your ability to incorporate your course material into your life experiences is related to your ability to derive personal meaning from theories and ideas (Hills, 1987). This personal meaning translates into your inside experience as you are doing counseling and facilitates many of the attitudes Rogers pointed to.

The personal meaning you ascribe to any element is a manifestation of the unique combination of life experiences you have had. By being aware of your personal meanings, you better understand how and why certain information pertains to you.

SUMMARY

We can most easily summarize the content of this chapter with the statement that self-awareness in the counselor is crucial for effective helping. One excellent way to develop self-awareness is to become engaged as a client in the counseling process. Regardless of whether you choose to enter personal counseling, be aware of the inevitability of your own internal reactions to concerns and issues clients bring to you. Those reactions may range from intensely positive to intensely negative. Well-developed self-awareness reduces the likelihood that those reactions will have a detrimental effect on the counseling you are able to do with your client.

ROPE ANALOGY EXERCISE

Note: Be aware that this exercise may generate some strong emotions. If you are concerned about being unable to cope with those emotions, wait to do this exercise until you have appropriate emotional support either from someone in your support system or from a counselor. The suggested method for engaging in this exercise is to first read the description completely, then find a quiet place to sit, relax, and then do the imagery. After engaging in the imagery, it might be helpful to journal some of your conclusions, or perhaps to draw a depiction of your own spiral and the personal conclusions and developments you have experienced as a result of your own strands of rope.

In your mind's eye visualize a rope that spirals upward. Imagine that each of your life experiences, both pleasant and unpleasant, are represented by a strand. As the rope ascends, it incorporates an increasing number of strands twisted together, so that each individual strand is virtually indistinguishable from the whole of the rope. Each spiral on the rope may represent a developmental period.

Imagine a point on the rope where a significant experience has been assimilated into your self-concept, the "you" that you present to others in the world. Consider how that experience influences your thoughts and perceptions. Imagine later situations you have encountered that resembled the original experience, and if possible, the extent to which you re-experienced some of the feelings that accompanied the original experience. Try to recall the most significant life experiences, both positive and negative, that have shaped who you are, how you respond to other people, and how you respond to life's stressors. Finally, praise yourself for attempting to raise your self-awareness before returning mentally to the room where you are sitting. Begin to jot down or draw images of your insights.

DISCUSSION ITEMS

1. What is your cultural background? What are some of the values of your cultural background that influence the way you experience the world? How might these values influence your work as a counselor?
2. With one word, describe the feeling you experience contemplating going into personal counseling. After sharing the one word, elaborate on this feeling.
3. Think of a time when you were helped by someone. What were you feeling before and after the help? What was the situation?

4. Discuss your motivations for wanting to enter community agency counseling. What are your expectations about the rewards? What do you imagine as the biggest challenge?
5. All of us have personal wounds that are resolved, current, or residual. What relationship do your wounds have to your desire to be a counselor?
6. What type of client or client issue do you imagine would be most difficult for you? Why?

REFERENCES

Altucher, N. (1969). Constructive use of the supervisory relationship. *Journal of Counseling Psychology, 14,* 165–170.

Bandura, A., Lipsher, D., & Miller, P. E. (1960). Psychotherapists' approach-avoidance reactions to patients' expressions of hostility. *Journal of Consulting Psychology, 24,* 1–8.

Banikiotes, P. (1975). Personal growth and professional training. *Counselor Education and Supervision, 15,* 149–151.

Baumgold, J. (1983, fall). In-house psychotherapy. *Voices,* 51–55.

Bergin, A. E. (1967). Some implications of psychotherapy research for therapeutic practice. *Journal of Abnormal Psychology, 71,* 235–246.

Blocher, D. H. (1983). Toward a cognitive developmental approach to counselor supervision. *The Counseling Psychologist, 11,* 27–34.

Bordin, E. S. (1979). The generalizability of the psychoanalytic concept of the working alliance. *Psychotherapy: Research and Practice, 16,* 252–260.

Combs, A. W. (1982). Affective education or none at all. *Educational Leadership, 39,* 495–497.

Corey, G. (1996). *Theory and practice of counseling and psychotherapy* (5th ed.). Pacific Grove, CA: Brooks/Cole.

Eliade, M. (1964). *Shamanism.* Princeton, NJ: Bolligen.

Fouad, N. A., Hains, A. A., & Davis, J. L. (1990). Factors in students' endorsement of counseling as a requirement for graduation from a counseling program. *Counselor Education and Supervision, 29,* 268–274.

Frankl, V. E. (1967). *Psychotherapy and existentialism.* New York: Washington Square Press.

Garfield, S. L., & Bergin, A. E. (1971). Personal therapy, outcome and some therapist variables. *Psychotherapy: Theory, Research and Practice, 8*(3), 251–253.

Hess, A. K. (1980). *Psychotherapy in supervision: Theory, research, and practice.* New York: John Wiley & Sons.

Hills, M. (1987). The discovery of personal meaning: A goal for counselor training. *Counselor Education and Supervision, 27*(1), 37–43.

Ivey, A. E. (1994). *Intentional interviewing and counseling: Facilitating client development in a multicultural society.* Pacific Grove, CA: Brooks/Cole.

Ivey, A. E., & Authier, J. (1971). *Microcounseling: Innovations in interviewing, counseling, psychotherapy, and psychoeducation.* Springfield, IL: Charles C. Thomas.

Kleinke, C. L. (1994). *Common principles of psychotherapy.* Pacific Grove, CA: Brooks/Cole.

Kottler, J. A. (1993). *On being a therapist.* San Francisco: Jossey-Bass.

Kottler, J. A., & Brown, R. W. (1996). *Introduction to therapeutic counseling* (3rd. ed.). Pacific Grove, CA: Brooks/Cole.

Leader, A. L. (1971). The argument against required personal analysis in training for psychotherapy. In R. Holt (Ed.), *New horizon for psychotherapy: Autonomy as a profession.* New York: International Universities Press.

Mahon, B. R.: Attman, H. A. (1977). Skill training: Cautions and recommendations. Counselor Education and Supervision, 17, 42–49.

Maslow, A. H. (1954). *Motivation and personality.* New York: Harper & Row.

May, R. (1953). *Man's search for himself.* New York: Norton.

Peck, M. S. (1978). *The road less traveled: A new psychology of love, traditional values, and spiritual growth.* New York: Simon & Schuster.

Peebles, M. J. (1980). Personal therapy and ability to display empathy, warmth and genuineness in psychotherapy. *Psychotherapy: Theory, Research and Practice, 17*(30), 258–262.

Post-Kammer, P., & Davis, J. (1986, winter). Are we systematically addressing the personal development of counselors-in-training? *The Wisconsin Counselor, 7*–10.

Ramsay, R. W. (1980). Goals of a personal therapy for trainees considered from a behavior viewpoint. In W. D. DeMoor & H. R. Wyngaarder (Eds.), *Psychotherapy, research, and training; Proceedings of the 11th International Congress of Psychotherapy.* Amsterdam; New York: Elsevier/North Holland Biomedical Press.

Rogers, C. R. (1957). The necessary and sufficient conditions of therapeutic personality change. *Journal of Consulting Psychology, 21*(2), 95–103.

Rogers, C. R. (1980). *A way of being.* Boston: Houghton Mifflin.

Rubinfine, D. L. (1971). The role of personal psychotherapy in the training of psychotherapists. In R. R. Holt (Ed.), *New Horizon for Psychotherapy: Autonomy as a Profession.* New York: International Universities Press.

Schaef, A. W. (1992). *Beyond therapy, beyond science: A new model for healing the whole person.* New York: HarperCollins.

Speight, S. L., Myers, L. J., Cox, C. I., & Highlen, P. S. (1991). A redefinition of multicultural counseling. *Journal of Counseling and Development, 70*(1), 29–36.

Vandenbos, G. R. & Karon, B.P. (1971). Pathogenesis: A new therapist personality dimension related to therapeutic effectiveness. *Journal of Personality Assessment, 35,* p. 252–260.

Visokey, E. A. (1987). Personal growth and therapy as a component of graduate training in counseling psychology programs. Unpublished dissertation, Chicago IL: Loyola University.

Ramsay, R. W. (1980). Goals of a personal therapy for trainees considered from a behavior viewpoint. In W. DeMoor and H.R. Wijngaarden (Eds.), *Psychotherapy, research, and training; Proceedings of the 11th International Congress of Psychotherapy.* Amsterdam; New York: Elsevier/North-Holland Biomedical Press.

Vandenbos, G. R. & Karon, B. P. (1971). Pathogenesis: A new therapist personality dimension related to therapeutic effectiveness. Journal of Personality Assessment, 35, p. 252–260.

Watts, A. W. (1966). *The book: On the taboo against knowing who you are.* New York: Vintage.

Wilber, K. (1980). *The Atman project: A transpersonal view of human development.* Wheaton, IL: Quest.

Wilber, K. (1995). *Sex, ecology, spirituality: The spirit of evolution.* Boston: Shambhala.

Wilber, K. (1996). *Eye to eye: The quest for the new paradigm* (3rd ed.). Boston: Shambhala.

Yalom, I. D. (1975). *The theory and practice of group psychotherapy.* New York: Basic Books.

ETHICAL ISSUES IN AGENCY COUNSELING

When in doubt, do the right thing.

Anonymous

Bursting Enthusiastically Through the Door to His Waiting Room, Irwin Unwittingly Violates the Prime Ethical Principle "First Do No Harm."

We begin this final chapter on inner exploration with a quote said to have been displayed on a wall plaque in a Washington, DC, law firm (Beiser, 1994). The point of the quote is not to encourage reliance on common sense in ethical decisions but, rather, to recognize that many of us possess a sense of ethical behavior, which must be supplemented through a study of ethics. This "sense" may be Kitchener's (1984) implicit moral rationale as opposed to an unreflective common sense. Indeed, relying solely on common sense (what is "familiar") has been said to be unwise and unproductive (Gladding, 1997). Brown University professor of ethics Edward Beiser (1994) noted that "one must not confuse the necessary with the familiar." Professional codes of ethics help us identify what is necessary, so that we do not overly rely on what is familiar. As Welfel (1998) asserted, no mental health professional is excused from doing "ethics homework" and must make decisions "based on more than intuition" (p. 25).

This chapter will begin with some definitions relevant to ethical concerns in agency counseling, will discuss the basis for ethical systems in general, will summarize key ethical principles, will review key principles in the American Counseling Association (ACA) ethical guidelines, and will review selected ethical issues in agency counseling. This chapter is designed to be an overview and is supplemented with the ethical code of the American Counseling Association. You may wish to read the entire ACA ethical code before continuing with this chapter. The code is included at the end of this chapter.

Each therapeutic profession mentioned in chapter 1 has its own ethical code. The American Psychological Association (APA), the National Association of Social Workers (NASW), and the American Association of Marriage and Family Therapists (AAMFT) ethical codes can be found at the web sites listed at the end of chapter 1. Space precludes an in-depth study of each ethical code in this chapter. Since this text is targeted toward students in counselor education, we will focus on the ACA code, but bear in mind that it is similar to the ethical codes of the other professions previously noted.

DEFINITIONS OF TERMS

Ethics is derived from a Greek word meaning "character" or "custom" and refers to standards of human conduct. These standards are often referred to as morals, (from the Latin, also meaning "customs"). As these etymological roots imply, ethics is a normative discipline concerned with what is good or right for specific groups of people (in this case, therapeutic professionals), or how people ought to treat one another. As Russell (1957) suggested, we may see ethics as the interdisciplinary study of which human desires and behavior are good, and which are bad and the justification and advocacy of the good ones. Russell noted that bad desires and behaviors can be described as those that "tend to thwart the desires of others, or, particularly, those which thwart more desires than they assist" (p. 77). Since desires influence behaviors, ethics is ultimately the study of good or proper behavior. Ethics has two primary purposes: (1) to establish the criteria to label "good" and "bad" behavior and (2) to promote the good and discourage the bad (Russell, 1945).

According to Rand (1982), ethics is one of five branches of philosophy (the others being epistemology, metaphysics, politics, and aesthetics). Perhaps what makes ethics more relevant for human services professionals is that a code of ethics is necessary for a group of practitioners to be considered a profession (Allen, 1986). In addition to having a code of ethics, professionals must receive guidance in using and abiding by that code (Welfel, 1998). Researchers have concluded that the ethical decision-making process is a weak area for many counseling professionals (Hayman & Covert, 1986), which further supports Welfel's (1998) admonition.

THE BASIS OF ETHICAL BEHAVIOR

[Ethical] analysis must be grounded in a commitment to virtues that the profession values.

Elizabeth Reynolds Welfel

Aside from consulting and understanding our professional code of ethics, what motivates our ethical practices? When we are in doubt, why do we bother seeking out the right thing, let alone deciding what the right thing is? What is the basis for our commitment to the virtues (good or admirable qualities) valued by our profession? Certainly, we may do the right thing out of fear of the consequences of doing the wrong thing. Many therapists have dutifully documented session notes motivated more by fear of lawsuits than a desire to be an ethical clinician, yet there is more to ethical practice than fearful motivation. Understanding your own motivation for ethical practice is valuable self-knowledge.

For centuries, philosophers have wrestled with the question of what is goodness in conduct. Two principles that have guided their efforts were things that were good or right (in and of themselves) and things that were good because they complied with certain standards relative to the group in question. A professional code of ethics provides standards relative to the therapeutic professions, but what about the other principle? Other than ethical standards that may point us to the right thing, why bother (other than to avoid lawsuits) seeking out that right thing? These questions are addressed in this chapter.

The Divine Model of Ethical Behavior

I have come to the conclusion that whether or not a person is a religious believer does not matter much. Far more important is that they be a good human being.

His Holiness the 14th Dalai Lama

Across cultures, human beings have invoked authority when trying to define and justify the good. In Western society, the authority invoked has spanned the extreme poles of God and nature. Initially, the authority invoked to recommend or enforce ethical behavior was assumed to be divine. This is particularly true in the West, where ethics has been regarded as having a religious foundation (Kaplan, 1961). Some writers even claim that ethics is based in a religious worldview (Ramsey, 1981). Including a god in one's ethical consciousness implies a supreme good *(summum bonum)*, which the god in question either endorses or commands. This "supreme good" then becomes the basis for an ethical code.

An ethical code rooted in a concept of a god may have shortcomings. For one thing, it may not extend to people belonging to groups that do not share a particular concept of God. The notion that certain people are part of an ingroup based on their concept of God has been a common root of religious warfare for thousands of years (Armstrong, 1993). Ultimately, we may find that ethical behavior as motivated by a particular sense of God can degenerate into parochial self-motivation.

Another problem with using divine authority as an ethical basis was outlined by Russell (1957). He noted that "as soon as it is held that any belief, no matter what, is important for some other reason than that it is true, a whole host of evils is ready to spring up" (p. 197). Russell's logic is that, if a particular theology is believed necessary for ethical behavior, regardless of the truth of that theology, it will breed unethical suppression of truthful inquiry into the theology in question. Despite these problems, many people, therapists included, both consciously and unconsciously use the model of divine authority as the basis for ethical behavior.

The Naturalistic Model of Ethical Behavior

In the nineteenth century, Western philosophers challenged their contemporary, literal images of God in what has been called the death of God movement (Armstrong, 1993). An increasing number of philosophers defined the good by focusing more on nature or human reason than on God. Freidrich Nietszche (the philosopher who gave the death of God movement its name) wrote during a period when Darwin's theory of evolution was upsetting traditional religious conceptions of humanity—conceptions that are still embedded in many notions of human services. In a nutshell, Darwin's notion of natural selection maintains that these creatures that best adapt are most likely to survive (the phrase "survival of the fittest" was not Darwin's but was stated by Herbert Spencer, one of his contemporaries). According to Nietszche, the good has no need of a divine decree but, rather, is embodied as anything that heightens a person's will to power. Nietzsche died before he was able to finish his philosophy of the will to power, but the will to power was equated with life itself and the power he referred to was the spiritual power of the artist or sage, rather than political or social power. Indeed, Nietzsche believed that political or social power merely leads people to betray their true destiny, which is to manifest the unique expression of the evolving life force coursing through them (Kaufmann, 1974; Soloman, 1974). In this sense, we can surmise that there is a similarity between living one's will to power, what Campbell (1949) referred to as "heeding the call" of the heroic life (p. 391) and what humanistic psychology refers to as self-actualization. To contrast Nietszche's will to power with social conformity is to paraphrase Fromm (1950), who identified two types of psychotherapy: one that heals the soul and one that merely produces good citizens.

We can view the notion of perfecting human nature through the will to power as consonant with the practice of counseling and psychotherapy. This is the authority at the naturalistic end of the ethics continuum. Helping human beings adapt to their environment and courageously face the existential givens of life, (such as aging, injustice, and death, is essential to the work of therapeutic professions. If such adaptation and courage increase the chance of survival, this naturalistic philosophy provides an ethical basis.

A naturalistic ethical basis might be summed up as follows. Life is difficult for most people. If life is a transitory, natural phenomenon, with no immortal or divine undercurrent, helping others adapt to life's challenges logically enhances the society we belong to, which also enhances our lives. This naturalistic ethical authority has some things in common with Ellis' (1973) discussion of human value. Like Ellis, we cannot prove it is a good thing to help others adapt and survive. We might conclude that, if we contribute to a society that does that, this increases the probability that perhaps someone will help us adapt when we need to. Thus, we may again come full circle to justifying a naturalistic ethic as ultimately rooted in self-interest. Such is the fate of any ultimate attempt to justify the good.

The Ideal Observer Model of Ethical Behavior

As the Western world secularized, another basis for ethical consciousness developed that blended those based in God and nature. The ideal observer outlook approaches right and wrong in terms of an ideal spectator (Taliaferro, 1988). According to Firth (1952), the goodness or badness of an action or a state can be explored and analyzed in terms of whether or not an ideal observer would approve or disapprove. Certainly, this sounds very similar to the theistic approach to ethics but, as Taliaferro pointed out, it does not matter whether such an ideal observer actually exists. The ideal observer is supposed to be omniscient, *omnipercipient* (able to empathize fully with all parties involved), dispassionate, and consistent. As such, the ideal observer could sanction assistance to the weak to help them better adapt to their environment. This could be a synthesis of the theistic and naturalistic bases for ethical behavior. This may seem like a variation of psychodynamic notions of conscience or a more secular anthropomorphic projection. Regardless, the ideal observer outlook does provide a common ground for answering the question "Why bother to find out what the right thing is?" Consider the following questions:

1. Imagine the basis for ethical behavior spanning the two poles of the naturalistic and the divine. Which of the two poles would you place yourself closest to? Why?
2. Suppose you had an experience that led you to drastically change your answer to question 1. What would that experience be? How might that experience and the resulting shift in your basis for ethical behavior affect your counseling of clients?

THE GOLDEN FIVE ETHICAL PRINCIPLES
OF THE THERAPEUTIC PROFESSIONS

If virtues are good or admirable qualities, what are the virtues or ethical principles that therapeutic professions value? Kitchner (1984) and Cottone and Tarvydas (1998) noted that counseling and psychology have traditionally endorsed the system of principle ethics, which is also dominant in medicine. In principle ethics, objectively applied ethical guidelines or rules are used to assess the right or the good in regard to ethical dilemmas. Kitchner (1984) identified five ethical principles from systems of principle ethics that are prominent guidelines for ethical decision making in the therapeutic professions. These "golden five" principles are autonomy, beneficence, nonmaleficence (the responsibility to avoid harm), justice, and fidelity. These can be thought of as attitudes and practices supported by a knowledge base.

Autonomy is honoring clients' right to independence and freedom, as well as their ability to make decisions about the course of their lives. Although counseling is not value-free, and therapists do seek to influence their clients, a commitment to autonomy can help preclude any undue influence by the counselor.

Beneficence is the doing of good to others. Obviously, the standards of the society in which it is done and the ethical code of the profession involved define the "good." In this regard, we can reflect back to Russell's (1957) notion that the good or good desires facilitate the desires of others, rather than thwart them. In this sense, beneficence is facilitating the good desires of others—in this case, clients.

Nonmaleficence is not doing harm through one's actions. This has been defined as one of the oldest ethical virtues dating to the formulation of the Hippocratic oath ("primum non nocere-"—"first do no harm") (Cottone & Tarvydas, 1998). As Welfel (1998) pointed out, thirty years ago counseling was portrayed as more benign than we now know it to be. We now know that we can do a great deal of harm through incompetence and unethical behavior.

The principle of justice requires therapists to be fair and to treat clients as equally as possible. It is interesting that a Hebrew definition of compassion includes "to do justice" (Fox, 1980). Understood in this sense, justice is an outgrowth of compassion for the client. This compassion, far from countertransference, is an egalitarian "suffering with" the client as a fellow traveler on the human journey, willing to use one's skills and experiences to ease that suffering (Jung, 1958). Justice also promotes security by recognizing the equal claims of all human beings (Russell, 1957). As such, justice rooted in compassion promotes security and trust in the counseling relationship.

Finally, fidelity is practicing honesty and loyalty in your relationships with clients. It is easy to see how each of the golden five virtues reinforces the others. We will now generally review the categories from the ACA code of ethics, looking at these principles in each category.

As previously stated, all therapeutic professions must have a code of ethics to be considered a profession proper. Most organizations such as the American Counseling Association (ACA) also have codes of ethics for specialty areas. Since there is no explicit specialty area for community agency counseling, there is no specialized ethical code for that setting. Hershenson, Power, and Waldo (1996) have maintained that the general ethical code of the American Counseling Association is broad enough to provide a foundation for ethical practice. The ethical categories of the American Counseling Association that we will examine are the counseling relationship, confidentiality, professional responsibility, relationships with other professionals, evaluation, and the resolution of ethical dilemmas. Our review will be cursory; you should also read the entire ACA ethical code, which is included at the end of this chapter.

The Counseling Relationship

> I remember the first Latino client I worked with. He was referred from his place of employment for a drinking problem. In the course of our sessions, it became clear that he had strong conflicts with his religion (which was Roman Catholic). When he mentioned the conflicts and I asked if he wanted to elaborate, he just shook his head and said, "There is nothing to be done." The client's drinking seemed to be related to his somewhat closeted identity as a gay man. This turned out to be the source of religious conflict as well. Two months into our sessions, the client said that, in his family, religious faith was everything and that no one ever questioned the teachings of the church. He said that to openly question his religion (something I had been trained to do from birth) would "scandalize" his parents and ostracize him from his family. In this case, the client autonomously chose to suffer his religious conflict and his closeted sexual orientation to maintain ties with his family and culture. What I had seen as lack of will was actually the living-out of a supreme act of will—albeit a difficult one.

A therapist must be very careful in defining autonomy for the client. This definition must come from both the client and the counselor, in dialogue with each other. Certainly, cultural differences play a large role in this type of caution, but individual differences are equally important. In the case just described, the client exercised his autonomy in choosing to identify closely with family and cultural norms at great expense. In addition, the client's fatalistic perspective ("there is nothing to be done") is common among Hispanic people (Ruiz & Langrod, 1982). The ACA code of ethics states that counselors must avoid encouraging dependent relationships, respect clients' cultural differences, and promote clients' interest and welfare. All of these require a commitment to the client's autonomy. It is assumed that beneficent actions will be one product of respecting a client's autonomy, whereas harmful actions (maleficence) will be the fruits of violating a client's autonomy.

Justice as rooted in compassion is certainly a powerful aspect of the therapeutic relationship. If justice is merely a form of "bean counting" whereby the therapist seeks to quantify that she or he has treated clients equally, it is at best an empty gesture. Justice that is linked to compassion is an outgrowth of a relationship of trust and equality. Certainly, the therapist always has power over the client who is in counseling voluntarily. The client discloses far more than the therapist, seeks the therapist's guidance, and, many times, uses the therapist as a role model. The therapist, on the other hand, has special skills and training she or he uses to help the client, ethical and legal obligations while endeavoring to help the client, and liability in the relationship that the client does not share. This does not mean, however, that the therapist cannot share power with the client. Seeing the client as a fellow sufferer in the existential sense heightens awareness of the client's dilemma, as well as of the client's need to the final judge of which choices to make.

Fidelity as honesty and loyalty is the basis of a healthy therapeutic relationship. One of the primary expectations therapists share with clients is that clients be honest. One of the primary promises therapists make to clients is that therapists will be honest in their dealings with clients. This fidelity is the basis of the trust that is so necessary to the type of work to be done. It can be surprisingly difficult to be honest with a client—particularly when the client's main problem is facing aspects of her- or himself. If you are to help the client, it is critical that you develop the skill of being honest in a way that is also compassionate. This is the type of feedback clients will be paying you to give them. The honesty necessary for a successful therapeutic relationship begins with the therapist's professional disclosure statement to clients, which is typically discussed in the first session. The professional disclosure statement should contain the therapist's professional education, including academic degrees, licenses, certifications, services offered, fees for services, and areas of competence.

Confidentiality

As noted by Welfel (1998), confidentiality is a therapist's ethical obligation to keep the identity of the clients they see in sessions and the content of those sessions secret. Session content includes recollections of dialogue as well as written records referring to that dialogue. Confidentiality is distinct from "privileged communication," which refers to clients' legal right to prevent a court from demanding the therapist disclose identity or session content.

There are limits to confidentiality, and part of valuing the client's autonomy is to explain clearly those limits to the client. As Welfel (1998) explained, therapeutic professionals are latecomers to the legal protection of confidentiality, and this protection is weaker for therapeutic professionals than for lawyers, physicians, or clerics. Be that as it may, all therapists should make every effort to explain confidentiality to clients in a manner the clients are likely to understand. A concise, honest, and developmentally appropriate dialogue with clients about confidentiality is an act of beneficence, whereas an incomplete or a developmentally inappropriate dialogue on confidentiality is maleficient. Being clear with the client about the limits of confidentiality is particularly important.

Confidentiality can be broken ethically under several circumstances. First, if the counselor believes that the client is a danger to her- or himself or others, the counselor may break confidentiality. Ideally, the counselor should make an effort to share these concerns directly with the client and to share her or his intentions to break confidentiality.

> As one of the primary clinicians who did crisis intervention at a mental health center, I evaluated and counseled many individuals who came into the center on an emergency basis to assess their level of suicidality. In the cases in which there was a high intent for self-harm and a clear plan, I strongly encouraged the client to tell a family member or another primary support person. I saw this as preferable to my breaking confidentiality to disclose the suicidality. This way allowed the client to remain in control of the course of treatment. I broke confidentiality only when the client flatly refused to make the disclosure her- or himself.

State laws vary regarding the degree of responsibility therapists have to warn an outside party that a client may be threatening but the ethical obligation is to make every effort to do so. Counselors are also obligated by law to break confidentiality if they suspect the client is abusing vulnerable individuals, such as children, elderly people, or people who are mentally retarded. Clients may not always see justice in these limitations on confidentiality. For example, one client, suffering from paranoid schizophrenia, believed that the counselor had violated his rights by having him placed in an inpatient setting following his statements of suicidal intent. In this case, the client (who had stopped taking the medication that was controlling his symptoms) insisted he had every right to take his own life. After a grueling session in which the client became increasingly suspicious of and hostile to the counselor, inpatient commitment was arranged. Not all instances necessitating the breaking of confidentiality are as neat as this. What about the client who suffers from HIV infection and states intent to practice unsafe sex if given the opportunity? This will be addressed more specifically at the end of the chapter, but the example points to the degree of complexity that can be involved in breaking confidentiality.

Abiding by the limits of confidentiality can be a practice in fidelity with clients. It is important that clients know they can trust what you say, even if they disagree with your actions at the time. We can reframe abiding by the limits of confidentiality as modeling consistency and boundary setting in the therapeutic relationship. Some clients may have had relationships in which there were inconsistent expectations or unclear rules and boundaries. By stating at the outset the limits of confidentiality, when you encounter a situation in which you must follow through on those limits, it communicates to the client that you are true to your word. Therefore, although it may seem like a betrayal, it can actually be helpful and therapeutic for the client to know the limits of your relationship.

> A co-worker was working with a 15-year-old boy who was depressed. After about three sessions, the boy disclosed that he had a plan to hang himself that weekend. The counselor had no choice but to notify the parents and arrange for a hospitalization. In this case, the counselor had neglected to discuss the limits of

confidentiality with the client ahead of time. After the hospitalization, the client refused to continue counseling because he felt betrayed by the counselor.

Professional Responsibility

Professional responsibility deals with the counselor's knowledge of ethical standards, boundaries of competence, honest disclosure of credentials, ethical practice in advertising services, and responsibility to the public and other professionals. The virtue of honoring the client's autonomy is practiced in this area by clearly knowing (and stating) what you can and cannot offer clients. It is important that you communicate clearly to clients (or potential clients when advertising or interacting with the public) what help you believe you can offer them. This must be based in your knowledge of your strengths and weaknesses as they relate to clients' problems. Two essential ingredients of therapeutic success are the client's belief that the therapist can help her or him and the therapist's belief that she or he can help the client (Frank, 1961; Yalom, 1995).

Therapists are ethically bound to evaluate realistically whether they have the competence to work with a particular client. All too often, clients are willing to perceive counselors as sages who can ease their suffering when, in fact, there may be no basis for this. Given this tendency and the somewhat abstract nature of therapy, it is always a temptation for therapists to delude themselves that they are able to work with all clients under all circumstances. The existential givens of finitude and temperament consistently say otherwise. In life, each of us has finite energies and talents. In counseling, this fact must be respected, so that you do not take on clients you have neither the energy nor the talent to help. In addition, your temperament will dictate the types of cases you are effective in working with. It is your duty to continually assess your skills and areas of expertise, while striving to maintain them, and to develop new ones through continuing education. It is beneficent and nonmaleficent to engage continually in this self-assessment.

What about professional responsibility and justice? If a counselor's sense of justice is rooted in compassion, there is a higher probability that the counselor will assess accurately what she or he can and cannot offer clients. For example, one therapist, a clinical social worker, worked for over a year with a man suffering from depression. This client did all his "homework" and worked dutifully through gestalt, cognitive, and client-centered techniques. Despite the best efforts of client and therapist, the client's symptoms persisted. The therapist had long suspected that the client may benefit from psychotropic medication, but the client resisted to the idea. Although the therapist enjoyed working with the client, the difficult day came when she stated that she did not believe the client was going to get better unless he supplemented their efforts with a trial of antidepressant medication. She no longer believed that her skills alone would help the client and knew it was her ethical duty to share that with the client. The client finally did acquiesce to a trial of paroxotine (Paxil), which alleviated many of his physical symptoms, freeing him to put even more energy into the therapeutic relationship. The therapist's compassion for the client guided her sense of what was right (most helpful) for the client. Clearly, this example also illustrates the therapist's practice of fidelity with the client. It was tempting for her to believe that, if she just kept working with the client, the depression would remit. She also knew that the client was suffering from his symptoms and that her primary concern was to use the knowledge available to her to ease that suffering. She consulted with two supervisors (one of whom was a psychiatrist), who both confirmed that the client's most problematic symptoms seemed to be vegetative (related to physical signs, such as disruption in sleep, appetite, and libido).

A final note on professional responsibility is in order. Chapter 1 stated that there are a variety of therapeutic professionals offering counseling or similar services and that there is often antagonism among these groups. Much of the enmity seems to be related to economic "turf battles," which are part of the structure of a free-market, capitalist system. Be that as it may, this does not reduce the clinician's ethical obligation to act responsibly in interactions with other professionals. This obligation includes honoring the fact that others have a right to choose their professional paths and to ethically earn their livelihood in the practice of those professions. Too much energy is wasted when members of one therapeutic profession criticize members of another. As noted in chapter 1, there is no evidence to support such an attitude.

Relationships with Other Professionals

Power, like the diamond, dazzles the beholder and the wearer equally.

C. C. Colten

This area of the ACA code addresses the therapist in professional relationships, particularly with employers and employees. It indicates the behaviors that are desirable in the organizational culture of the workplace. This section of the ethical code addresses the formal expectations within the organizational culture. However, there are also informal aspects to the workplace that may be more influential and more difficult to discern (Alle-Corliss & Alle-Corliss, 1999). The golden five principles we have been examining can give a newcomer to any organizational culture the basic tools to build ethical work relationships.

Respect for autonomy extends beyond clients to peers, employees, and employers. Part of honoring others' autonomy is crafting clear agreements between you and those whom you employ, supervise, or consult with. Just as in a counseling relationship we distinguish the client's "job" from the counselor's "job", in professional relationships we clearly communicate the parameters of the work situation. Since human services are not highly valued in American society, their funding depends on the political climate. As discussed in chapter 2, the combination of stressful workload and low pay has always been an occupational hazard. Agency supervisors and administrators can model respect for employees by paying attention to the stresses their employees are under and to the ways in which agency resources are allocated. Clearly worded agreements related to employment and job description can preclude a great deal of frustration.

> In my one of my earlier jobs in community mental health, I had a supervisor whose only knowledge of my job description was "other duties as assigned." Our agency worked on a thin budget, and we all pitched in to keep the physical structure running, but it seemed that every day she was asking me to do some non-counseling duty, such as unplugging drains, moving furniture in the recreation area, and assisting with cleaning tasks. To make matters worse, I had never really been given a job description and was beginning to understand why that was so important. Under that arrangement, my ability to move large pieces of furniture seemed more important to my supervisor than my counseling skills.

In terms of work arrangements, beneficence and nonmaleficence can be practiced through fair employment practices and healthy relationships with co-workers and employees. This section of the ACA ethical code includes positions on exploitative relationships and discrimination. Clearly, the presence of either of these in the workplace is detrimental, and practices that bring about or contribute to these situations are unethical. Similarly, justice can be practiced with regard to the ethical guidelines on fair employment and ethical professional conduct. Again, a sense of justice rooted in compassion can cultivate a healthy work climate in which employees feel they are compensated fairly for their work and receive some satisfaction from that work. A sense of justice rooted in fear of reprisal will more likely create a work environment that is fraught with underlying frustration and paralyzed by a rigid hierarchy. Unhealthy work environments are almost always correlated with the presence of such a hierarchy. These organizations seem to be characterized by a lack of trust of the co-workers in one another and in themselves. Such a work climate is also highly correlated with burnout, which we discussed in chapter 2. Practicing fidelity in work relationships is as important as practicing it with clients. Such practices need to be rooted consistently in your sense of self in order to be effective. The best place to start any work relationship is to do what you say you are going to do. This is not always easy, especially in human service agencies, where increases in workloads may not be matched by increases in pay.

The context of ethical behavior relates to McGregor's (1960) two theories of organizational culture (theory "X" and theory "Y"). Theory "X" is somewhat pessimistic about human nature. It postulates that people work only for profit and to survive. This theory recommends treating people in this manner, expecting them to work as little as they can get away with. Theory "Y," in contrast, is more optimistic. It postulates that people work for the intrinsic enjoyment of the work, independent of the money they make. In most cases, there is probably a little of both theories in each organizational climate. The more an organizational culture tends toward a theory "Y" philosophy, the more likely the employees will be treated in an ethical manner.

> I worked for a governmental agency that was managed from a theory "X" perspective. One day, after moving to an unfamiliar city and being employed at the agency for two weeks, I accidentally took the wrong bus to work and arrived at 7:36 A.M. rather than 7:30. My supervisor called me into his office and informed me that I would be charged one-half day of vacation time ("leave time") because I had not observed my work schedule. Despite my profuse apologies and offer to work through my lunch hour to make up the lost minutes, he insisted that I be charged vacation time. This had a detrimental effect on my morale and increased my sensitivity to other management decisions that seemed to have a negative impact on co-workers.

Cultural Issues in Evaluation, Assessment, and Interpretation

Looking to science alone is as narrow as clinging to parables.

Mitsugi Saotome

As the counseling field becomes increasingly clinical, there are more and more assessment and evaluation instruments used in practice. This not only requires counselors to master a more challenging knowledge base but also an awareness of the appropriate and ethical use of those tools available. Hood and Johnson (1997) emphasized the importance of asking "Who is making the assessment?" and "What is being assessed?" Another important question is "What tool is being used to assess the client?"

These three questions have particular importance regarding cultural differences between the clinician doing the assessment and the client being assessed. We will now explore the importance of cultural awareness in the ethical practice of assessment. By maintaining cultural awareness as you engage in ethical assessment practices, you can adequately meet all five golden principles. Since this section focuses on the practice of the five golden principles through cultural awareness, you should again refer to the ACA code of ethics at the end of this chapter for a complete treatment of ethical assessment.

Who Is Making the Assessment?   First and foremost, this question simply asks if the assessment is a self-assessment (*s* or subjective data), an assessment by another person (*o* or objective data), or a combination of the two. An important dimension to the question is whether there are important cultural differences between the clinician doing the assessment and the client being assessed. This topic is receiving increasing consideration in all the therapeutic professions.

The ACA (1995) code of ethics states that "counselors recognize that culture affects the manner in which clients' problems are defined." When you assess a client, you will usually attempt to ascertain the degree of disturbance that person is experiencing. You also will try to differentiate between normal and abnormal behavior, evaluations based on normative data, meaning that, informally, you are comparing your client with your mental representation of the general population. Counselors base their definitions of abnormal partially on the rate of occurrence of certain symptoms; people with abnormal symptoms have symptoms that are infrequent in the population. During an assessment, it is important to be aware of the extent to which your definition of normal is based on a population that is culturally homogeneous. For example, the term *co-dependent* has appeared in the popular literature and media. It is a term that was originally used in the context of substance abuse. However, the construct of co-dependency grew out of the dominant U.S. culture and is not appropriate for culturally "different" people, such as Hispanics or Asians (Gonzalez, Griffith, & Ruiz, 1994). Thus, if a statistical base is used to determine what is normal, that base cannot be generalized beyond the demographics in the sample used to compile it.

Recognizing the limits of constructs, samples, and statistical bases increases the probability that you will help rather than harm the client in the assessment phase. All five golden principles are practiced in cultural awareness during assessment. Respect for the client's autonomy extends to the awareness that the client may make choices based on premises that differ from your own. It is beneficent and nonmaleficent to honor both the client's choices and the premises they are based on. The question of who is making the assessment also calls into question the qualifications of that person. Clinicians not only need to be educated about the intended uses, psychometric properties, and appropriate uses of instruments but also should have supervised practicum/internship experience in using those tools before ending their formal training.

What Is Being Assessed?   This question refers to how the client is being defined (individual, couple, family) and what domain (affect, cognition, behavior) is being assessed. Affect may be temperamental or motivational. Cognitive variables include achievement and aptitude. Behavioral measures include both voluntary and nonvoluntary responses.

Ethical assessment includes identifying the client appropriately, identifying the proper domain of assessment, and being flexible about theories of etiology. The practice of family therapy has highlighted many important limitations in diagnosing and assessing only individuals. The degree to which family dynamics play the prominent role in symptom manifestation is the degree to which the family, not just the individual, needs to be the target of assessment. Again, cultural differences play a major role in the degree to which individuals see themselves as either separating from the family or individuating in the context of the family (Gonzalez et al., 1994). The former is more typically North American and the latter more typically Asian.

Regarding the domain of assessment, it is very difficult to isolate affect, cognition, and behavior. The three go together, much the same way coffee grounds, water, and a container constitute a cup of coffee. The best we can do is understand which domain we are aiming at, while accepting that the other two will encroach on that domain. In addition, it is important to take into account the influence of environment on the client and the domain. Mezzich, Kleinman, and Fabrega (1993) summarized several environmental influences that need to be included in the assessment of clients being considered for certain diagnoses. One example is that diagnoses such as substance abuse, learning disorders, and disruptive disorders may be a function of an environment of cultural dislocation and oppressive surroundings.

Regarding flexibility in interpreting etiology, the *Diagnostic and Statistical Manual of Mental Disorders* (American Psychiatric Association, 1994) is a good tool but does have certain limitations. For one thing, it does not explain why certain disorders manifest the way they do. In this sense, the manual is *aetiological,* meaning it endorses no theories of what causes disorders. Cultural differences play an important role in the explanations given for certain disorders. Cultures vary to the degree that they stigmatize mental and emotional problems. When the stigma is high, it is common to find people in these cultures offering somatic or environmental explanations for symptoms. In a study by White (1982), Hong Kong Chinese students were compared with North American students in the types of explanations they gave for particular behaviors or somatic complaints. By and large, the Chinese students relied more on explanations involving situational or environmental factors, whereas the North American students relied more on explanations involving psychological factors.

What Tool Is Being Used to Assess the Client?   If clinicians are to practice ethically while assessing clients, they must know the characteristics of the tools they are using to conduct the assessment. With regard to psychological testing, the therapeutic professions seem to have reached two conclusions that can be viewed as contradictory.

First, there is no such thing as a culture-free test. There are tests that are more "culture-fair" than others, but even this distinction has severe limitations. Second, culture permeates the environment, and the effect of one's environment always influences test results. This leads to the conclusion that "every test tends to favor persons from the culture in which it was developed" (Anastasi & Urbina, 1997, p. 342). Anastasi and Urbina noted that cultural differences become cultural handicaps when a person leaves one culture or subculture and tries to live—that is, tries to compete and succeed—in a different culture. These authors noted that, although this type of intercultural exchange stimulates the advance of civilizations, it can be difficult for the individuals involved.

There are important cultural limitations in any tool used to assess clients. The best way to guard against the inappropriate use of an assessment instrument is to understand the norming population of the instrument and its psychometric properties. If your client fits the demographic span of the norming population, there is less chance that the tool will mistake cultural differences for pathology.

The Resolution of Ethical Dilemmas

Therapeutic professionals are required to know and follow the guidelines for ethical practice. Despite this, violations and uncertainties occur in practice, and professionals must know the basic steps in resolving ethical issues. These are covered in a section of the ACA ethical code. First and foremost, counselors are expected to have training in understanding and applying their ethical code in practice settings. As the code of ethics states, ignorance or misunderstanding of the code is no defense against unethical conduct.

When a counselor is uncertain about the ethics of her or his actions (or those of a colleague), the counselor should first seek out consultation with other professionals who are knowledgeable about the actions in question. If the conflict is between the code of ethics and the organization for which the counselor works, the counselor should seek out a supervisor, explain the conflict, and express her or his commitment to the ethical code. The ACA code of ethics reinforces that, when possible, the counselor should work toward change in the organization, so that it complies with the ethical code.

If you are concerned that another counselor is practicing unethically, and you judge that the degree of harm being done is minimal, the ethics code encourages you first to resolve the situation informally. Note that you can do this only if the act of informal resolution is not going to violate confidentiality. Informal resolution entails approaching the colleague, explaining your concern, and suggesting a more appropriate course of action that is in line with the ethical code. This approach can be well received by colleagues who may not be aware they are violating the ethical code. If a colleague's unethical practice is doing harm to others (including clients and co-workers), you must report the suspected violation to the state or national ethics committee. Again, this action should not conflict with confidentiality rights. Finally, counselors are not to make unwarranted or frivolous complaints and are expected to cooperate with ethics committees in their investigations of complaints.

SELECTED ETHICAL ISSUES

In this section, we will deal with some ethical situations important to agency counseling: sexual contact with clients, work with involuntary clients, work with clients suffering from human immunodeficiency virus (HIV) infection or acquired immune deficiency syndrome (AIDS), and therapy and technology. We will end this section with a discussion of ethical issues related to managed care and third-party billing. Managed care in general is treated in detail in chapter 8.

Sexual Contact with Clients

The prohibition against sexual contact with clients is at least as old as the 2,500-year-old Hippocratic oath, which demands that practitioners work only for the good of the patient. Despite the longevity of the prohibition, it was not incorporated into the various helping professions until modern times (Koocher & Keith-Speigel, 1998). Welfel (1998) noted that, despite clear prohibitions in all mental health professions, sexual misconduct with clients continues. The ACA, APA, NASW, and AAMFT all unequivocally prohibit sexual contact with clients. Sexual misconduct is an ethical violation committed by mental health professionals ranging from newcomers to the field to established figures who have served in leadership positions (Pope, 1990), and only recently has it gotten the attention it deserves from professional organizations and the legal system (Welfel, 1998). Recent surveys indicate that clients whose therapists have breached this ethical boundary still have to struggle to obtain satisfactory assistance with their complaints (Luepker, 1999).

In summarizing the data on sexual misconduct by therapists, Welfel noted the following:

- Male therapists are most often the offenders and female clients most often the victims.
- Therapist characteristics other than gender have not been reliable predictors of who will commit sexual misconduct with a client.
- The problem is increasingly reported worldwide, not just in North America.
- The sexual contact is not limited to adults and includes children.
- Efforts in rehabilitating professionals who commit this ethical violation have not been very successful.

Sexual misconduct by therapists is one of the most common ethical complaints handled by the state boards that license mental health professionals (Neukrug, Healy, & Herlihy, 1992). Many studies suggest that therapists from social workers to psychologists do not feel that they received adequate training in dealing responsibly with this problem (Blanchard & Lichtenberg, 1998; Sehl, 1998). National efforts are being made to include education related to the prevention of sexual misconduct as part of the preparation of mental health professionals (Samuel & Gorton, 1998). According to Plaut (1997), effective prevention requires understanding the nature of trust-based relationships and the damage that sexual misconduct can cause.

Both therapists and clients feel the negative effects of sexual misconduct, but clients are affected far more than is the offending therapist. Luepker (1999) found in one sample of women increased posttraumatic stress symptoms, depressive symptoms, suicidality, the use of prescription drugs and alcohol, and disrupted work and personal relationships following practitioner sexual misconduct. In addition, such offenses tarnish the reputation of the profession in the community.

Dealing with sexual attraction to clients requires a good supervisory relationship in which these feelings can be explored. You should consider personal counseling for yourself if you experience such feelings and they disrupt your ability to work with clients. Dealing with sexual feelings for a client can be one of the most difficult self-exploration tasks a person can engage in, but, if they become an issue, it is imperative to deal with them for both client safety and counselor self-care.

Work with Involuntary Clients

Another ethical (and procedural) paradox in the therapeutic professions involves counseling clients who are coerced into treatment. On the one hand, most counseling theories (with the exception of behavior therapy) assume that the client is, generally, cooperative in the sense of wanting the clinician's services to make a change in her or his life (Gladding, 1997; Ritchie, 1986). On the other hand, in agency settings many clients are there by court order, and their only alternative is incarceration. Consider the following case.

> Rick was a 19-year-old male who was ordered by the court to counseling at the agency where I worked. He had a history of substance abuse, one driving while intoxicated (DWI) conviction, one conviction for drunk and disorderly conduct, and a recent court conviction for assault for which he was placed on probation. After the assault conviction, Rick was diagnosed with major depression and polysubstance abuse. He was hospitalized for a short period, prescribed medication, and mandated to take part in counseling and partial hospitalization and to reside in a group home or face incarceration for violation of probation. Rick was quite angry that he had to live in a semisupervised group home and come to counseling. He said we could make him come but he wasn't going to change. I first told Rick that he was right, that there was nothing I could do to make him change. Then I shared that I did not like treating people in Rick's situation and that I seriously doubted I could help him make changes without some cooperation on his part. More than affirming what power Rick did have, I think there was some countertransference on my part, as this was the sixth involuntary client to whom I was assigned that month. We spent the first five sessions just discussing his anger and his options. He could feign the "right" behaviors and stay in treatment long enough to get off probation, refuse counseling and face incarceration, or engage in counseling to examine some of the issues that had landed him in his situation. Rick wanted to avoid prison at all costs. He had been sexually abused as a child and knew that sexual assault was a common occurrence in prison. This left two choices. Certainly, Rick was less than the "ideal" client. He did, however, have

enough dread of prison as an aversive stimulus to engage in behavioral treatment, with remaining out of prison as the prime reinforcer. In time, enough of a therapeutic alliance developed, and Rick began engaging in cognitive work, examining some of the cognitive distortions that only escalated his anger.

In Rick's case, the aversive stimulus was strong enough and his reality testing intact enough for a favorable outcome, but such is not always the case. What are the ethical implications for treating involuntary clients and what is the best way to proceed? These are the two questions we will address in this section.

The involuntary client either is required by law to attend counseling sessions or is otherwise pressured to attend counseling. In involuntary counseling relationships, the client feels forced to remain in the relationship because of the lack of an attractive alternative (Rooney, 1992). In these instances, the power differential between counselor and client increases. This raises the ethical question about whether such relationships are appropriate. "Freedom of choice" is defined in the ACA ethical code as the freedom to choose whether or not to enter into a relationship with a counseling professional. Does the client truly have freedom of choice? In Rick's case, legally and technically, he had a choice (albeit the alternative was prison). Philosophically, we could probably debate how much the conditions really constituted a choice. On the other hand, Rick's behavior got him involved with the criminal justice system; in that involvement, he lost some of the rights retained by people who are not involved with the criminal justice system. The question still remains as to whether or not the referral of people like Rick to counseling is appropriate. In addition, the ACA ethical code states that clients are supposed to consent to the treatment described by the counselor. Under the involuntary conditions described, is the client truly consenting? Despite the positive aspects of Rick's treatment, the research has yielded mixed results on treatment outcome with involuntary clients. In some studies, treatment outcomes in involuntary relationship fall far behind outcomes in voluntary relationships (Paradise & Wilder, 1979). Other researchers, such as Gove and Fain (1977) and Bastien and Adelman (1984), found that the notion that voluntary clients will progress more than nonvoluntary clients was not supported.

"Involuntariness" may involve reluctance, resistance, or both. Ritchie (1986) summarized the difference between *reluctance* and *resistance*. Whereas *reluctance* is associated with "involuntariness," *resistance* is an unwillingness to change. If they were given a choice, reluctant clients would not seek out the services of a counselor. Resistant clients may seek counseling but then put all their energy into staying the same rather than risking a change. A client entering treatment with reluctance typically does so because of external demands from an organization or individual. Virtually all clients, even those who have a high degree of readiness to make changes, experience and express some amount of resistance (Ritchie, 1986). One way of thinking about resistance is to think of the familiarity of maintaining the status quo, even if it means continuing to have one's symptoms. In some ways, this can be more comforting than embarking on making changes and focusing on the issues that caused the problem in the first place. Obviously, a client could be reluctant and resistant. In the case of Rick, he started out as both reluctant and resistant but decreased his resistance to the point at which some valuable work could be done. The therapeutic alliance is a key to overcoming reluctance and resistance, but, as the name implies, it takes both the clinician and the client to establish and develop it. As in the case of Rick, one cornerstone of counseling involuntary clients is to start where the client is. In these cases, the client is usually feeling frightened, angry, and somewhat powerless. By acknowledging the anger, you can at least address it while validating the power the client has and, at the same time, not exacerbate the feelings of powerlessness.

A continuum of techniques can be used with involuntary clients, depending on the degree of their unwillingness to change (reluctance). The continuum moves from the least intrusive techniques, relying on persuasion methods, to the most intrusive, compliance-oriented methods. Cialdini (1993) outlined the methods of persuasion. These include the foot-in-the-door principle (asking clients for a small concession increases the probability that they will acquiesce to a larger concession) and the door-in-the-face principle (asking for an outrageously large concession increases the probability that clients will acquiesce to a considerably smaller one —the one you really wanted all along). Compliance-oriented methods are designed to directly influence actions and attitudes by punishing undesirable behaviors and rewarding desirable behaviors (Rooney, 1992). These include the use of chemical or physical restraint. The following are some types of punishment commonly used:

- Positive punishment: the use of an aversive consequence after an unwanted behavior occurs. An example is the use of Antabuse (disulfiram) to induce vomiting in alcoholics who drink.
- Response cost punishment: withholding reinforcements when an unwanted behavior occurs. An example is withholding a smoking client's cigarette ration when the client violates the behavior contract.
- Negative reinforcement: removal of an aversive stimulus when an unwanted behavior stops and then applying a positive reinforcer when the desired behavior appears. An example is placing a client in a more supervised setting following an undesired behavior (if, indeed, the client desires the least supervised setting). This is followed with a move to a less supervised setting after the inappropriate behavior stops, followed by the appearance of the desired behavior.

Skinner (1953) pointed out that punishment is not as effective as an appropriately planned schedule of reinforcement. Obviously, one of the keys to reinforcement management with resistant, involuntary clients is that you must have control over something the client wants, which makes it a reinforcer. Some court-ordered clients who know that overcrowded prisons are the only reason they are diverted to counseling. They also know there is a slim chance of being incarcerated due to that condition. With these clients, it is very difficult to establish any therapeutic rapport and to find a reinforcer adequate to motivating them if your attempts at rapport totally fail. If you are considering entering an area of human services that uses punishment with involuntary clients, you need to investigate fully the types of punishment being used and the ethical implications of them. Further, you need to compare this with your vision of how you feel most effective working with clients. As in other areas we have discussed in this text, self-knowledge increases the probability of a good fit.

It is interesting that counseling involuntary clients is often assumed to imply that the status of the therapist is lower than the status of a therapist treating voluntary clients. Rooney (1992) noted that greater prestige is projected onto therapists who treat voluntary clients. These are the clients that are usually written about in case studies, talked about at conferences, and most desired in practice. Rooney also noted the following:

- Practitioners often lack the theoretical concepts for understanding what occurs in involuntary sessions, since most clinicians are trained with models based on voluntary relationships.
- The use of authority (as in getting control of something the client desires for use as a reinforcer) has not been fashionable in the therapeutic professions. There is a delicate line between respecting the client and taking the position of court-sanctioned authority figure. Carl Rogers (1942) even went so far as to say that the counselor cannot maintain a relationship with the client if the counselor has authority over the client.
- Models of service provision for involuntary clients can conflict with an agency's public statements of how it is serving the community. Most communities do not want to house agencies that are treating involuntary clients. Most agencies want to justify their funding by demonstrating that they offer services relevant to the community but find that there is more funding if they treat involuntary clients. Also, remaining is the question of whether an involuntary relationship can be freely chosen.
- Often, therapeutic professionals question the worth of rehabilitation efforts for involuntary clients.

According to Rooney, counseling involuntary clients does not have to be distasteful social control nor ethically questionable. The three aspects of involuntary treatment that must be balanced are (1) practice within the legal guidelines with adequate concern for client protections, (2) work for an ethical blend of self-determination (client autonomy) and paternalism, and (3) practice in a manner that meets the goals of treatment.

Regarding the first aspect of involuntary treatment, adequate concern for the client may be expressed in advocating for, what research points to, as enabling conditions for success in therapy. One such condition is pretherapy training. This is time taken with the involuntary client to explain what the therapy is about, what the alternatives are, and how the client can best use the sessions. Rooney noted that this can reduce the client's ambiguity about the counselor's role.

Regarding the second aspect of involuntary treatment, one way to balance self-determination with paternalism is to separate negotiable from nonnegotiable treatment elements. Nonnegotiable treatment elements are conditions for remaining in treatment such as submitting to and passing drug tests and refraining from violence. The client must perceive the negotiable elements as desirable things he or she can work toward. Contracting for an appropriate increase in autonomy or privileges contingent on agreed upon measures of progress can enhance the client's motivation.

The third aspect of involuntary treatment, practicing in a manner that meets the goals of treatment, is the ideal win-win situation. The client's behavior is modified to fulfill the goal of social control that underlies the client's commitment to treatment, while the client re-enters society with some tools that decrease the probability of recidivism. Although far more research is needed, that also raises the ethical dilemma of informed consent. Many therapists fear that requesting research consent from involuntary clients will increase their resistance to treatment.

Work with Clients with HIV or AIDS

The Centers for Disease Control (CDC) define acquired immune deficiency syndrome (AIDS) in an adolescent over age 13 or in an adult as the presence of one or more opportunistic diseases, such as Kaposi's sarcoma, or an HIV-infected person with a CD4+ T-helper cell count less than 200 cells per cubic millimeter of blood. In children, the definition is similar but includes more diseases and bacterial infections. Since clinical investigators on both U.S. coasts began seeing the disorder in 1981, AIDS has had an impact on our culture like no other epidemic. Estimates of the number of AIDS cases and cases of HIV infection are difficult to come by. The American Association for World Health (1998) noted that, currently, reported practices vary from state to state. Only 30 states report the numbers of known HIV cases to the CDC; only 27 states report adult, adolescent, and pediatric cases; and 20 states do not report HIV cases. This situation, combined with the latency period for HIV (10 years or more) and newer effective treatments, further complicates estimating the number of Americans affected. Although estimates of infection vary, it is increasingly likely that therapists will treat clients suffering from AIDS or HIV infection or who are affected through the infection of a significant other.

The increasing incidence of HIV transmission has forced the allied health professions to modify some aspects of service delivery for clients and patients who are HIV positive. The AIDS epidemic has raised broad ethical questions for therapeutic professionals about protecting client confidentiality and the extent of a therapist's duty to warn third parties who may become infected through certain types of contact with the client. The idea of coerced partner notification stems from a U.S. Health Department policy called "contact tracing," which was initially implemented in the 1930s to stem the spread of syphilis and gonorrhea. The American Civil Liberties Union (ACLU) (1998) argued that this was dramatically different, since a cure exists for both syphilis and gonorrhea, whereas the current lack of a cure for HIV infection decreases the chance that such a policy would be effective in decreasing transmission. The ACLU has noted that the original contact tracing failed to slow the spread of syphilis and gonorrhea. Currently, states vary regarding reporting practices in health-care settings.

While the debate continues over whether health-care professionals should be required by law to report HIV-positive patients, therapeutic professionals must face similar issues. As Welfel (1998) noted, only the ACA code of ethics has made explicit reference to the limits of confidentiality when the client has a contagious, fatal disease. The ACA ethical stance is that, before the counselor breaks client confidentiality to warn a third party who will be infected in the future by the client, the counselor needs to know that the third party is identifiable and at risk for contracting the disease from the client. In addition, the counselor needs to be certain that the client has not informed the third party or has no intention to do so in the near future. The ethical principle of beneficence is the primary principle underlying a counselor's duty to warn in these situations (Melchert & Patterson, 1999).

In 1988, Ryan and Rowe predicted the following ethical problems in counseling clients with HIV or AIDS:

- Therapists experiencing serious countertransference in response to client behaviors and values
- Increased conflict with colleagues who have unresolved issues and biases related to HIV/AIDS
- Concerns about whether to reveal HIV status to clients' sexual partners
- Conflicts with agencies that do not have or do not follow proper protocol regarding HIV-infected clients and employees
- Concerns about the degree to which the counselor should act as a client advocate

Gray and Harding (1988) outlined the limits of confidentiality that came to be reflected in the ACA ethical guidelines. They stated that therapists are justified in breaking confidentiality when three conditions are met: (1) a therapeutic relationship exists between the counselor and the client, (2) the client is known to have a medically verified diagnosis of HIV infection or AIDS and refuses to make contacts aware of the situation, and (3) the risk to other identifiable victims is (or seems) imminent. Gray and Harding added that, when these criteria are met and the counselor knows that the client is engaging in unsafe sexual contact with anonymous partners, that counselor is justified in contacting the state public health office. As noted earlier, what happens from that point depends on the state law. These positions are similar to those outlined for psychologists by Melchert and Patterson (1999), but it is also important to understand the state guidelines as they vary state to state.

Erickson (1990) also offered three levels of guidelines around confidentiality and HIV-infected clients. The first level includes telling the client the limits of confidentiality in the initial counseling session. If the client's HIV status is then disclosed in the therapeutic relationship, the counselor should begin to educate and counsel the client toward the goal of responsible sexual behavior and should secure permission to contact the medical professional who confirmed the client's HIV status. Part of this education is to encourage the client to notify sexual partners. Counselors then assist clients in clarifying the values related to decisions they make about health practices. Erickson noted that an often neglected component, that of helping the client with any denial or grieving, should be included in the first level. In addition, level 1 guidelines include gaining access to appropriate referrals, such as groups for HIV-infected people and support for significant others.

Erickson's second level begins with the counselor's securing permission from the client and contacting relevant medical personnel. If the client has not agreed to the importance of safe sex practices, the counselor can ask the medical personnel for assistance in effecting a change in the client's behavior. This practice will change from state to state, depending on what state law requires of medical personnel in terms of reporting practices. Both the therapeutic professional and the medical professionals involved are encouraged to work together at this level to get the client to change her or his behavior.

The third level assumes that the client has still not agreed to safe sexual practices and/or notifying sexual or needle sharing partners. At this level, the client is informed that if she or he will not act appropriately, the counselor will break confidentiality to protect vulnerable others in the client's life. If the client's contacts are anonymous, the counselor reports to the state health department. If the identity of the contacts is known, the counselor informs them directly. Erickson also noted that counselors can contact local law enforcement personnel to report probable harm to others. In extreme cases in which the victims are identifiable, police powers of quarantine may be applicable. In cases in which clients inform their partners of their HIV status, it is best if the therapist can be onhand, whether the contact is made in person or over the phone. Therapists can then know that the appropriate information is being communicated and can be there to offer interventions if needed (Knapp & VandeCreek, 1990).

Melchert and Patterson (1999) developed a protocol similar to Erickson's based on the client's risk level for HIV transmission. They outline four levels: no risk, negligible risk, high risk, and severe risk. "No risk" is designated for activity in which casual contact (such as handshakes) is made with an HIV infected person. Negligible risk includes clean needle sharing and safer sex practices, such as mutual masturbation. High risk includes unprotected sexual intercourse, the sharing of unclean needles, and higher frequencies of these types of behaviors. Severe risk is reserved for those who intend to harm others by infecting them with HIV.

Despite the concern for counseling irresponsible clients infected with HIV, another aspect of the AIDS crisis is the way in which therapeutic professionals are trained to work with responsible clients who are infected. Allers and Katrin (1988) developed an outline for an AIDS psychosocial counseling model, which has five phases relevant to preparing mental health professionals to work effectively with HIV-infected clients. The first component of the model is overcoming one's fear of HIV and AIDS. This phase of training focuses on gaining basic knowledge of the diseases and their psychosocial implications, including the possible negative reactions of the infected persons' significant others. The second phase focuses on redefining relationships. This emphasizes an examination (and strengthening, if necessary) of the client's current support system. The third phase focuses on helping the client modify her or his lifestyle. Aside from the obvious modifications related to the client's sexual practices and intravenous drug use, helping the client adjust to a lifestyle steeped in involvement with medical professionals should be addressed. The fourth phase of the model focuses on the existential and spiritual aspects of HIV/AIDS. This phase focuses on helping the client find meaning in the situation, as well as new ways to say "yes" to life in the midst of it. If the client develops AIDS and experiences debilitation, the final phase is designed to train counselors to help clients cope with these new limitations.

Obviously, therapeutic professionals can also offer interventions designed to prevent the spread of HIV. Kelly and Murphy (1992) noted that prevention efforts begin with the recognition of behaviors that put clients more at risk to contract HIV. These behaviors include engaging in heavy substance use before sexual activity, having low self-efficacy, receiving high reinforcement for unsafe sexual practices, and perceiving that unsafe sexual practices are a peer norm. Therapeutic professionals have numerous opportunities to heighten clients' awareness of behaviors that put them at higher risk for HIV infection.

Therapy and Technology

As Cottone and Tarvydas (1998) noted, the ethical codes of the mental health professions have scarcely been able to keep pace with the dramatic changes in computer and electronic technology. If you keep case notes on a computer and your hard drive crashes, is that an ethical violation? Are you violating confidentiality by communicating with a client or supervisee via e-mail? Can counseling really be done over the Internet? These are just some of the issues that are unresolved.

Sturges (1998) noted that the appropriate use of technology could result in a more cost-effective clinical practice, yet it is still unclear how much mental health professionals rely on technology. McMinn et al., (1999) studied a sample of psychologists and their uses of technology. The researchers categorized the behaviors that the respondents endorsed as "common" (meaning occurring for 90 percent or more of the sample), "equivocal" (meaning one of two conditions were met on ethics ratings indicating ethical uncertainty), and "rare" (meaning the behaviors only occurred for 10 percent or less of the sample). The common uses were related to using the telephone for crisis or other consultation; These were rated as generally ethically acceptable. Equivocal behaviors related to the areas of client confidentiality, technology failure, computer applications, and teleconferencing; there was great ethical uncertainty in these areas. Rare behaviors that were also rated unethical included listening to a client's phone message in the presence of another client, leaving confidential information displayed on a computer screen, faxing confidential information to the wrong destination, and allowing unauthorized access to client records. McMinn and colleagues concluded that psychologists are uncertain about the ethical uses of many technologies and that this is an area that mental health professionals need to develop through research and relevant publications.

Many mental health therapists use computers for word processing elements of case notes and case records. Concerning case records, Cottone and Tarvydas 1998) noted that it is far easier to steal a floppy disk or CD-ROM than with a full-sized chart, and the disk or CD could contain exponentially more case records. Data stored on floppy disks, CD-ROMs, zip-disks, and hard drives must be controlled. Professionals using their computers or computer-related elements to store client records should purchase and install security software that limits access to users with the appropriate codes. The American Psychological Association (1992) Ethical Principles and Code of Conduct note that client information not stored in secure computers must be coded anonymously, so that client identification is not possible. Gellman and Frawley (1996) described a secure computer as one that (1) does not permit unauthorized access to information, (2) retains a record of communications to and from the system, (3) prevents alterations in or loss of the data entered, (4) recovers completely and effectively from unexpected disruptions ("crashes" and power surges).

Ethics and Managed Care

Despite commonly held sentiments among service providers, the phrase "ethics and managed care" is not an oxymoron. There are managed care organizations (MCOs) that offer high-quality care at a reasonable cost as their primary goal. Even mental health providers, when surveyed, make the distinction between good and bad MCOs (Thompson et al., 1991). Although we will take an in-depth look at managed mental health care in chapter 8, we will conclude this chapter by considering ethical issues germane to managed mental health care.

A number of scenarios occur between service providers and managed care companies that, for the provider, constitute ethical dilemmas. The following are some of those scenarios:

- A client is depressed. The insurance company has authorized four sessions but no more because she is not imminently suicidal. After four sessions, she is still depressed but has no more session coverage. The insurer states, "We pay for crisis intervention and stabilization, not therapy."
- The insurance company allows for *x* number of sessions to be completed by a specified date. The counselor misses seeing the client for the authorized number of sessions by the deadline the insurance company has allowed.
- The client signs a waiver granting the counselor permission to speak with insurance and managed care companies about the diagnosis, so confidentiality per se is not an issue. However, the insurer must communicate with the client's employer about insurance use; therefore, confidentiality is compromised.
- The client must sometimes speak on the phone to an insurance company care manager. Some clients find it intrusive and upsetting to have to repeat their "story" to people over the phone, who will not be doing the counseling work with them.
- Some managed care companies do not like a particular treatment and will not pay for that treatment, despite evidence that the treatment strategy is effective (for example, eye movement desensitization and reprocessing).
- Many managed care companies have gag clauses as part of their contractual agreement with service providers. Therefore, the clinicians are prohibited from telling a client with a particular diagnosis that treatment coverage was denied because of the diagnosis—they can tell the client only that the claim was denied.

Ethics and ethical behavior have always been an important component of the provision of services to clients. However, with the emergence of managed care in mental health, new challenges appear for the sensitive and ethical provision of services. Indeed, some authors have observed, "The bioethical principles of autonomy, beneficence, non-maleficence, and justice are being strongly pressured by the current forces in the market" (Lazarus & Pollack, 1997, p. 30). This is not to imply that managed care is unethical care; only that in the context of managed care, the motives for decision making are primarily economic. Economic parsimony does not necessarily constitute unethical behavior, unless it sacrifices the sufficiency or quality of care in the process. This is precisely where some observers have criticized managed care and MCO companies in general.

> One psychologist, employed by an HMO, was asked to consult on an adolescent being treated as an inpatient for severe depression and seizures in a psychiatric unit. After a careful neuropsychological screening of the teen, the psychologist wrote in the teen's medical chart that an MRI was recommended to rule out a brain tumor. (MRIs are very precise and can detect tissue pathology that a CT scan misses.) Later that day, the psychologist was severely reprimanded by the supervising M.D. because the MRI suggestion had been written in the boy's chart. The HMO owned only CT equipment, not MRI. Since it was in the chart, the boy would need to be sent "out of network," at a higher cost to the HMO, to get the procedure. The psychologist was told to never again put a recommendation for a particular procedure in a chart but, instead, to discuss it only verbally with the medical staff.

As many politicians in the past several years have observed, there are fundamental problems with the health-care industry in the United States. To summarize the problem, the concept of free enterprise and political freedom are essential components of what has made the United States the land of promise for so many people from other countries. However, when the concept of free enterprise is applied to the delivery of health care, there are inevitable outcomes, one of which is that selected people profit. The selected people in this case are the people who set the fees for mental health services. They may be service providers who are setting their fees competitively or multiple providers in a specialty setting fees at a particular level so that, if patients want that service, they have no choice but to pay the set fee. More and more, it is the MCO that sets the fees paid to the provider and the percentage of profit paid to the MCO.

The notion of set fees brings us to another outcome of combining free enterprise and health care: some people will not be able to access care due to lack of resources. Obviously, only patients who have the money to pay for the service can get the service. These are usually people who are functioning highly enough to work at a job that provides insurance coverage, since most people do not have the money to pay out-of-pocket medical care. Because the federal and state money allocated for health care is limited, there are strict guidelines established for the medical and financial conditions that must be met in order for people to get public assistance to help with their medical care. This becomes an ethical issue upon closer examination.

Federal law requires employers who employ people full-time (40 hours per week) to provide certain benefits. As health-care costs have risen, the premiums employers must pay have also increased. One way employers have dealt with increasing health-care costs is to employ people less than full-time.

It is not unusual to see employees, particularly those who need minimal train-ing to do the job they are in, working 35 or 37 hours a week—essentially full-time but less than the number of hours at which the employer is mandated to provide benefits. Often, these people are working for hourly wages at or around minimum wage. This is the category referred to as "the working poor"—generating enough income that they do not qualify for federal or state assistance, but not generating enough income to be able to afford the medical care they have to pay for out-of-pocket, since they do not have insurance. The result is that many people have no medical coverage and go without preven-tive care because they simply cannot afford it.

The bottom line is that health-care professionals, counselors included, must face certain questions: Is everyone entitled to access to health care (in-cluding mental health)? If so, who should pay for it? One perspective is that adequate health care is a basic human right, an integral aspect of respecting the essential dignity of all individuals. If we, as a society, embrace this premise, we imply that some people in health care "should" be willing to work for oth-ers. These people may be the service providers who "should" be willing to do work at a reduced fee or pro bono (for free). The people who "should" work for others may be every employed individual who will pay more tax dollars for government-sponsored health care. Are the people who "should" work for others be the wealthier people, since they possess more fiscal resources? There are no easy answers to these questions.

Sabin (1996) presented four additional ethical principles to augment the golden five and stated that, when all these principles are met, counselors can confidently provide managed care services that are on solid ethical ground. The additional ethical principles are helpful in that they help shift the focus to broader issues than service provision to individual clients or even an individ-ual counselor's caseload. The principles are as follows:

- *Principle 1: Ethical clinicians should dedicate themselves to providing services to their clients with fidelity while respecting their stewardship for the collective resources of society.* Implied in this is a prohibition against overtreatment. This idea of protecting collective resources of society is one that is not mentioned often. If mental health professionals desire to offer services to the greatest possible number of people, then they must use their resources prudently. Dwyer and Shih (1998), Bilynsky and Vernaglia (1998), and Wineburgh (1998) have all discussed the ethical responsibility of mental health professionals not to overtreat clients or tailor client charts to what is reimbursable.
- *Principle 2: Ethical clinicians should recommend the least costly treatment choice unless there exists substantial evidence that a more expensive treatment would likely yield a more favorable outcome for the client.* Sabin (1996) observed that, although the connection between

financial resources and service delivery seems fragmented in the United States, the case is very different in Canada and the United Kingdom. In these countries, the public votes to increase taxes to finance health care for the entire population (although their tax burden is far greater). In those countries, the relationship between service to individual patients and collective resources is quite clear. American providers of medical and mental health services need to also acknowledge that, although our system is not socialized, we need to decide whether we have a responsibility to conserve money that can be used to help treat others. The problem is that, now that managed care has emerged on the scene, the payment for services has been reduced and fewer services are being paid for. Have the savings resulted in better care for all people? The jury is still out on this question.

- *Principle 3: Ethical clinicians must advocate for justice in the health-care system, and in their clinical role they must advocate for their clients.* Important perspectives must be considered by all service providers in order for principle 3 to be realized. First, clinicians and the general public need to insist that managed care systems prove that they really do enhance the effectiveness of health care. As noted in chapter 1, this is an area in which all the therapeutic professions can band together. Therapists, clients, and the employers who subscribe to managed care systems need to demand accountability for the fees the managed care systems are setting. Second, clinicians and the public need to insist on true informed consent. This means that insurance companies should be able to articulate in writing their philosophy of care and basis for deciding what will be covered and what will not. The purchasers of insurance coverage need to be able to compare the coverage and philosophy of several companies, so they can make an informed choice about the type of coverage they get.

- Principle 4: *Ethical clinicians insist that beneficial interventions should be withheld only on the basis of explicit standards.* This is an issue of informed consent. Wineburgh (1998) wrote that clinicians are ethically responsible for knowing the type and extent of services offered and for clearly communicating this to potential clients. If potentially helpful treatment procedures are going to be denied by the insurance company, explicit standards need to be established with the affected population. Moreover, individual patients need to acknowledge and agree with these standards. There are several ways managed care companies have accomplished cost containment (discussed in detail in chapter 8), all of which amount to the rationing of health-care services. One method by which cost containment has been achieved is by setting arbitrary benefit limits. For example, most MCO plans allow for 20 outpatient counseling/psychotherapy visits per year, but insurance providers may request justification for further treatment after only 5 sessions (Herron & Adlerstein, 1994). Although 20 outpatient sessions has been generally deemed an adequate number (Richardson & Austad, 1991), there are ethical and legal risks to these limitations (Herron & Adlerstein, 1994). There are clearly some people who could benefit by more than 20 sessions but, because of the cap, they are denied coverage. Since they cannot afford to pay out-of-pocket for more than 20 sessions, they essentially are denied service. In addition, caps on the number of sessions force clinicians to be competent at brief therapeutic interventions, although such interventions may not benefit all clients. Wineburgh (1998) noted that "one shoe does not fit all" (p. 440).

Other ethical dilemmas are also related to managed care in Sabin's four principles. One is the impact on the therapeutic relationship described by Blum (1992) and Edward (1999). In a sense, the therapeutic relationship involves not only the client and the clinician but the MCO overseeing services. As Bilynsky and Vernaglia (1998) noted, this complicates the transference and countertransference dynamics of the relationship, as well as compromises confidentiality (Edward, 1999). In addition to the competence issues raised by forcing a brief therapy model onto clinicians, therapists working in MCOs typically see a broader array of clients, some of whom they may not be competent to treat. Since many MCOs are closed systems, these therapists may not be able to refer the clients to more competent therapists.

A final ethical dilemma in managed care settings is the criticism that managed care practices neglect the cultural diversity of clients and force a Euro-American model on all clients, regardless of their background (Dana, 1998). The first issue involves who decides what services are required for culturally diverse clients. Dana (1998) argued that it is only recently that mental health professionals have encouraged the voice of diverse clients in deciding what type of care they should receive and that managed care arrangements have decreased the autonomy of both clinicians and clients, thus stifling this emergent voice. It has also been noted that even medical treatments for mental/emotional disorders have differential effects, depending on the client's race (Tien, 1984), as well as that different cultures may be less compliant with medication regimens than others (Chan, 1984). This new interest in ethnopharmacology is not represented in most managed care models.

Diagnosis and Third-Party Payors

Related to managed care ethical dilemmas are questions regarding diagnosis and third-party payors in general. Bilynsky and Vernaglia (1998) noted that managed care models put pressure on clinicians for quick diagnoses to justify payments for services. This is related to abuses in diagnosing as well as ne-glect in client care.

> In the community mental health agency where I was employed, we were required to generate a diagnosis on clients after the intake session. Sometimes when I would submit my billing sheet to our billing clerk, she would ask me if I was cer-tain of the diagnosis and if there were any more severe diagnosis I could assign. An example is adjustment disorder with depressed mood as opposed to major de-pression. This occurred because a given client's insurance carrier would provide coverage for major depression but not for adjustment disorder.

There may be times when what a clinician is required to do in order to get paid is in conflict with what is ethical and right. This example of "over-diagnosing,"—that is, making a diagnosis more severe than symptoms warrant to get reimbursement—is just such an instance. Although some clinicians view this as helping the client, it is insurance fraud and punishable in a court of law. In the previous example, the agency was under pressure to collect as much as possible from private insurance companies because the funds com-ing in from the state were decreasing. Consequently, there was more pressure on clinicians to generate billable hours, and to get those billable hours with clients whose insurance would pay well. The clinicians were not encouraged to overdiagnose; on the other hand, if there was a differential diagnosis deci-sion to be made, they were encouraged to give the most serious diagnosis pos-sible in order to increase the chances of reimbursability for services.

There are many financial situations in managed care in which clinicians can get into ethical trouble, if they are not careful. Welfel (1998) identified some considerations and questions clinicians need to ask themselves or their employers in order to stay on solid ethical ground. First, consider whether the financial agreement with the payor allows the practitioner to make indepen-dent professional judgment based on the client's goals and needs. Also con-sider whether the people conducting the utilization review have the appropriate clinical background to make informed decisions, taking into ac-count the idiosyncratic aspects of individual cases.

> I once had to contact a case manager to get authorization for emergency hospital-ization. As the suicidal client was sitting in my office, I called the case manager and proceeded to answer her questions about the client's history of depression and suicide attempts. The case manager was unclear on how to spell "Prozac" and was uninformed as to the difference between major depression and dys-thymia; I explained it to her during our conversation.

Many therapists are frequently frustrated by the amount of power third-party payers can exert over clinicians and clients' access to treatment. In fact, Welfel (1998) observed that, between the years 1990 and 1993, a full 15 per-cent of the ethics complaints filed with the American Psychological Associa-tion against psychologists were based on therapists' allegedly misrepresenting clients' diagnoses.

Welfel (1998) further asserted that clinicians need to consider what resources are available to meet special client needs and to allow for unique variables affecting the client's need for services. For example, one worried mother had a 12-year-old boy who acted very effeminate and was sometimes cross-dressing to go to school. Her HMO had a mental health department, but there were no clinicians who specialized in gender identity disorders of adolescence. It would be within reason to ask the HMO to authorize her to go out of network to work with a therapist who had gender identity issues as a specialty area. A related concern is whether the benefits plan responds to clients who are culturally diverse. There also need to be reasonable protections in place to guard the confidential therapeutic information. One of the biggest issues is whether the insurance plan recognizes that professionals have a duty to disclose the potential impact of managed care on treatment. This includes the possibility that the termination of benefits might occur before the problem has been resolved to the client's satisfaction.

One of the biggest problems with determining medical necessity in the mental health field is the ambiguity of desired outcomes. Is symptom remission or reduction sufficient? This brings us around again to the question of quality of life and, for example, whether someone who is in an unhappy marriage is as entitled to mental health care as someone who has bipolar disorder.

SUMMARY

We began this chapter with the idea that, when in doubt, do the right thing. Although many of us have a sense of "the right thing," that sense needs to be supplemented with a thorough knowledge of professional ethics combined with good supervision. As noted, you should study the ACA ethical code that constitutes the appendix to this chapter. Before going on to chapter 5, on services, consider the following discussion questions.

DISCUSSION ITEMS

1. What do you see as the guiding force in your life regarding ethical behavior? When you do the right thing, why do you do it?
2. Assume you are trying to find employment as an agency counselor. You interview with a managed care organization that asks if you are willing to set up brief therapy protocols with all your clients. How do you respond to this?
3. Imagine working in your internship, and a close friend, also in an agency counseling internship, tells you he has fallen in love with one of his clients

and they have begun dating. What is your response to this friend? What actions might you take?

4. What type of client do you think you would have the most difficulty working with because of countertransference issues? How would you deal with your issues if you were assigned such a client in an MCO and there was no mechanism for referral?

REFERENCES

Alle-Corliss, L., & Alle-Corliss, R. (1999). *Advanced practice in human services agencies: Issues, trends, and treatment perspectives.* Pacific Grove, CA: Brooks/Cole.

Allen, V. B. (1986). A historical perspective of the AACD ethics committee. *Journal of Counseling and Development, 64,* 293.

Allers, C. T., & Katrin, S. E. (1988). AIDS counseling: A psychosocial model. *Journal of Mental Health Counseling 10,* 235–244.

American Association for World Health. (1998). *Be a force for change. Resource booklet.* Washington, DC: Author.

American Civil Liberties Union (1998). HIV partner notification: Why coercion won't work. Internet Document found at *http://www.aclu.org/issues/aids/hiv_partner.html.*

American Counseling Association. (1995). *Code of ethics and standards of practice.* Alexandria, VA: Author.

American Psychiatric Association. (1994). *Diagnostic and statistical manual of mental disorders* (4th ed.). Washington, DC: Author.

American Psychological Association. (1992). Ethical principles of psychologists and code of conduct. *American Psychologist, 47,* 1597–1611.

Anastasi, A., & Urbina, S. (1997). *Psychological testing* (7th ed.). Upper Saddle River, NJ: Prentice Hall.

Armstrong, K. (1993). *A history of God: The 4000 year-old quest of Judaism, Christianity, and Islam.* New York: Alfred Knopf.

Bastien, R. T., & Adelman, H. S. (1984) Noncompulsory versus legally mandated placement, perceived choice, and response to treatment among adolescents. *Journal of Consulting & Clinical Psychology Vol 52,* 171–179.

Beisner, E. N. (Speaker). (1994). *Ethics and public policy.* Superstar Teaching Series. Springfield, VA: The Teaching Company.

Bilynsky, N. S., & Vernaglia, E. R. (1998). The ethical practice of psychology in a managed-care framework. *Psychotherapy, 35,* 54–68.

Blanchard, C. A., & Lichtenberg, J. W. (1998). Counseling psychologists' training to deal with their sexual feelings in therapy. *Counseling Psychologist, 26,* 624–639.

Blum, S. (1992). Ethical issues in managed mental health. In S. Feldman (Ed.), *Managed mental health services* (pp. 245–265). Springfield, IL: Charles C Thomas.

Campbell, J. (1949). *The hero with a thousand faces:* Princeton, NJ: Princeton University Press.

Chan, D. W. O. (1984). Medication compliance in a Chinese psychiatric outpatient setting. *British Journal of Medical Psychology, 57,* 81–89.

Cialdini, R. (1993). *Influence: The psychology of persuasion* (rev. ed.). New York: Quill.

Cottone, R. R., & Tarvydas, V. M. (Eds.). (1998). *Ethical and professional issues in counseling.* Upper Saddle River, NJ: Prentice Hall.

Dana, R. H. (1998). Problems with managed mental health care for multicultural populations. *Psychological Reports, 83,* 283–294.

Dwyer, J., & Shih, A. (1998). The ethics of tailoring the patient's chart. *Psychiatric Services, 49,* 1309–1312.

Edward, J. (1999). Is managed mental health treatment psychotherapy? *Clinical Social Work Journal, 27,* 87–102.

Ellis, A. (1973). *Humanistic psychotherapy.* New York: McGraw-Hill.

Erickson, S. H. (1990). Counseling the irresponsible AIDS client: Guidelines for decision making. *Journal of Counseling and Development, 68,* 454–455.

Firth, R. (1952). Ethical absolutism and the ideal observer. *Philosophy and Phenomenological Research, 12,* 317–345.

Fox, M. (1980). *Breakthrough: Meister Eckhart's creation spirituality in new translation.* New York: Doubleday.

Frank, J. D. (1961). *Persuasion and healing: A comparative study of psychotherapy.* Baltimore: The Johns Hopkins Press.

Fromm, E. (1950). *Psychoanalysis and religion.* New York: Bantam.

Gellman, R., & Frawley, K. (1996). The need to know versus the right to privacy. In T. Trabin (Ed.), *The computerization of behavioral health care.* San Francisco: Jossey-Bass.

Gladding, S. T. (1997). *Community and agency counseling.* Upper Saddle River, NJ: Prentice Hall.

Gonzalez, C. A., Griffith, E. E., & Ruiz, P. (1994). Cross-cultural issues in psychiatric treatment. In G. Gabbard (Ed.), *Treatments of psychiatric disorders* (2nd ed., pp. 55–90). Washington DC: American Psychiatric Press.

Gove, W. R., & Fain, T. A. (1977). A comparison of voluntary and committed psychiatric patients. *Archives of General Psychiatry, 34,* 669–676.

Gray, L. A., & Harding, A. K. (1988). Confidentiality limits with clients who have the AIDS virus. *Journal of Counseling and Development, 66,* 219–223.

Hayman, P. M., & Covert, J. A. (1986). Ethical dilemmas in college counseling centers. *Journal of Counseling & Development, 64,* 318–320.

Herron, W. G., & Adlerstein, L. K. (1994). The dynamics of managed mental health care. *Psychological Reports, 75,* 723–741.

Hershenson, D. B., Power, P. W., & Waldo, M. (1996). *Community counseling: Contemporary theory and practice.* Boston: Allyn & Bacon.

Hood, A. B., & Johnson, R. W. (1997). *Assessment in counseling: A guide to the use of psychological assessment procedures.* (2nd Ed.) Alexandria, VA: American Counseling Association.

Jung, C. G. (1958). The practice of psychotherapy. *Collected works, volume 16.* Princeton, NJ: Bollingen.

Kaplan, A. (1961). *The new world of philosophy.* New York: Vintage.

Kaufmann, W. (1974). *Nietzsche: Philosopher, psychologist, antichrist.* Princeton, NJ: Princeton University Press.

Kelly, J. A., & Murphy, D. A. (1992). Psychological interventions with AIDS and HIV: Prevention and treatment. *Journal of Consulting and Clinical Psychology, 60,* 376–385.

Kitchener, K. S. (1984). Intuition, critical evaluation, and ethical principles: The foundation for ethical decisions in counseling psychology. *The Counseling Psychologist, 12,* 43–55.

Knapp, S., & VandeCreek, L. (1990). Application of the duty to protect HIV- positive patients. *Professional Psychology: Research and Practice, 21,* 161–166.

Koocher, G. P., & Keith-Speigel, P. (1998). *Ethics in psychology: Professional standards and cases* (2nd ed.). New York: Random House.

Lazarus, J., & Pollack, D. (1997). Ethical aspects of public sector managed care. In K. Minkoff and D. Pollack, (Eds) *Managed mental health care in the public sector,* 25–36. Amsterdam, The Netherlands: Harwood Academic Publishers.

Leupker, E. T. (1999). Effects of practitioners' sexual misconduct: A follow-up study. *Journal of the American Academy of Psychiatry and the Law, 27,* 51–63.

McGregor, D. (1960). *The human side of enterprise.* New York: McGraw-Hill.

McMinn, M. R., Buchanan, T., Ellens, B. M., & Ryan, M. K. (1999). Technology, professional practice, and ethics: Survey findings and implications. *Professional Psychology: Research and Practice, 30,* 165–172.

Melchert, T. P., & Patterson, M. M. (1999). Duty to warn and interventions with HIV-positive clients. *Professional Psychology: Research and Practice, 30,* 180–186.

Mezzich, J. E., Kleinman, A., & Fabrega, H. (Eds). (1993, September). *Revised cultural proposals for* DSM-IV. Submitted to the *DSM-IV* Task Force by the Steering Committee, NIMH-sponsored Group on Culture and Diagnosis.

Neukrug, E. S., Healy, M., & Herlihy, B. (1992). Ethical practices of licensed professional counselors: An updated survey of state licensing boards. *Counselor Education and Supervision, 32,* 130–141.

Paradise, L. C., & Wilder, D. H. (1979). The relationship between client reluctance and counseling effectiveness. *Counselor Education and Supervision, 19,* 35–41.

Plaut, S. M. (1997). Boundary violations in professional-client relationships: Overview and guidelines for prevention. *Sexual and Marital Therapy, 12,* 77–94.

Pope, K. S. (1990). Therapist-patient sex as sex abuse: Six scientific, professional and practical dilemmas in addressing victimization and rehabilitation. *Professional Psychology: Research and Practice, 21,* 227–239.

Ramsey, P. (1981). Kant's moral theology or a religious ethics? In D. Callahan & H. T. Englehardt, Jr. (Eds.), *The roots of ethics: Science, religion and values.* New York: Plenum Press.

Rand, A. (1982). *Philosophy: Who needs it?* New York: Doubleday.

Richardson, L. M. & Austad, C. S. (1991). Realities of mental health practice in managed-care settings. *Professional Psychology: Research & Practice, 22,* 52–59.

Ritchie, M. H. (1986). Counseling the involuntary client. *Journal of Counseling and Development, 64,* 516–518.

Riuz, P., & Langrod, J. (1982). Cultural issues in the mental health of Hispanics in the United States. *American Journal of Social Psychiatry, 2,* 35–38.

Rogers, C. R. (1942). *Counseling and psychotherapy.* Boston: Houghton Mifflin.

Rooney, R. H. (1992). *Strategies for work with involuntary clients.* New York: Columbia University Press.

Russell, B. (1945). *A history of Western philosophy.* New York: Simon & Schuster.

Russell, B. (1957). *Why I am not a Christian: And other essays on religion and related subjects.* New York: George Allen & Unwin.

Ryan, C. C., & Rowe, M. J. (1988). AIDS: Legal and ethical issues. *Social Casework, 69,* 324–333.

Sabin, J. E. (1996). Is managed care ethical care? In A. Lazarus (Ed.) *Controversies in managed mental health care,* 115–128. Washington, DC: American Psychiatric Press.

Samuel, S. E., & Gorton, G. E. (1998). National survey of psychology internship directors regarding education for prevention of psychologist-patient sexual exploitation. *Professional Psychology: Research and Practice, 29,* 86–90.

Sehl, M. R. (1998). Erotic countertransference and clinical social work practice: A national survey of psychotherapists' sexual feelings, attitudes, and responses. *Journal of Analytical Social Work, 5,* 39–55.

Skinner, B. F. (1953). *Science and human behavior.* New York: Free Press.

Soloman, R. C. (Ed.). (1974). *Existentialism.* New York: The Modern Library.

Sturges, J. W. (1998). Practical uses of technology in professional practice. *Professional Psychology: Research and Practice, 29,* 183–188.

Taliaferro, C. (1988). The environmental ethics of an ideal observer. *Environmental Ethics, 10,* 232–250.

Thompson, J. W., Smith, J., Burns, B. J., & Berg, R. (1991). How mental health providers see managed care. *Journal of Mental Health Administration, 18,* 284–291.

Tien, J. L. (1984). Do Asians need less medication? *Journal of Psychosocial Nursing and Mental Health Services, 22,* 19–22.

Welfel, E. R. (1998). *Ethics in counseling and psychotherapy: Standards, research, and emerging issues.* Pacific Grove, CA: Brooks/Cole.

White, G. M. (1982). The role of cultural explanations in "somatization" and "psycholization." *Social Science Medicine, 16,* 1519–1530.

Wineburgh, M. (1998). Ethics, managed care, and outpatient psychotherapy. *Clinical Social Work Journal, 26,* 433–443.

Yalom, I. D. (1995). *The theory and practice of group psychotherapy* (4th ed.). New York: Basic Books.

American Counseling Association

CODE OF ETHICS AND STANDARDS OF PRACTICE

PREAMBLE

The American Counseling Association is an educational, scientific and professional organization whose members are dedicated to the enhancement of human development throughout the life span. Association members recognize diversity in our society and embrace a cross-cultural approach in support of the worth, dignity, potential, and uniqueness of each individual.

The specification of a code of ethics enables the association to clarify to current and future members, and to those served by members, the nature of the ethical responsibilities held in common by its members. As the code of ethics of the association, this document establishes principles that define the ethical behavior of association members. All members of the American Counseling Association are required to adhere to the Code of Ethics and the Standards of Practice. The Code of Ethics will serve as the basis for processing ethical complaints initiated against members of the association.

SECTION A: THE COUNSELING RELATIONSHIP

A.1. Client Welfare

   a. Primary Responsibility.
      The primary responsibility of counselors is to respect the dignity and to promote the welfare of clients.
   b. Positive Growth and Development.
      Counselors encourage client growth and development in ways that foster the clients' interest and welfare; counselors avoid fostering dependent counseling relationships.

113

c. Counseling Plans.

Counselors and their clients work jointly in devising integrated, individual counseling plans that offer reasonable promise of success and are consistent with abilities and circumstances of clients. Counselors and clients regularly review counseling plans to ensure their continued viability and effectiveness, respecting clients' freedom of choice. (See A.3.b.)

d. Family Involvement.

Counselors recognize that families are usually important in clients' lives and strive to enlist family understanding and involvement as a positive resource, when appropriate.

e. Career and Employment Needs.

Counselors work with their clients in considering employment in jobs and circumstances that are consistent with the clients' overall abilities, vocational limitations, physical restrictions, general temperament, interest and aptitude patterns, social skills, education, general qualifications, and other relevant characteristics and needs. Counselors neither place nor participate in placing clients in positions that will result in damaging the interest and the welfare of clients, employers, or the public.

A.2. *Respecting Diversity*

a. Nondiscrimination.

Counselors do not condone or engage in discrimination based on age, color, culture, disability, ethnic group, gender, race, religion, sexual orientation, marital status, or socioeconomic status. (See C.5.a., C.5.b., and D.1.i.)

b. Respecting Differences.

Counselors will actively attempt to understand the diverse cultural backgrounds of the clients with whom they work. This includes, but is not limited to, learning how the counselor's own cultural/ethnic/racial identity impacts her/his values and beliefs about the counseling process. (See E.8. and F.2.i.)

A.3. *Client Rights*

a. Disclosure to Clients.

When counseling is initiated, and throughout the counseling process as necessary, counselors inform clients of the purposes, goals, techniques, procedures, limitations, potential risks and benefits of services to be performed, and other pertinent information. Counselors take steps to ensure that clients understand the implications of diagnosis, the intended use of tests and reports, fees, and billing arrangements. Clients have the right to expect confidentiality and to be provided with an explanation of its limitations, including supervision and/or treatment team professionals; to obtain clear information about their case records; to participate in the ongoing counseling plans; and to refuse any recommended services and be advised of the consequences of such refusal. (See E.5.a. and G.2.)

b. Freedom of Choice.

Counselors offer clients the freedom to choose whether to enter into a counseling relationship and to determine which professional(s) will provide counseling. Restrictions that limit choices of clients are fully explained. (See A.1.c.)

c. Inability to Give Consent.

When counseling minors or persons unable to give voluntary informed consent, counselors act in these clients' best interests. (See B.3.)

A.4. Clients Served by Others

If a client is receiving services from another mental health professional, counselors, with client consent, inform the professional persons already involved and develop clear agreements to avoid confusion and conflict for the client. (See C.6.c.)

A.5. Personal Needs and Values

a. Personal Needs.
   In the counseling relationship, counselors are aware of the intimacy and responsibilities inherent in the counseling relationship, maintain respect for clients, and avoid actions that seek to meet their personal needs at the expense of clients.
b. Personal Values.
   Counselors are aware of their own values, attitudes, beliefs, and behaviors and how these apply in a diverse society, and avoid imposing their values on clients. (See C.5.a.)

A.6. Dual Relationships

a. Avoid When Possible.
   Counselors are aware of their influential positions with respect to clients, and they avoid exploiting the trust and dependency of clients. Counselors make every effort to avoid dual relationships with clients that could impair professional judgment or increase the risk of harm to clients. (Examples of such relationships include, but are not limited to, familial, social, financial, business, or close personal relationships with clients.) When a dual relationship cannot be avoided, counselors take appropriate professional precautions such as informed consent, consultation, supervision, and documentation to ensure that judgment is not impaired and no exploitation occurs. (See F.1.b.)
b. Superior/Subordinate Relationships.
   Counselors do not accept as clients superiors or subordinates with whom they have administrative, supervisory, or evaluative relationships.

A.7. Sexual Intimacies with Clients

a. Current Clients.
   Counselors do not have any type of sexual intimacies with clients and do not counsel persons with whom they have had a sexual relationship.
b. Former Clients.
   Counselors do not engage in sexual intimacies with former clients within a minimum of two years after terminating the counseling relationship. Counselors who engage in such relationships after two years following termination have the responsibility to thoroughly examine and document that such relations did not have an exploitative nature, based on factors such as duration of counseling, amount of time since counseling, termination circumstances, client's personal history and mental status, adverse impact on the client, and actions by the counselor suggesting a plan to initiate a sexual relationship with the client after termination.

A.8. Multiple Clients

When counselors agree to provide counseling services to two or more persons who have a relationship (such as husband and wife, or parents and children), counselors clarify at the outset which person or persons are clients and the nature of the relationships they will have with each involved person. If it becomes apparent that counselors may be called upon to perform potentially conflicting roles, they clarify, adjust, or withdraw from roles appropriately. (See B.2. and B.4.d.)

A.9. Group Work

a. Screening.
   Counselors screen prospective group counseling/therapy participants. To the extent possible, counselors select members whose needs and goals are compatible with goals of the group, who will not impede the group process, and whose well-being will not be jeopardized by the group experience.
b. Protecting Clients.
   In a group setting, counselors take reasonable precautions to protect clients from physical or psychological trauma.

A.10. Fees and Bartering

(See D.3.a. and D.3.b.)

a. Advance Understanding.
   Counselors clearly explain to clients, prior to entering the counseling relationship, all financial arrangements related to professional services including the use of collection agencies or legal measures for nonpayment. (A.11.c.)
b. Establishing Fees.
   In establishing fees for professional counseling services, counselors consider the financial status of clients and locality. In the event that the established fee structure is inappropriate for a client, assistance is provided in attempting to find comparable services of acceptable cost. (See A.10.d., D.3.a., and D.3.b.)
c. Bartering Discouraged.
   Counselors ordinarily refrain from accepting goods or services from clients in return for counseling services because such arrangements create inherent potential for conflicts, exploitation, and distortion of the professional relationship. Counselors may participate in bartering only if the relationship is not exploitive, if the client requests it, if a clear written contract is established, and if such arrangements are an accepted practice among professionals in the community. (See A.6.a.)
d. Pro Bono Service.
   Counselors contribute to society by devoting a portion of their professional activity to services for which there is little or no financial return (pro bono).

A.11. Termination and Referral

a. Abandonment Prohibited.
   Counselors do not abandon or neglect clients in counseling. Counselors assist in making appropriate arrangements for the continuation of treatment, when necessary, during interruptions such as vacations, and following termination.
b. Inability to Assist Clients.
   If counselors determine an inability to be of professional assistance to clients, they avoid entering or immediately terminate a counseling relationship. Counselors are

knowledgeable about referral resources and suggest appropriate alternatives. If clients decline the suggested referral, counselors should discontinue the relationship.

c. Appropriate Termination.

Counselors terminate a counseling relationship, securing client agreement when possible, when it is reasonably clear that the client is no longer benefiting, when services are no longer required, when counseling no longer serves the client's needs or interests, when clients do not pay fees charged, or when agency or institution limits do not allow provision of further counseling services. (See A.10.b. and C.2.g.)

A.12. Computer Technology

a. Use of Computers.

When computer applications are used in counseling services, counselors ensure that: (1) the client is intellectually, emotionally, and physically capable of using the computer application; (2) the computer application is appropriate for the needs of the client; (3) the client understands the purpose and operation of the computer applications; and (4) a follow-up of client use of a computer application is provided to correct possible misconceptions, discover inappropriate use, and assess subsequent needs.

b. Explanation of Limitations.

Counselors ensure that clients are provided information as a part of the counseling relationship that adequately explains the limitations of computer technology.

c. Access to Computer Applications.

Counselors provide for equal access to computer applications in counseling services. (See A.2.a.)

SECTION B: CONFIDENTIALITY

B.1. Right to Privacy

a. Respect for Privacy.

Counselors respect their clients' right to privacy and avoid illegal and unwarranted disclosures of confidential information. (See A.3.a. and B.6.a.)

b. Client Waiver.

The right to privacy may be waived by the client or their legally recognized representative.

c. Exceptions.

The general requirement that counselors keep information confidential does not apply when disclosure is required to prevent clear and imminent danger to the client or others or when legal requirements demand that confidential information be revealed. Counselors consult with other professionals when in doubt as to the validity of an exception.

d. Contagious, Fatal Diseases.

A counselor who receives information confirming that a client has a disease commonly known to be both communicable and fatal is justified in disclosing information to an identifiable third party, who by his or her relationship with the client is at a high risk of contracting the disease. Prior to making a disclosure the counselor should ascertain that the client has not already informed the third party about his or her disease and that the client is not intending to inform the third party in the immediate future. (See B.1.c and B.1.f.)

e. Court Ordered Disclosure.
   When court ordered to release confidential information without a client's permission, counselors request to the court that the disclosure not be required due to potential harm to the client or counseling relationship. (See B.1.c.)

f. Minimal Disclosure.
   When circumstances require the disclosure of confidential information, only essential information is revealed. To the extent possible, clients are informed before confidential information is disclosed.

g. Explanation of Limitations.
   When counseling is initiated and throughout the counseling process as necessary, counselors inform clients of the limitations of confidentiality and identify foreseeable situations in which confidentiality must be breached. (See G.2.a.)

h. Subordinates.
   Counselors make every effort to ensure that privacy and confidentiality of clients are maintained by subordinates including employees, supervisees, clerical assistants, and volunteers. (See B.1.a.)

i. Treatment Teams.
   If client treatment will involve a continued review by a treatment team, the client will be informed of the team's existence and composition.

B.2. Groups and Families

a. Group Work.
   In group work, counselors clearly define confidentiality and the parameters for the specific group being entered, explain its importance, and discuss the difficulties related to confidentiality involved in group work. The fact that confidentiality cannot be guaranteed is clearly communicated to group members.

b. Family Counseling.
   In family counseling, information about one family member cannot be disclosed to another member without permission. Counselors protect the privacy rights of each family member. (See A.8., B.3., and B.4.d.)

B.3. Minor or Incompetent Clients

When counseling clients who are minors or individuals who are unable to give voluntary, informed consent, parents or guardians may be included in the counseling process as appropriate. Counselors act in the best interests of clients and take measures to safeguard confidentiality. (See A.3.c.)

B.4. Records

a. Requirement of Records.
   Counselors maintain records necessary for rendering professional services to their clients and as required by laws, regulations, or agency or institution procedures.

b. Confidentiality of Records.

Counselors are responsible for securing the safety and confidentiality of any counseling records they create, maintain, transfer, or destroy whether the records are written, taped, computerized, or stored in any other medium. (See B.1.a.)

c. Permission to Record or Observe.

Counselors obtain permission from clients prior to electronically recording or observing sessions. (See A.3.a.)

d. Client Access.

Counselors recognize that counseling records are kept for the benefit of clients, and therefore provide access to records and copies of records when requested by competent clients, unless the records contain information that may be misleading and detrimental to the client. In situations involving multiple clients, access to records is limited to those parts of records that do not include confidential information related to another client. (See A.8., B.1.a., and B.2.b.)

e. Disclosure or Transfer.

Counselors obtain written permission from clients to disclose or transfer records to legitimate third parties unless exceptions to confidentiality exist as listed in Section B. 1. Steps are taken to ensure that receivers of counseling records are sensitive to their confidential nature.

B.5. Research and Training

a. Data Disguise Required.

Use of data derived from counseling relationships for purposes of training, research, or publication is confined to content that is disguised to ensure the anonymity of the individuals involved. (See B.1.g. and G.3.d.)

b. Agreement for Identification.

Identification of a client in a presentation or publication is permissible only when the client has reviewed the material and has agreed to its presentation or publication. (See G.3.d.)

B.6. Consultation

a. Respect for Privacy.

Information obtained in a consulting relationship is discussed for professional purposes only with persons clearly concerned with the case. Written and oral reports present data germane to the purposes of the consultation, and every effort is made to protect client identity and avoid undue invasion of privacy.

b. Cooperating Agencies.

Before sharing information, counselors make efforts to ensure that there are defined policies in other agencies serving the counselor's clients that effectively protect the confidentiality of information.

SECTION C: PROFESSIONAL RESPONSIBILITY

C.1. Standards Knowledge

Counselors have a responsibility to read, understand, and follow the Code of Ethics and the Standards of Practice.

C.2. Professional Competence

a. Boundaries of Competence.

Counselors practice only within the boundaries of their competence, based on their education, training, supervised experience, state and national professional credentials, and appropriate professional experience. Counselors will demonstrate a commitment to gain knowledge, personal awareness, sensitivity, and skills pertinent to working with a diverse client population.

b. New Specialty Areas of Practice.

Counselors practice in specialty areas new to them only after appropriate education, training, and supervised experience. While developing skills in new specialty areas, counselors take steps to ensure the competence of their work and to protect others from possible harm.

c. Qualified for Employment.

Counselors accept employment only for positions for which they are qualified by education, training, supervised experience, state and national professional credentials, and appropriate professional experience. Counselors hire for professional counseling positions only individuals who are qualified and competent.

d. Monitor Effectiveness.

Counselors continually monitor their effectiveness as professionals and take steps to improve when necessary. Counselors in private practice take reasonable steps to seek out peer supervision to evaluate their efficacy as counselors.

e. Ethical Issues Consultation.

Counselors take reasonable steps to consult with other counselors or related professionals when they have questions regarding their ethical obligations or professional practice. (See H.1.)

f. Continuing Education.

Counselors recognize the need for continuing education to maintain a reasonable level of awareness of current scientific and professional information in their fields of activity. They take steps to maintain competence in the skills they use, are open to new procedures, and keep current with the diverse and/or special populations with whom they work.

g. Impairment.

Counselors refrain from offering or accepting professional services when their physical, mental, or emotional problems are likely to harm a client or others. They are alert to the signs of impairment, seek assistance for problems, and, if necessary, limit, suspend, or terminate their professional responsibilities. (See A.11.c.)

C.3. Advertising and Soliciting Clients

a. Accurate Advertising.

There are no restrictions on advertising by counselors except those that can be specifically justified to protect the public from deceptive practices. Counselors advertise or represent their services to the public by identifying their credentials in an accurate manner that is not false, misleading, deceptive, or fraudulent. Counselors may only advertise the highest degree earned which is in counseling or a closely related field from a college or university that was accredited when the degree was awarded by one of the regional accrediting bodies recognized by the Council on Postsecondary Accreditation.

b. Testimonials.

Counselors who use testimonials do not solicit them from clients or other persons who, because of their particular circumstances, may be vulnerable to undue influence.

c. Statements by Others.

Counselors make reasonable efforts to ensure that statements made by others about them or the profession of counseling are accurate.

d. Recruiting through Employment.

Counselors do not use their places of employment or institutional affiliation to recruit or gain clients, supervisees, or consultees for their private practices. (See C.5.e.)

e. Products and Training Advertisements.

Counselors who develop products related to their profession or conduct workshops or training events ensure that the advertisements concerning these products or events are accurate and disclose adequate information for consumers to make informed choices.

f. Promoting to Those Served.

Counselors do not use counseling, teaching, training, or supervisory relationships to promote their products or training events in a manner that is deceptive or would exert undue influence on individuals who may be vulnerable. Counselors may adopt textbooks they have authored for instruction purposes.

g. Professional Association Involvement.

Counselors actively participate in local, state, and national associations that foster the development and improvement of counseling.

C.4. Credentials

a. Credentials Claimed.

Counselors claim or imply only professional credentials possessed and are responsible for correcting any known misrepresentations of their credentials by others. Professional credentials include graduate degrees in counseling or closely related mental health fields, accreditation of graduate programs, national voluntary certifications, government issued certifications or licenses, ACA professional membership, or any other credential that might indicate to the public specialized knowledge or expertise in counseling.

b. ACA Professional Membership.

ACA professional members may announce to the public their membership status. Regular members may not announce their ACA membership in a manner that might imply they are credentialed counselors.

c. Credential Guidelines.

Counselors follow the guidelines for use of credentials that have been established by the entities that issue the credentials.

d. Misrepresentation of Credentials.

Counselors do not attribute more to their credentials than the credentials represent, and do not imply that other counselors are not qualified because they do not possess certain credentials.

e. Doctoral Degrees from Other Fields.

Counselors who hold a master's degree in counseling or a closely related mental health field, but hold a doctoral degree from other than counseling or a closely related field do not use the title "Dr." in their practices and do not announce to the public in relation to their practice or status as a counselor that they hold a doctorate.

C.5. Public Responsibility

a. Nondiscrimination.
Counselors do not discriminate against clients, students, or supervisees in a manner that has a negative impact based on their age, color, culture, disability, ethnic group, gender, race, religion, sexual orientation, or socioeconomic status, or for any other reason. (See A.2.a.)

b. Sexual Harassment.
Counselors do not engage in sexual harassment. Sexual harassment is defined as sexual solicitation, physical advances, or verbal or nonverbal conduct that is sexual in nature, that occurs in connection with professional activities or roles, and that either: (1) is unwelcome, is offensive, or creates a hostile workplace environment, and counselors know or are told this; or (2) is sufficiently severe or intense to be perceived as harassment to a reasonable person in the context. Sexual harassment can consist of a single intense or severe act or multiple persistent or pervasive acts.

c. Reports to Third Parties.
Counselors are accurate, honest, and unbiased in reporting their professional activities and judgments to appropriate third parties including courts, health insurance companies, those who are the recipients of evaluation reports, and others. (See B.1.g.)

d. Media Presentations.
When counselors provide advice or comment by means of public lectures, demonstrations, radio or television programs, prerecorded tapes, printed articles, mailed material, or other media, they take reasonable precautions to ensure that (1) the statements are based on appropriate professional counseling literature and practice; (2) the statements are otherwise consistent with the Code of Ethics and the Standards of Practice; and (3) the recipients of the information are not encouraged to infer that a professional counseling relationship has been established. (See C.6.b.)

e. Unjustified Gains.
Counselors do not use their professional positions to seek or receive unjustified personal gains, sexual favors, unfair advantage, or unearned goods or services. (See C.3.d.)

C.6. Responsibility to Other Professionals

a. Different Approaches.
Counselors are respectful of approaches to professional counseling that differ from their own. Counselors know and take into account the traditions and practices of other professional groups with which they work.

b. Personal Public Statements.
When making personal statements in a public context, counselors clarify that they are speaking from their personal perspectives and that they are not speaking on behalf of all counselors or the profession. (See C.5.d.)

c. Clients Served by Others.
When counselors learn that their clients are in a professional relationship with another mental health professional, they request release from clients to inform the other professionals and strive to establish positive and collaborative professional relationships. (See A.4.)

SECTION D: RELATIONSHIPS WITH OTHER PROFESSIONALS

D.1. Relationships with Employers and Employees

a. Role Definition.
   Counselors define and describe for their employers and employees the parameters and levels of their professional roles.

b. Agreements.
   Counselors establish working agreements with supervisors, colleagues, and subordinates regarding counseling or clinical relationships, confidentiality, adherence to professional standards, distinction between public and private material, maintenance and dissemination of recorded information, workload, and accountability. Working agreements in each instance are specified and made known to those concerned.

c. Negative Conditions.
   Counselors alert their employers to conditions that may be potentially disruptive or damaging to the counselor's professional responsibilities or that may limit their effectiveness.

d. Evaluation.
   Counselors submit regularly to professional review and evaluation by their supervisor or the appropriate representative of the employer.

e. In-Service.
   Counselors are responsible for in-service development of self and staff.

f. Goals.
   Counselors inform their staff of goals and programs.

g. Practices.
   Counselors provide personnel and agency practices that respect and enhance the rights and welfare of each employee and recipient of agency services. Counselors strive to maintain the highest levels of professional services.

h. Personnel Selection and Assignment.
   Counselors select competent staff and assign responsibilities compatible with their skills and experiences.

i. Discrimination.
   Counselors, as either employers or employees, do not engage in or condone practices that are inhumane, illegal, or unjustifiable (such as considerations based on age, color, culture, disability, ethnic group, gender, race, religion, sexual orientation, or socioeconomic status) in hiring, promotion, or training. (See A.2.a. and C.5.b.)

j. Professional Conduct.
   Counselors have a responsibility both to clients and to the agency or institution within which services are performed to maintain high standards of professional conduct.

k. Exploitive Relationships.
   Counselors do not engage in exploitive relationships with individuals over whom they have supervisory, evaluative, or instructional control or authority.

l. Employer Policies.
   The acceptance of employment in an agency or institution implies that counselors are in agreement with its general policies and principles. Counselors strive to reach agreement with employers as to acceptable standards of conduct that allow for changes in institutional policy conducive to the growth and development of clients.

D.2. Consultation (See B.6.)

a. Consultation as an Option.
   Counselors may choose to consult with any other professionally competent persons
   about their clients. In choosing consultants, counselors avoid placing the consultant in
   a conflict of interest situation that would preclude the consultant being a proper party
   to the counselor's efforts to help the client. Should counselors be engaged in a work
   setting that compromises this consultation standard, they consult with other professionals whenever possible to consider justifiable alternatives.
b. Consultant Competency.
   Counselors are reasonably certain that they have or the organization represented has the
   necessary competencies and resources for giving the kind of consulting services needed
   and that appropriate referral resources are available.
c. Understanding with Clients.
   When providing consultation, counselors attempt to develop with their clients a clear
   understanding of problem definition, goals for change, and predicted consequences of
   interventions selected.
d. Consultant Goals.
   The consulting relationship is one in which client adaptability and growth toward self-
   direction are consistently encouraged and cultivated. (See A.1.b.)

D.3. Fees for Referral

a. Accepting Fees from Agency Clients.
   Counselors refuse a private fee or other remuneration for rendering services to persons who are entitled to such services through the counselor's employing agency or institution. The policies of a particular agency may make explicit provisions for agency
   clients to receive counseling services from members of its staff in private practice. In
   such instances, the clients must be informed of other options open to them should
   they seek private counseling services. (See A.10.a., A.11.b., and C.3.d.)
b. Referral Fees.
   Counselors do not accept a referral fee from other professionals.

D.4. Subcontractor Arrangements

When counselors work as subcontractors for counseling services for a third party, they have
a duty to inform clients of the limitations of confidentiality that the organization may place
on counselors in providing counseling services to clients. The limits of such confidentiality
ordinarily are discussed as part of the intake session. (See B.1.e. and B.1.f.)

SECTION E: EVALUATION, ASSESSMENT, AND INTERPRETATION

E.1. General

a. Appraisal Techniques.
   The primary purpose of educational and psychological assessment is to provide measures that are objective and interpretable in either comparative or absolute terms.
   Counselors recognize the need to interpret the statements in this section as applying
   to the whole range of appraisal techniques, including test and nontest data.

b. Client Welfare.

Counselors promote the welfare and best interests of the client in the development, publication, and utilization of educational and psychological assessment techniques. They do not misuse assessment results and interpretations and take reasonable steps to prevent others from misusing the information these techniques provide. They respect the client's right to know the results, the interpretations made, and the bases for their conclusions and recommendations.

E.2. *Competence to Use and Interpret Tests*

a. Limits of Competence.

Counselors recognize the limits of their competence and perform only those testing and assessment services for which they have been trained. They are familiar with reliability, validity, related standardization, error of measurement, and proper application of any technique utilized. Counselors using computer-based test interpretations are trained in the construct being measured and the specific instrument being used prior to using this type of computer application. Counselors take reasonable measures to ensure the proper use of psychological assessment techniques by persons under their supervision.

b. Appropriate Use.

Counselors are responsible for the appropriate application, scoring, interpretation, and use of assessment instruments, whether they score and interpret such tests themselves or use computerized or other services.

c. Decisions Based on Results.

Counselors responsible for decisions involving individuals or policies that are based on assessment results have a thorough understanding of educational and psychological measurement, including validation criteria, test research, and guidelines for test development and use.

d. Accurate Information.

Counselors provide accurate information and avoid false claims or misconceptions when making statements about assessment instruments or techniques. Special efforts are made to avoid unwarranted connotations of such terms as IQ and grade equivalent scores. (See C.5.c.)

E.3. *Informed Consent*

a. Explanation to Clients.

Prior to assessment, counselors explain the nature and purposes of assessment and the specific use of results in language the client (or other legally authorized person on behalf of the client) can understand, unless an explicit exception to this right has been agreed upon in advance. Regardless of whether scoring and interpretation are completed by counselors, by assistants, or by computer or other outside services, counselors take reasonable steps to ensure that appropriate explanations are given to the client.

b. Recipients of Results.

The examinee's welfare, explicit understanding, and prior agreement determine the recipients of test results. Counselors include accurate and appropriate interpretations with any release of individual or group test results. (See B.1.a. and C.5.c.)

E.4. Release of Information to Competent Professionals

a. Misuse of Results.
   Counselors do not misuse assessment results, including test results, and interpretations, and take reasonable steps to prevent the misuse of such by others. (See C.5.c.)
b. Release of Raw Data.
   Counselors ordinarily release data (e.g. protocols, counseling or interview notes, or questionnaires) in which the client is identified only with the consent of the client or the client's legal representative. Such data are usually released only to persons recognized by counselors as competent to interpret the data. (See B.1.a.)

E.5. Proper Diagnosis of Mental Disorders

a. Proper Diagnosis.
   Counselors take special care to provide proper diagnosis of mental disorders. Assessment techniques (including personal interview) used to determine client care (e.g., locus of treatment, type of treatment, or recommended follow-up) are carefully selected and appropriately used. (See A.3.a. and C.5.c.)
b. Cultural Sensitivity.
   Counselors recognize that culture affects the manner in which clients' problems are defined. Clients' socioeconomic and cultural experience is considered when diagnosing mental disorders.

E.6. Test Selection

a. Appropriateness of Instruments.
   Counselors carefully consider the validity, reliability, psychometric limitations, and appropriateness of instruments when selecting tests for use in a given situation or with a particular client.
b. Culturally Diverse Populations.
   Counselors are cautious when selecting tests for culturally diverse populations to avoid inappropriateness of testing that may be outside of socialized behavioral or cognitive patterns.

E.7. Conditions of Test Administration

a. Administration Conditions.
   Counselors administer tests under the same conditions that were established in their standardization. When tests are not administered under standard conditions or when unusual behavior or irregularities occur during the testing session, those conditions are noted in interpretation, and the results may be designated as invalid or of questionable validity.
b. Computer Administration.
   Counselors are responsible for ensuring that administration programs function properly to provide clients with accurate results when a computer or other electronic methods are used for test administration. (See A.12.b.)
c. Unsupervised Test-Taking.
   Counselors do not permit unsupervised or inadequately supervised use of tests or assessments unless the tests or assessments are designed, intended, and validated for self administration and/or scoring.

d. Disclosure of Favorable Conditions.
Prior to test administration, conditions that produce most favorable test results are made known to the examinee.

E.8. *Diversity in Testing*

Counselors are cautious in using assessment techniques, making evaluations, and interpreting the performance of populations not represented in the norm group on which an instrument was standardized. They recognize the effects of age, color, culture, disability, ethnic group, gender, race, religion, sexual orientation, and socioeconomic status on test administration and interpretation and place test results in proper perspective with other relevant factors. (See A.2.a.)

E.9. *Test Scoring and Interpretation*

a. Reporting Reservations.
In reporting assessment results, counselors indicate any reservations that exist regarding validity or reliability because of the circumstances of the assessment or the inappropriateness of the norms for the person tested.
b. Research Instruments.
Counselors exercise caution when interpreting the results of research instruments possessing insufficient technical data to support respondent results. The specific purposes for the use of such instruments are stated explicitly to the examinee.
c. Testing Services.
Counselors who provide test scoring and test interpretation services to support the assessment process confirm the validity of such interpretations. They accurately describe the purpose, norms, validity, reliability, and applications of the procedures and any special qualifications applicable to their use. The public offering of an automated test interpretations service is considered a professional-to-professional consultation. The formal responsibility of the consultant is to the consultee, but the ultimate and overriding responsibility is to the client.

E.10. *Test Security*

Counselors maintain the integrity and security of tests and other assessment techniques consistent with legal and contractual obligations. Counselors do not appropriate, reproduce, or modify published tests or parts thereof without acknowledgment and permission from the publisher.

E.11. *Obsolete Tests and Outdated Test Results*

Counselors do not use data or test results that are obsolete or outdated for the current purpose. Counselors make every effort to prevent the misuse of obsolete measures and test data by others.

E.12. *Test Construction*

Counselors use established scientific procedures, relevant standards, and current professional knowledge for test design in the development, publication, and utilization of educational and psychological assessment techniques.

SECTION F: TEACHING, TRAINING, AND SUPERVISION

F.1. Counselor Educators and Trainers

a. Educators as Teachers and Practitioners.
   Counselors who are responsible for developing, implementing, and supervising educational programs are skilled as teachers and practitioners. They are knowledgeable regarding the ethical, legal, and regulatory aspects of the profession, are skilled in applying that knowledge, and make students and supervisees aware of their responsibilities. Counselors conduct counselor education and training programs in an ethical manner and serve as role models for professional behavior. Counselor educators should make an effort to infuse material related to human diversity into all courses and/or workshops that are designed to promote the development of professional counselors.

b. Relationship Boundaries with Students and Supervisees.
   Counselors clearly define and maintain ethical, professional, and social relationship boundaries with their students and supervisees. They are aware of the differential in power that exists and the student's or supervisee's possible incomprehension of that power differential. Counselors explain to students and supervisees the potential for the relationship to become exploitive.

c. Sexual Relationships.
   Counselors do not engage in sexual relationships with students or supervisees and do not subject them to sexual harassment. (See A.6. and C.5.b.)

d. Contributions to Research.
   Counselors give credit to students or supervisees for their contributions to research and scholarly projects. Credit is given through coauthorship, acknowledgment, footnote statement, or other appropriate means, in accordance with such contributions. (See G.4.b. and G.4.c.)

e. Close Relatives.
   Counselors do not accept close relatives as students or supervisees.

f. Supervision Preparation.
   Counselors who offer clinical supervision services are adequately prepared in supervision methods and techniques. Counselors who are doctoral students serving as practicum or internship supervisors to master's level students are adequately prepared and supervised by the training program.

g. Responsibility for Services to Clients.
   Counselors who supervise the counseling services of others take reasonable measures to ensure that counseling services provided to clients are professional.

h. Endorsement.
   Counselors do not endorse students or supervisees for certification, licensure, employment, or completion of an academic or training program if they believe students or supervisees are not qualified for the endorsement. Counselors take reasonable steps to assist students or supervisees who are not qualified for endorsement to become qualified.

F.2. Counselor Education and Training Programs

a. Orientation.
   Prior to admission, counselors orient prospective students to the counselor education or training program's expectations, including but not limited to the following: (1) the type and level of skill acquisition required for successful completion of the training,

(2) subject matter to be covered, (3) basis for evaluation, (4) training components that encourage self-growth or self-disclosure as part of the training process, (5) the type of supervision settings and requirements of the sites for required clinical field experiences, (6) student and supervisee evaluation and dismissal policies and procedures, and (7) up-to-date employment prospects for graduates.

b. Integration of Study and Practice.
   Counselors establish counselor education and training programs that integrate academic study and supervised practice.

c. Evaluation.
   Counselors clearly state to students and supervisees, in advance of training, the levels of competency expected, appraisal methods, and timing of evaluations for both didactic and experiential components. Counselors provide students and supervisees with periodic performance appraisal and evaluation feedback throughout the training program.

d. Teaching Ethics.
   Counselors make students and supervisees aware of the ethical responsibilities and standards of the profession and the students' and supervisees' ethical responsibilities to the profession. (See C.1. and F.3.e.)

e. Peer Relationships.
   When students or supervisees are assigned to lead counseling groups or provide clinical supervision for their peers, counselors take steps to ensure that students and supervisees placed in these roles do not have personal or adverse relationships with peers and that they understand they have the same ethical obligations as counselor educators, trainers, and supervisors. Counselors make every effort to ensure that the rights of peers are not compromised when students or supervisees are assigned to lead counseling groups or provide clinical supervision.

f. Varied Theoretical Positions.
   Counselors present varied theoretical positions so that students and supervisees may make comparisons and have opportunities to develop their own positions. Counselors provide information concerning the scientific bases of professional practice. (See C.6.a.)

g. Field Placements.
   Counselors develop clear policies within their training program regarding field placement and other clinical experiences. Counselors provide clearly stated roles and responsibilities for the student or supervisee, the site supervisor, and the program supervisor. They confirm that site supervisors are qualified to provide supervision and are informed of their professional and ethical responsibilities in this role.

h. Dual Relationships as Supervisors.
   Counselors avoid dual relationships such as performing the role of site supervisor and training program supervisor in the student's or supervisee's training program. Counselors do not accept any form of professional services, fees, commissions, reimbursement, or remuneration from a site for student or supervisee placement.

i. Diversity in Programs.
   Counselors are responsive to their institution's and program's recruitment and retention needs for training program administrators, faculty, and students with diverse backgrounds and special needs. (See A.2.a.)

F.3. *Students and Supervisees*

a. Limitations.
   Counselors, through ongoing evaluation and appraisal, are aware of the academic and personal limitations of students and supervisees that might impede performance.

Counselors assist students and supervisees in securing remedial assistance when needed, and dismiss from the training program supervisees who are unable to provide competent service due to academic or personal limitations. Counselors seek professional consultation and document their decision to dismiss or refer students or supervisees for assistance. Counselors assure that students and supervisees have recourse to address decisions made, to require them to seek assistance, or to dismiss them.

b. Self-Growth Experiences.

Counselors use professional judgment when designing training experiences conducted by the counselors themselves that require student and supervisee self-growth or self-disclosure. Safeguards are provided so that students and supervisees are aware of the ramifications their self-disclosure may have on counselors whose primary role as teacher, trainer, or supervisor requires acting on ethical obligations to the profession. Evaluative components of experiential training experiences explicitly delineate predetermined academic standards that are separate and not dependent on the student's level of self-disclosure. (See A.6.)

c. Counseling for Students and Supervisees.

If students or supervisees request counseling, supervisors or counselor educators provide them with acceptable referrals. Supervisors or counselor educators do not serve as counselor to students or supervisees over whom they hold administrative, teaching, or evaluative roles unless this is a brief role associated with a training experience. (See A.6.b.)

d. Clients of Students and Supervisees.

Counselors make every effort to ensure that the clients at field placements are aware of the services rendered and the qualifications of the students and supervisees rendering those services. Clients receive professional disclosure information and are informed of the limits of confidentiality. Client permission is obtained in order for the students and supervisees to use any information concerning the counseling relationship in the training process. (See B.1.e.)

e. Standards for Students and Supervisees.

Students and supervisees preparing to become counselors adhere to the Code of Ethics and the Standards of Practice. Students and supervisees have the same obligations to clients as those required of counselors. (See H.1.)

SECTION G: RESEARCH AND PUBLICATION

G.1. Research Responsibilities

a. Use of Human Subjects.

Counselors plan, design, conduct, and report research in a manner consistent with pertinent ethical principles, federal and state laws, host institutional regulations, and scientific standards governing research with human subjects. Counselors design and conduct research that reflects cultural sensitivity appropriateness.

b. Deviation from Standard Practices.

Counselors seek consultation and observe stringent safeguards to protect the rights of research participants when a research problem suggests a deviation from standard acceptable practices. (See B.6.)

c. Precautions to Avoid Injury.

Counselors who conduct research with human subjects are responsible for the subjects' welfare throughout the experiment and take reasonable precautions to avoid causing injurious psychological, physical, or social effects to their subjects.

d. Principal Researcher Responsibility.

The ultimate responsibility for ethical research practice lies with the principal researcher. All others involved in the research activities share ethical obligations and full responsibility for their own actions.

e. Minimal Interference.

Counselors take reasonable precautions to avoid causing disruptions in subjects' lives due to participation in research.

f. Diversity.

Counselors are sensitive to diversity and research issues with special populations. They seek consultation when appropriate. (See A.2.a. and B.6.)

G.2. *Informed Consent*

a. Topics Disclosed.

In obtaining informed consent for research, counselors use language that is understandable to research participants and that: (1) accurately explains the purpose and procedures to be followed; (2) identifies any procedures that are experimental or relatively untried; (3) describes the attendant discomforts and risks; (4) describes the benefits or changes in individuals or organizations that might be reasonably expected; (5) discloses appropriate alternative procedures that would be advantageous for subjects; (6) offers to answer any inquiries concerning the procedures; (7) describes any limitations on confidentiality; and (8) instructs that subjects are free to withdraw their consent and to discontinue participation in the project at any time. (See B.1.f.)

b. Deception.

Counselors do not conduct research involving deception unless alternative procedures are not feasible and the prospective value of the research justifies the deception. When the methodological requirements of a study necessitate concealment or deception, the investigator is required to explain clearly the reasons for this action as soon as possible.

c. Voluntary Participation.

Participation in research is typically voluntary and without any penalty for refusal to participate. Involuntary participation is appropriate only when it can be demonstrated that participation will have no harmful effects on subjects and is essential to the investigation.

d. Confidentiality of Information.

Information obtained about research participants during the course of an investigation is confidential. When the possibility exists that others may obtain access to such information, ethical research practice requires that the possibility, together with the plans for protecting confidentiality, be explained to participants as a part of the procedure for obtaining informed consent. (See B.1.e.)

e. Persons Incapable of Giving Informed Consent.

When a person is incapable of giving informed consent, counselors provide an appropriate explanation, obtain agreement for participation and obtain appropriate consent from a legally authorized person.

f. Commitments to Participants.

Counselors take reasonable measures to honor all commitments to research participants.

g. Explanations After Data Collection.

After data are collected, counselors provide participants with full clarification of the nature of the study to remove any misconceptions. Where scientific or human values justify delaying or withholding information, counselors take reasonable measures to avoid causing harm.

h. Agreements to Cooperate.
Counselors who agree to cooperate with another individual in research or publication incur an obligation to cooperate as promised in terms of punctuality of performance and with regard to the completeness and accuracy of the information required.

i. Informed Consent for Sponsors.
In the pursuit of research, counselors give sponsors, institutions, and publication channels the same respect and opportunity for giving informed consent that they accord to individual research participants. Counselors are aware of their obligation to future research workers and ensure that host institutions are given feedback information and proper acknowledgment.

G.3. Reporting Results

a. Information Affecting Outcome.
When reporting research results, counselors explicitly mention all variables and conditions known to the investigator that may have affected the outcome of a study or the interpretation of data.

b. Accurate Results.
Counselors plan, conduct, and report research accurately and in a manner that minimizes the possibility that results will be misleading. They provide thorough discussions of the limitations of their data and alternative hypotheses. Counselors do not engage in fraudulent research, distort data, misrepresent data, or deliberately bias their results.

c. Obligation to Report Unfavorable Results.
Counselors communicate to other counselors the results of any research judged to be of professional value. Results that reflect unfavorably on institutions, programs, services, prevailing opinions, or vested interests are not withheld.

d. Identity of Subjects.
Counselors who supply data, aid in the research of another person, report research results, or make original data available take due care to disguise the identity of respective subjects in the absence of specific authorization from the subjects to do otherwise. (See B.1.g. and B.5.a.)

e. Replication Studies.
Counselors are obligated to make available sufficient original research data to qualified professionals who may wish to replicate the study.

G.4. Publication

a. Recognition of Others.
When conducting and reporting research, counselors are familiar with and give recognition to previous work on the topic, observe copyright laws, and give full credit to those to whom credit is due. (See F.1.d. and G.4.c.)

b. Contributors.
Counselors give credit through joint authorship, acknowledgment, footnote statements, or other appropriate means to those who have contributed significantly to research or concept development in accordance with such contributions. The principal contributor is listed first and minor technical or professional contributions are acknowledged in notes or introductory statements.

c. Student Research.
For an article that is substantially based on a student's dissertation or thesis, the student is listed as the principal author. (See F.1.d. and G.4.a.)

d. Duplicate Submission.
Counselors submit manuscripts for consideration to only one journal at a time. Manuscripts that are published in whole or in substantial part in another journal or published work are not submitted for publication without acknowledgment and permission from the previous publication.

e. Professional Review.
Counselors who review material submitted for publication, research, or other scholarly purposes respect the confidentiality and proprietary rights of those who submitted it.

SECTION H: RESOLVING ETHICAL ISSUES

H.1. Knowledge of Standards

Counselors are familiar with the *Code of Ethics* and the *Standards of Practice* and other applicable ethics codes from other professional organizations of which they are members, or from certification and licensure bodies. Lack of knowledge or misunderstanding of an ethical responsibility is not a defense against a charge of unethical conduct. (See F.3.e.)

H.2. Suspected Violations

a. Ethical Behavior Expected.
Counselors expect professional associates to adhere to the *Code of Ethics*. When counselors possess reasonable cause that raises doubts as to whether a counselor is acting in an ethical manner, they take appropriate action. (See H.2.d. and H.2.e.)

b. Consultation.
When uncertain as to whether a particular situation or course of action may be in violation of the *Code of Ethics,* counselors consult with other counselors who are knowledgeable about ethics, with colleagues, or with appropriate authorities.

c. Organization Conflicts.
If the demands of an organization with which counselors are affiliated pose a conflict with the *Code of Ethics,* counselors specify the nature of such conflicts and express to their supervisors or other responsible officials their commitment to the *Code of Ethics.* When possible, counselors work toward change within the organization to allow full adherence to the *Code of Ethics.*

d. Informal Resolution.
When counselors have reasonable cause to believe that another counselor is violating an ethical standard, they attempt to first resolve the issue informally with the other counselor if feasible, providing that such action does not violate confidentiality rights that may be involved.

e. Reporting Suspected Violations.
When an informal resolution is not appropriate or feasible, counselors, upon reasonable cause, take action such as reporting the suspected ethical violation to state or national ethics committees, unless this action conflicts with confidentiality rights that cannot be resolved.

f. Unwarranted Complaints.
Counselors do not initiate, participate in, or encourage the filing of ethics complaints that are unwarranted or intend to harm a counselor rather than to protect clients or the public.

H.3. *Cooperation with Ethics Committees*

Counselors assist in the process of enforcing the *Code of Ethics*. Counselors cooperate with investigations, proceedings, and requirements of the ACA Ethics Committee or ethics committees of other duly constituted associations or boards having jurisdiction over those charged with a violation. Counselors are familiar with the ACA Policies and Procedures and use it as a reference in assisting the enforcement of the *Code of Ethics*.

STANDARDS OF PRACTICE

All members of the American Counseling Association (ACA) are required to adhere to the *Standards of Practice* and the *Code of Ethics*. The *Standards of Practice* represent minimal behavioral statements of the *Code of Ethics*. Members should refer to the applicable section of the *Code of Ethics* for further interpretation and amplification of the applicable Standard of Practice.

Section A: *The Counseling Relationship*

Standard of Practice One (SP-1)
Nondiscrimination
Counselors respect diversity and must not discriminate against clients because of age, color, culture, disability, ethnic group, gender, race, religion, sexual orientation, marital status, or socioeconomic status. (See A.2.a.)

Standard of Practice Two (SP-2)
Disclosure to Clients
Counselors must adequately inform clients, preferably in writing, regarding the counseling process and counseling relationship at or before the time it begins and throughout the relationship. (See A.3.a.)

Standard of Practice Three (SP-3)
Dual Relationships
Counselors must make every effort to avoid dual relationships with clients that could impair their professional judgment or increase the risk of harm to clients. When a dual relationship cannot be avoided, counselors must take appropriate steps to ensure that judgment is not impaired and that no exploitation occurs. (See A.6.a. and A.6.b.)

Standard of Practice Four (SP-4)
Sexual Intimacies with Clients
Counselors must not engage in any type of sexual intimacies with current clients and must not engage in sexual intimacies with former clients within a minimum of two years after terminating the counseling relationship. Counselors who engage in such relationship after two years following termination have the responsibility to thoroughly examine and document that such relations did not have an exploitative nature.

Standard of Practice Five (SP-5)
Protecting Clients During Group Work
Counselors must take steps to protect clients from physical or psychological trauma resulting from interactions during group work. (See A.9.b.)

Standard of Practice Six (SP-6)

Advance Understanding of Fees

Counselors must explain to clients, prior to their entering the counseling relationship, financial arrangements related to professional services. (See A.10. a.-d. and A.11.c.)

Standard of Practice Seven (SP-7)

Termination

Counselors must assist in making appropriate arrangements for the continuation of treatment of clients, when necessary, following termination of counseling relationships. (See A.11.a.)

Standard of Practice Eight (SP-8)

Inability to Assist Clients

Counselors must avoid entering or immediately terminate a counseling relationship if it is determined that they are unable to be of professional assistance to a client. The counselor may assist in making an appropriate referral for the client. (See A.11.b.)

Section B: Confidentiality

Standard of Practice Nine (SP-9)

Confidentiality Requirement

Counselors must keep information related to counseling services confidential unless disclosure is in the best interest of clients, is required for the welfare of others, or is required by law. When disclosure is required, only information that is essential is revealed and the client is informed of such disclosure. (See B.1. a.-f.)

Standard of Practice Ten (SP-10)

Confidentiality Requirements for Subordinates

Counselors must take measures to ensure that privacy and confidentiality of clients are maintained by subordinates. (See B.1.h.)

Standard of Practice Eleven (SP-11)

Confidentiality in Group Work

Counselors must clearly communicate to group members that confidentiality cannot be guaranteed in group work. (See B.2.a.)

Standard of Practice Twelve (SP-12)

Confidentiality in Family Counseling

Counselors must not disclose information about one family member in counseling to another family member without prior consent. (See B.2.b.)

Standard of Practice Thirteen (SP-13)

Confidentiality of Records

Counselors must maintain appropriate confidentiality in creating, storing, accessing, transferring, and disposing of counseling records. (See B.4.b.)

Standard of Practice Fourteen (SP-14)

Permission to Record or Observe

Counselors must obtain prior consent from clients in order to electronically record or observe sessions. (See B.4.c.)

Standard of Practice Fifteen (SP-15)
Counselors must obtain client consent to disclose or transfer records to third parties, unless exceptions listed in SP-9 exist. (See B.4.e.)

Standard of Practice Sixteen (SP-16)
Data Disguise Required
Counselors must disguise the identity of the client when using data for training, research, or publication. (See B.5.a.)

Section C: Professional Responsibility

Standard of Practice Seventeen (SP-17)
Boundaries of Competence
Counselors must practice only within the boundaries of their competence. (See C.2.a.)

Standard of Practice Eighteen (SP-18)
Continuing Education
Counselors must engage in continuing education to maintain their professional competence. (See C.2.f.)

Standard of Practice Nineteen (SP-19)
Impairment of Professionals
Counselors must refrain from offering professional services when their personal problems or conflicts may cause harm to a client or others. (See C.2.g.)

Standard of Practice Twenty (SP-20)
Accurate Advertising
Counselors must accurately represent their credentials and services when advertising. (See C.3.a.)

Standard of Practice Twenty-one (SP-21)
Recruiting Through Employment
Counselors must not use their place of employment or institutional affiliation to recruit clients for their private practices. (See C.3.d.)

Standard of Practice Twenty-two (SP-22)
Credentials Claimed
Counselors must claim or imply only professional credentials possessed and must correct any known misrepresentations of their credentials by others. (See C.4.a.)

Standard of Practice Twenty-three (SP-23)
Sexual Harassment
Counselors must not engage in sexual harassment. (See C.5.b.)

Standard of Practice Twenty-four (SP-24)
Unjustified Gains
Counselors must not use their professional positions to seek or receive unjustified personal gains, sexual favors, unfair advantage, or unearned goods or services. (See C.5.e.)

Standard of Practice Twenty-five (SP-25)
Clients Served by Others
With the consent of the client, counselors must inform other mental health professionals serving the same client that a counseling relationship between the counselor and client exists. (See C.6.c.)

Standard of Practice Twenty-six (SP-26)
Negative Employment Conditions
Counselors must alert their employers to institutional policy or conditions that may
be potentially disruptive or damaging to the counselor's professional
responsibilities, or that may limit their effectiveness or deny clients' rights.
(See D.1.c.)

Standard of Practice Twenty-seven (SP-27)
Personnel Selection and Assignment
Counselors must select competent staff and must assign responsibilities compatible
with staff skills and experiences. (See D.1.h.)

Standard of Practice Twenty-eight (SP-28)
Exploitive Relationships with Subordinates
Counselors must not engage in exploitive relationships with individuals over whom
they have supervisory, evaluative, or instructional control or authority.
(See D.1.k.)

Section D: Relationship with Other Professionals

Standard of Practice Twenty-nine (SP-29)
Accepting Fees from Agency Clients
Counselors must not accept fees or other remuneration for consultation with persons
entitled to such services through the counselor's employing agency or institution.
(See D.3.a.)

Standard of Practice Thirty (SP-30)
Referral Fees
Counselors must not accept referral fees. (See D.3.b.)

Section E: Evaluation, Assessment, and Interpretation

Standard of Practice Thirty-one (SP-31)
Limits of Competence
Counselors must perform only testing and assessment services for which they are
competent. Counselors must not allow the use of psychological assessment
techniques by unqualified persons under their supervision. (See E.2.a.)

Standard of Practice Thirty-two (SP-32)
Appropriate Use of Assessment Instruments
Counselors must use assessment instruments in the manner for which they were
intended. (See E.2.b.)

Standard of Practice Thirty-three (SP-33)
Assessment Explanations to Clients
Counselors must provide explanations to clients prior to assessment about the nature
and purposes of assessment and the specific uses of results. (See E.3.a.)

Standard of Practice Thirty-four (SP-34)
Recipients of Test Results
Counselors must ensure that accurate and appropriate interpretations accompany any
release of testing and assessment information. (See E.3.b.)

Standard of Practice Thirty-five (SP-35)

Obsolete Tests and Outdated Test Results

Counselors must not base their assessment or intervention decisions or recommendations on data or test results that are obsolete or outdated for the current purpose. (See E.11.)

Section F: Teaching, Training, and Supervision

Standard of Practice Thirty-six (SP-36)

Sexual Relationships with Students or Supervisees

Counselors must not engage in sexual relationships with their students and supervisees. (See F.1.c.)

Standard of Practice Thirty-seven (SP-37)

Credit for Contributions to Research

Counselors must give credit to students or supervisees for their contributions to research and scholarly projects. (See F.1.d.)

Standard of Practice Thirty-eight (SP-38)

Supervision Preparation

Counselors who offer clinical supervision services must be trained and prepared in supervision methods and techniques. (See F.1.f.)

Standard of Practice Thirty-nine (SP-39)

Evaluation Information

Counselors must clearly state to students and supervisees in advance of training, the levels of competency expected, appraisal methods, and timing of evaluations. Counselors must provide students and supervisees with periodic performance appraisal and evaluation feedback throughout the training program. (See F.2.c.)

Standard of Practice Forty (SP-40)

Peer Relationships in Training

Counselors must make every effort to ensure that the rights of peers are not violated when students and supervisees are assigned to lead counseling groups or provide clinical supervision. (See F.2.e.)

Standard of Practice Forty-one (SP-41)

Limitations of Students and Supervisees

Counselors must assist students and supervisees in securing remedial assistance, when needed, and must dismiss from the training program students and supervisees who are unable to provide competent service due to academic or personal limitations. (See F.3.a.)

Standard of Practice Forty-two (SP-42)

Self-growth Experiences

Counselors who conduct experiences for students or supervisees that include self-growth or self-disclosure must inform participants of counselors' ethical obligations to the profession and must not grade participants based on their nonacademic performance. (See F.3.b.)

Standard of Practice Forty-three (SP-43)

Standards for Students and Supervisees

Students and supervisees preparing to become counselors must adhere to the *Code of Ethics* and the *Standards of Practice* of counselors. (See F.3.e.)

Section G: Research and Publication

Standard of Practice Forty-four (SP-44)
Precautions to Avoid Injury in Research
Counselors must avoid causing physical, social, or psychological harm or injury to
  subjects in research. (See G.1.c.)

Standard of Practice Forty-five (SP-45)
Confidentiality of Research Information
Counselors must keep confidential information obtained about research participants.
  (See G.2.d.)

Standard of Practice Forty-six (SP-46)
Information Affecting Research Outcome
Counselors must report all variables and conditions known to the investigator that
  may have affected research data or outcomes. (See G.3.a.)

Standard of Practice Forty-seven (SP-47)
Accurate Research Results
Counselors must not distort or misrepresent research data, nor fabricate or
  intentionally bias research results. (See G.3.b.)

Standard of Practice Forty-eight (SP-48)
Publication Contributors
Counselors must give appropriate credit to those who have contributed to research.
  (See G.4.a. and G.4.b.)

Section H: Resolving Ethical Issues

Standard of Practice Forty-nine (SP-49)
Ethical Behavior Expected
Counselors must take appropriate action when they possess reasonable cause that
  raises doubts as to whether counselors or other mental health professionals are
  acting in an ethical manner. (See H.2.a.)

Standard of Practice Fifty (SP-50)
Unwarranted Complaints
Counselors must not initiate, participate in, or encourage the filings of ethics
  complaints that are unwarranted or intended to harm a mental health professional
  rather than to protect clients or the public. (See H.2.f.)

Standard of Practice Fifty-one (SP-51)
Cooperation with Ethics Committees
Counselors must cooperate with investigations, proceedings, and requirements of the
  ACA Ethics Committee or ethics committees of other duly constituted associations
  or boards having jurisdiction over those charged with a violation. (See H.3.)

SERVICES FROM INTAKE TO TERMINATION

"The more mentally healthy the person becomes, the more he or she is able to mold creatively the materials of life, and hence the more appropriate the potentiality of freedom."

Rollo May

Which One Is the "Real" Emergency?

An important part of professional exploration is examining the types of services you might provide as an agency counselor. The activities described in this chapter focus around outpatient services and cover a range from intensive individual assessment and counseling through prevention and outreach—services that are offered before emotional difficulties begin to emerge in a person. One means of conceptualizing the range of services you might provide is based on the public health concept of primary, secondary, and tertiary levels of prevention (Lewis, Lewis, Daniels, & D'Andrea, 1998).

Primary prevention involves offering community service to large groups of people who are not in distress and do not demonstrate any risk factors. This is the broadest level of prevention, aimed at developing awareness and teaching skills long before any specific problems emerge. Secondary prevention includes offering services to clients who are clearly at risk of developing emotional difficulties because of some salient characteristic. One example is to facilitate a support group for children whose parents are divorcing, even though those children may not currently be expressing distress. Tertiary prevention is the level at which individual counseling is provided to a client who is experiencing emotional difficulties. We will explore more about secondary and tertiary prevention later in the chapter. Although tertiary prevention most closely fits the prototypic picture of "individual counseling," community agency counselors also may be called on to provide primary and secondary prevention services.

The following disclaimer must be emphasized: reading descriptions about such services is only the introductory step in becoming skilled. Trainees who wish to become competent in any of the described areas need to complete additional coursework in theory and do counseling under the supervision of a practitioner who is certified, licensed, or otherwise qualified to supervise trainees.

This chapter introduces material on a variety of topics you might encounter in other content courses of your graduate program in counseling.

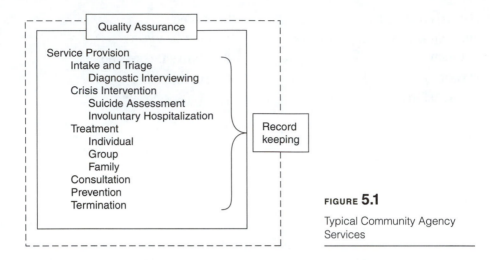

FIGURE **5.1**

Typical Community Agency Services

Specifically, we will examine a range of services that follow the agency counseling process from intake to termination of the therapeutic relationship. Our topics include intake and psychosocial history, mental status exams, crisis intervention, suicide assessment, diagnostic interviewing, and case documentation. One element common to all these services is that they should be documented in the client record.

Many practitioners note that paperwork—that is, case documentation—can become a time-consuming (and occasionally stressful) aspect of their work. The first clinical activity we will discuss in this chapter is record keeping, because documenting your work with a client is the one common denominator across all clinical activities that involve client contact. Those activities range from something as benign as a phone call through something as serious as a suicide assessment and hospitalization.

Figure 5.1 identifies the types of services commonly offered in community mental health agencies. In the case of an agency that specializes in a particular clientele, such as substance-abusing adolescents, there might be some services listed here that are not necessarily provided or other services unique to that agency or treatment program. However, this diagram is a broad, generic presentation of the services in a typical community mental health agency. Moving beyond the innermost box of "Service Provision," the bracket labeled "Record Keeping" denotes the fact that the listed services usually must be documented carefully. The outermost box, "Quality Assurance," is the process by which the agency and outside bodies monitor the quality of all the services and the documentation of those services. We will explore these service areas in descending order, beginning with quality assurance, followed by record keeping and the subsequent components of service provision.

QUALITY ASSURANCE

The basic purpose of quality assurance (QA) is just what the name implies—
to ensure that clients or intended recipients of services are, in fact, receiving
services that are of acceptable and appropriate quality. In the manufacturing
world, there is a production component called quality control, in which random samples of the product are taken off an assembly line and inspected carefully to monitor the quality of assembly. Quality assurance in agencies serves
precisely the same purpose.

Some agencies use a system of internal review, in which certain staff members are designated as QA workers. QA workers might have a portion of their
worktime allocated for chart review, in which they randomly select client
charts and scrutinize them carefully. Chart features that a QA worker might
look for include the proper inclusion of appropriate documents—such as consent to treatment, treatment plans, releases of information that are up-to-
date, and dates of billed service that should coincide with dates of service
documented in the progress notes.

Although it can be somewhat uncomfortable having one's work scruti-
nized for thoroughness, QA serves several important functions. First, when
outside accrediting bodies, such as the Joint Commission of Accreditation of
Healthcare Organizations (JCAHO), visit the agency and audit its records, if
the internal QA people have done their jobs well, site visits should go well.
Anyone working in an agency when an external reviewer has come in to in-
spect it knows how stressful it can be to everyone who works there.

> Prior to the agency's using QA staff, we were reviewed by Medicare and Medic-
> aid to check the adequacy and accuracy of record keeping and billing. For months
> prior to the scheduled visit, the only topic of discussion at staff meetings was how
> critical our charts were. Staff members worked evenings and weekends to get
> their charts in order. Although the agency was closed on Saturdays, I went in one
> Saturday to find four other clinicians spending the day updating treatment plans
> and progress notes.

Many direct care staff members tend to neglect paperwork in favor of
seeing clients. Most people choose the human service professions because
they enjoy human contact, and human contact is, for many, far preferable to
sitting alone at one's desk doing paperwork. In the previous example, the paperwork neglect had accumulated over several years since the previous site
visit. With the advent of QA, the staff members were given feedback on a
more regular basis if they were letting their paperwork slip, so that they were
not faced with trying to catch up with two years' worth of documentation.

External accreditation is important for agencies because it indicates that
they have met certain minimum criteria for service delivery. When clients
present at that agency for service, they know that a large, widely respected

body has endorsed the agency that scrutinizes health-care agencies. Additionally, agencies are better able to negotiate contracts with third-party providers if they have been endorsed by accrediting bodies such as JCAHO.

Another benefit of QA is that it sometimes sheds light on agencywide trends in service delivery or client type that might otherwise go unnoticed. Being aware of changes or shifts in clientele can help the agency adapt to better serve the community.

As you may have surmised, the major part of the quality assurance process involves the review of case documentation. The following section identifies the rationales for good case documentation and explores the features of a well-documented client record.

RECORD KEEPING AND THE CLIENT RECORD

The weakest ink lasts longer than the strongest memory.
                                        L. Glass

In their respective codes of ethics, both the American Counseling Association (ACA) and the American Psychological Association (APA) have specific reference to record-keeping guidelines. The ACA Code of Ethics Section B.4.a: Requirement of Records states the following: "Counselors maintain records necessary for rendering professional services to their clients and as required by laws, regulations, or agency or institutional procedures." The American Psychological Association (1993) has issued specific guidelines for psychologists on adequate case records. The guidelines stipulate that there must be information about the type of services provided, how the client responded to the services, and other information that includes identifying data, dates and types of service, tests or other assessment data, records of consultations, and releases of information with other parties.

It is important for you to document, for your own records, what you have done with a client in a counseling session. Perhaps you will not be seeing that client again for several weeks, or perhaps your caseload will be so heavy that you will be seeing 25 or 30 clients per week (which is not recommended). When you work with many clients, it can become difficult to remember who said what, or what you did and with whom. Still another reason for the documentation is that your client might have a mental health emergency at a time when you are not available. By documenting the case history and history of treatment, you can help not only the client but also a fellow counselor who might be treating the client. Agencies vary with respect to the specifics of how cases are documented.

Having the time to type, write, or dictate an interview or a session immediately afterward is a luxury many counselors do not have. Often, a workday is so busy that a whole day can go by with minimal, if any, case documentation.

If you find yourself in that predicament, you should take the time to at least scribble a few brief notes to yourself. This will help jog your memory when the time comes to actually write the progress note (just keep the scribbled note in a secure place). The details of a counseling session—or, more particularly, an assessment interview—will be fresher and more accurate if you document at the time of your contact with the client. On a Friday afternoon at the end of a busy week, it can be very difficult to recall what you did with a particular client on the previous Monday morning.

In the world of agency counseling, few things take on the importance of the client's record or file. The client record is not only the documentation of the therapeutic relationship but also highly personal information about the client's history. In addition to providing a useful history on clients, good client records are essential due to their use in legal proceedings. When clients have released their records to courts or courts have successfully subpoenaed their records, it is imperative that the records be complete and up-to-date.

In the clinical literature on case documentation, there seems to be much more written about medical records than about counseling records. Among the mental health professional literature, social work journals most frequently publish articles on case documentation. But, in the cases in which negligence and/or liability in counseling are being considered in a court of law, the treatment records are the first place a judge will look. Snider (1987) stated that the primary reason for good documentation is to avoid civil suits, and Schutz (1982) identified the five areas of therapy management that carry the highest risk for lawsuits:

1. Response to patient dissatisfaction
2. Charges of undue influence
3. The duty to get consultation or supervision
4. The duty to terminate
5. Adequate record keeping

The quality of care to your clients is greatly enhanced by good record keeping. The following are some scenarios in which case documentation is critical:

- You have a client with whom you have been working for several months. In the past several weeks, she has begun to decompensate (experience increasingly severe symptoms). You go on vacation and another counselor in the agency must provide crisis intervention services to her.
- You met with a client a few times. Following a disclosure he made about perpetrating physical abuse on a child, you were required by law to report him to the Department of Human Services (DHS). After the abuse case was determined to be "unfounded" by the DHS, the client discontinued treatment with you. Five years later, he returns to the agency, requesting services.

- A client comes to you for counseling, having worked with another counselor at the agency who is no longer employed there. The client states, that although she cannot remember exactly what the earlier counselor did with her in treatment, she recalls that the intervention was extremely helpful in reducing anxiety symptoms. You need to go back and review the treatment records from the previous counselor.
- A client, with whom you had worked several years before, committed suicide. As part of the coroner's investigation of the client's death, his treatment records from the mental health center are subpoenaed.
- Your client is hospitalized for an acute psychotic episode. The staff at the inpatient unit are requesting a summary of the treatment you have provided thus far.

Counselors already employed in agencies may tell you that the paperwork required in an agency job is overwhelming. There is another side to the argument, however. In the context of the previously listed scenarios, it quickly becomes apparent why case documentation is so important. Besides the reasons previously listed, case documentation is important because managed care companies or other third-party payors, may refuse to pay for services until treatment has been documented to the specifications of the third-party payor. (More will be said about this issue in chapter 8, in the context of managed care.) Moreover, if you have evaluated a client and have determined the diagnosis, you need to detail in writing or on a computer record what you have assessed and why, the symptoms and evidence you saw, and your conclusions based on that evidence.

Another important element of record keeping is legible handwriting. We have all made jokes about physicians' handwriting, but frequently counselors are guilty of the same hieroglyphic scribbling for which we castigate medical doctors. It is true, that legible handwriting takes more time, but it is a courtesy for others who need information from the chart. Illegible notes, according to Snider (1987), "constitute a reckless disregard for the client's safety" (p. 136). Weiner (1995) further expanded on this concept, noting that illegible writing suggests carelessness, which could be extrapolated to indicate general carelessness in providing services to a client. In a court of law, if the practitioner were being sued for negligence, such carelessness would likely be a contributing piece of evidence of neglect. A correct client record has the client's name on each page, all entries are signed and dated, and there are no lines left blank between entries.

Summarizing the work of Shutz (1982) and Piazza and Baruth (1990), the following is a list of the elements of a good client record:

- Intake/identifying information. This includes demographic information, cultural variables of diversity, home address and phone number, date of birth, marital status, type and place of employment, date of initial contact, emergency contacts, information about insurance and payment for services, and the client's history of mental health interventions. If the client is a minor, the record must include identifying information about the parents or primary caregivers, their employment status, and day-care provision when relevant. In addition, for minors, information should be included regarding anyone living in the home who is not a member of the immediate family.

- Presenting problem. This is a paraphrase of the client's own description of the reason for seeking counseling. You should note the manner and degree to which the presenting problem is interfering with the client's life.

- Assessment information. This includes the client's psychosocial history, medical history, current allergies and medications, and symptom picture leading to the diagnosis. This section of the client record also includes any assessment of mental status, personality, or cognitive functioning that was done. The client's diagnosis is also entered in this section of the client record. Cohen (1979) cautioned that any diagnoses should not be colloquial or abstract but in accordance with the accepted nosology (*DSM-IV*). Also, the person making the diagnosis must be licensed by the state to perform that function.

- Treatment plan. As with many aspects of the client record, the agency or practice you are with will have its own form for the treatment plan. The first elements are the presenting problem and the diagnosis. In other words, why is the client there? The second element of the treatment plan is the goals of the counseling relationship. These need to be stated in measurable terms to the degree that this is possible. In other words, since we know what the problem is, how will we know when it has been adequately resolved? Many counseling sessions founder because the counselor and client do not agree on clear, measurable goals. The goals provide the map for the counselor and client. Without such a map, neither will know where she or he is trying to go. The final element of the treatment plan is the list of steps that will be taken to reach the goal, including the theoretical approach and interventions to be used.

- Case notes. These include notes on all treatment contacts made, either in person or by telephone, including descriptions of significant events. Agencies vary with regard to the extent and format of the treatment records they require. Some might use the SOAP format, based on medical record keeping. The categories of the SOAP format are as follows (Tuthill, 1997):

  S—Subjective: the client's main complaint

  O—Objective: objective evidence for counseling

  A—Assessment: your assessment of the client's condition at the time of the visit

  P—Plan: your plan for treatment on that visit

Another format used by agencies is the DAP format. DAP stands for data, assessment, and plan. Data involve an objective account of what transpired in the counseling session. If a video/audio recording of the session was made, this is what that recording would contain. The data description might include the client's stated complaints; an objective report of client nonverbals and other behaviors; and the client's mental status, level of functioning, symptoms (duration and intensity), and quotes. Assessment is the clinician's account of what the data mean. Here you include what you think the client's symptoms mean, your interpretations of how the client's history might have contributed to the symptom picture, and your prognosis for the client. Based on the data and the assessment, the plan is what you and the client agree to do next. It may include homework assignments, a date for follow-up, and possible goal expansion. The plan may include the counselor and client's goals for the next session. Notice on both of the SOAP and DAP formats that the counselor is asked to make an objective report as the client's current disposition. You should stick to objective descriptions of the client's behavior. It can be very helpful to use direct quotes, including quotation marks, in your notes, as descriptions of the client's state. Remember that the client may, at some point, see those notes. Others may see them as well. The quality and content of your case documentation need to be professional. A good guideline to bear in mind is not to write anything you would not say out loud directly to the client.

- Termination summary. This should provide a clinical résumé of the course of treatment and the outcome at the time of termination. Termination ideally occurs as a result of a mutual decision by client and counselor. In many cases, though, clients stop going to sessions for other reasons. Each agency should have a protocol for when to draw up the termination summary in these situations. The termination summary recapitulates the assessment, identified problem, final outcome regarding each identified problem, the client's current functioning, and the reason for termination.
- Other data. The client record may also include written and signed consent forms for treatment and the transmission of confidential information and any instructions or suggestions made to the client that she or he failed to follow through on.

The agency or private practitioner has a professional responsibility to secure client records. Snider (1987) noted that a locked file cabinet is an absolutely minimal storage system. Since most agencies do not have access to a Wells-Fargo truck, keeping the locked cabinet in a locked room may be the best possible arrangement. Beis (1984) recommended retaining files for 10 years. Due to the statute of limitations in most states, it is unlikely that lawsuits would be filed after this period.

SERVICE PROVISION: INTAKE AND TRIAGE

As noted, virtually all community agencies have a procedure for initiating services with a new client. Depending on whether the client is self-referred or referred by someone else, the client or referring person might call the agency to schedule the first appointment. Some agencies obtain intake information over the phone, whereas others schedule the intake as the first face-to-face session. A client is sometimes asked, at the time she or he is scheduling the first appointment, what the presenting concern is. If the staff member taking the phone call determines that the presenting concern is of a pressing nature, the client may be scheduled as an "emergency intake" and seen within a day or two. On the other hand, sometimes agencies have waiting lists of several weeks between the client's request for an intake and the actual appointment time. This is clearly not a desirable situation, if the client is in distress. If the client is ambivalent about going for counseling, the extra waiting time might be just enough time for the client to decide not to follow through with the counseling. Ideally, a client should be able to see a counselor within no more than a few days of calling to schedule the appointment.

The intake procedure typically involves getting identifying information, such as name, date, age, and address, and getting financial or insurance information. The intake is the initial interview conducted at agencies for the purpose of gathering basic data on the client, understanding the client's presenting problem, and matching the client with a counselor. Following acquisition of the preliminary data, a staff member (either an "intake worker" or a counselor) conducts an initial interview. In an initial interview, the staff member asks about the presenting problem and how long it has been occurring, as well as the client's treatment history, family of origin, educational history, occupational history, medical history, and relationship history.

In some agencies, all the counselors do the intakes, and, in other agencies, specific intake workers do them. Some agencies have very specific formats to follow in conducting the intake interview. One style of interviewing includes an unstructured component, beginning with what the client has been experiencing most recently which prompted her or him to schedule an appointment. It seems to be more comfortable and conducive to establishing rapport to ask some broad, open-ended questions and let the client talk. Often the other data that you need will come to light in the client's story.

As the initial contact with the client, the intake worker provides crucial client data as well as serves as a triage point at which clients in crisis can be referred for immediate assistance. The concept of triage comes from the medical field, in which services are delivered to patients on the basis of a practitioner's evaluation as to how life-threatening the patient's condition is.

Faiver (1988) designed an initial client contact form (ICCF) that can be part of the intake interview or be filled out during an initial telephone contact. In the latter situation, if the client were then referred for an intake, the ICCF would be forwarded to the intake worker. Faiver noted that, in many cases, initial contacts are quite brief, but counselors must still maintain a record of observations and conclusions. The ICCF can provide data on many of the elements recommended for a complete chart and includes the following 11 sections:

- Client description/problem description
- Relevant history
- Mental status
- Suicidal/homicidal ideation/plans
- Medical history
- Current medications
- Allergies
- Drug/alcohol/tobacco/caffeine use
- Previous mental health contacts
- Diagnostic impressions
- Recommendations

Another schema for gathering the data necessary to assess a client's presenting problem was developed by Lazarus (1989) and is the basis of his multimodal therapy approach. Multimodal therapy was one of the first attempts at comprehensive assessment and treatment. Lazarus saw it as a more effective way of tailoring the treatment to the client instead of the other way around. Multimodal assessment focuses on seven elements of the client's experience, summarized in the acronym BASIC ID. Lazarus (1989) considered these elements "the fundamental vectors of human personality" (p. 16). The elements, which should be interrelated as the interview progresses, are as follows:

- *B*—Behavior. This element, or vector, includes behaviors that the client sees as getting in her or his way, behaviors she or he would like to increase or decrease, and behaviors that she or he views as strengths or assets.
- *A*—Affect. This vector deals with the client's emotional life—finding out not just how the client feels but what things make the client laugh and cry, how the client behaves when feeling a particular emotion, and whether or not the client feels troubled by negative emotions, such as depression and anxiety.
- *S*—Sensations. This vector deals with the client's sensory experiences. In this vector, the clinician tries to ascertain what the client likes (and dislikes) seeing, hearing, smelling, touching, and tasting. In this vector, the clinician inquires about persistent troubling sensations (headache,

dizziness, other pains). This is also the vector in which the client's sexual functioning can be explored. Here the clinician also addresses what bearing the client's sensations have on her or his behavior and feelings.

- *I*—Imagery. In this vector, the clinician tries to find out how the client images her- or himself in the past, present, and future. The clinician also explores what the client's image is of her or his body. The clinician can inquire what the client likes or dislikes about the way the client perceives her- or himself. Finally, the clinician finds out how these images influence the client's behavior, emotions, and sensations.
- *C*—Cognitions. In this vector, the clinician finds out what the client's cherished thoughts, beliefs, and values are. The clinician can listen for irrational or automatic thoughts that may unduly influence the client's behavior, moods, sensations, and images.
- *I*—Interpersonal relationships. In this vector, the clinician finds out who the important people are in the client's life, in addition to what the client expects from those people and what the client believes they expect of her or him. Again, the clinician tries to link this to the other vectors, finding out how interpersonal relationships interact with the client's behavior, emotions, sensations, images, and cognitions.
- *D*—Drug (or biological). In this vector, the clinician explores any concerns that the client has about health, including drug use. Lazarus noted that the *D* vector provides a much more compelling acronym than using the *B* (for *biological,* which would change the acronym to BASIC IB). This vector also includes information on fitness, diet, and prescription medication. As with the others, the clinician then tries to find out how this vector relates to all the others.

An advantage of using a multimodal assessment approach is that the data you acquire is conducive to proceeding with counseling using any of several counseling models. If you also supplement the presenting problem data with history in each of the same categories, you will have the additional information you need to make an educated guess about the level of risk the client poses to self and others, and therefore the urgency of making an immediate intervention. You will also have the information to help the client identify the most troubling symptoms of the presenting problem and to subsequently develop a treatment plan that will sufficiently address those symptoms and underlying issues (if there are any).

As you can see, several methods can be used to create a high-quality intake report. It is important to gather these data from the client. However, while gathering the intake information, you need to be listening not only to what the client says but also to how she or he says it, as well as to what the client *does not* say. You should be observing the client's behavior and emotion, monitoring the amount and quality of the client's speech, and noting if the speech is goal directed (Zimmerman, 1994). This requires observation skills that can only be acquired with practice. The combination of establishing rapport through dialogue and keenly observing the client constitutes the heart of a mental status exam. It is to the mental status exam that we will now turn.

Diagnostic Interviewing and Mental Status Exams   A mental status exam (MSE) is a component of diagnostic interviewing. The MSE is used to assess mental and emotional disorders; as such, it has been likened to the physical examination physicians use in assessing physical disorders (Zimmerman, 1994). The focus of the MSE is on "current signs, symptoms, affect, behavior, and cognition" (p. 120), and it has been outlined into areas that the clinician may need to address (Faiver, 1986; Strub & Black, 1988; Trzepacz & Baker, 1993; Zimmerman, 1994). There are slight variations from author to author but, generally, the areas outlined in the following sections are universal to the MSE.

As with the intake interview, the MSE is not to be conducted in a rigid, formal manner; rather, many of the items can be observed while the client is talking and telling her or his story. Zimmerman (1994) noted that good interviewers let the client do most of the talking and are able to gather relevant data while following the client's leads in dialogue. You will learn more about this process in the courses you take on diagnosis and case studies, as well as in the coursework you do in psychopathology. You will get more practice with the process in your practicum and internship courses. Following are some of the core areas addressed in the MSE.

Appearance, Attitude, Activity   *Appearance* means making a close, but unobtrusive, visual inspection of the client from the moment she or he enters your office. Look at whether the client is dressed appropriately for the season and temperature in your area, whether the clothing and person appear to be clean, and how much attention seems to have been paid to appearance. You need to assess hygiene as well. For obvious reasons, neglect in this area is easy to detect. You also should note the client's posture in the chair during the interview—for instance, is the client slumped or sitting perched on the edge of the chair? Is the client able to initiate and maintain eye contact with you? If not, are there aspects of the client's cultural background that would explain averted eye contact or staring? Also make note of any apparent physical abnormality and any other bizarre or striking features.

Attitude refers to the level of cooperation and attentiveness the client demonstrates. Is the client guarded, hostile, or suspicious? Sometimes a client is defensive or angry because of the circumstances under which she or he is being brought to see a counselor. Depending on your place of employment, you may see clients who have decompensated significantly, and the client's attitude toward you as a counselor may reflect that decompensation.

I remember the second intake I did at my internship. The client's name was Frank, and he had been seen at our agency two years previously. He suffered from paranoid schizophrenia and, up until 10 days before, had been stable on medication. Frank had gone off his medication. Having decompensated, Frank was in need of inpatient treatment. Our protocol was to do an intake with an MSE in order to refer him to an inpatient unit. Frank was very suspicious of me and insisted on searching the office for hidden microphones prior to answering my questions. He was dressed in a winter coat, boots, coveralls, and a fur-lined winter hat, despite the sixty-degree temperature that day. He smelled as if he hadn't bathed for a while and, when asked, noted that the government had poisoned his water supply, so it wasn't safe. Throughout the interview, Frank stared directly at me and appeared highly vigilant, as if I would "jump" him at any moment. After a very tense hour, he seemed to relax a bit, although it would be three hours after that before he was safely transported to a local inpatient unit.

As with so many other aspects of human life, activity level occurs on a continuum. The client's activity during your interview may range from hyperactivity to bradykinesia (slow movement). There also can be a general slowing down due to emotional state; this slowing down, which literally looks as though the client is moving in molasses, is known as psychomotor retardation. There are other symptoms of movement disorders, such as tremor. Many conditions, some of which are psychological and some of which are biological, can cause tremor. A tremor is certainly worth noting, as further evaluation may be necessary if it is a new symptom. Tics, involuntary movements or vocalizations that range from simple to complex, are usually psychological. They may be vocal or involve limbs or body parts.

I had a client, an 18-year-old young man, who had Tourette's disorder and obsessive-compulsive disorder. He exhibited several tics during our initial interview. One tic would occur immediately after he had made a statement, and he would whisper or mumble the statement again. The other tic was drawing numbers in the air with his index finger. He seemed to be unaware that he was doing either.

Besides tics, you also need to note any peculiar mannerisms—consistent, characteristic, distinctive, apparently purposeful, highly stylized ways of doing things. Compulsions—a subset of mannerisms—are actions that parallel obsessions and may be the motoric product of similar thoughts and urges as obsessions. Compulsive behaviors are usually related to counting, checking, or contamination. The film *As Good As It Gets,* starring Jack Nicholson, offers an excellent portrayal of compulsive behavior. Nicholson's character suffers from obsessions and compulsions, which center mainly on a fear of contamination. He behaviorally manifests this contamination fear by washing his hands only with a new bar of soap, six or seven washings at a time, and by using only sealed plastic silverware he takes with him when eating in restaurants.

Affect   We move now to affect and mood. *Affect* refers specifically to moment-to-moment changes in one's emotional state, perhaps in the course of a conversation, and the way those feelings are expressed. As a counselor is evaluating and observing a client's outwardly expressed emotions, there are multiple aspects of those expressions that are diagnostically important. One of those aspects is appropriateness, whether or not the feelings expressed in conversation are consistent (congruent) and of the type one would expect, given the conversational content. An example of inappropriate, incongruent affect is to have a client smiling or laughing while discussing the death of a loved family pet. Another important aspect of affect is its intensity. Exaggerated or heightened affect is reacting to a situation more strongly than most people would under similar circumstances.

> In my work as a counselor in a mental health agency, I received an emergency phone call one day from a mother who was in crisis about her adolescent son's behavior. She shrilly described her 16-year-old son who had refused to continue attending Sunday school, dyed his hair blue, and just bought tickets to a concert performed by a group called Jesus Lizard. This mother was so distraught that she was yelling into the phone and speaking so rapidly I couldn't get a word in. To me, she seemed to be demonstrating an exaggerated affective reaction to the rebellion many parents experience with their adolescent children.

Blunted and *flat* are similar affective attributes. In blunted affect, the client demonstrates reduced intensity of affective expression and reduced reactivity. *Reactivity* refers to how a client responds to something someone else says. Loss of mirth, for example, means that the client does not smile or laugh when you make a joke. In the case of flat affect, the client speaks without inflection in her or his voice, showing no change in emotional demeanor throughout the interview. This type of affective expression is most commonly seen when a client is depressed, suffers from schizophrenia, or has suffered brain trauma, such as stroke or closed head injury.

Yet another aspect of affect to which a clinician must pay attention is the mobility of the affective expression. *Affective lability* means that the client's emotional expression changes drastically and frequently in the course of a conversation. This is seen sometimes in a client experiencing an episode of mania and sometimes in a client having a psychotic episode. It also is common in someone who is intoxicated with alcohol or street drugs, such as "crack." Lability can be somewhat threatening in that the client can be unpredictable in her or his reactions, and anger can rapidly escalate into rage and subsequent impulsive actions that could be dangerous to self or others. It can be quite disconcerting to do an interview with a client who is extremely labile, in that it is hard to know what topics might engender an exaggerated response, or what that response will be. In clients who are more disturbed, the affective lability may also be situationally inappropriate, which obviously makes for a very interesting interview.

Speech and Language   There are two aspects of speech and language—semantic and motoric—to which a clinician must attend. In semantic language functions, you are looking at how well the client is choosing her or his words to communicate. There are a variety of language disorders that can indicate brain dysfunction. Particular types of dementia, for example, often are marked by specific peculiarities of language usage that can help psychiatrists and neuropsychologists pinpoint the type of dementia process from which a client suffers. We will not explore the nuances of expressive language disorders in this chapter, but is important to note, that poor or the peculiar use of language can be a "soft sign" for organic disorders as well as mental disorders. Therefore, you do need to be aware of how your client uses language.

One of the ways you can assess language usage is to paraphrase and summarize periodically for the client what you believe she or he has said, which also helps you establish rapport. A caveat here is that you need to be aware of the client's cultural background. It is very important to know whether English is the person's first or second language. If English is the person's second language, you cannot assume that inappropriate use of language is the result of a mental disorder. The motoric aspects of language are also of importance. The motoric aspects of language production include articulation (pronunciation), assembly (according to the rules of grammar), the building blocks of words (phonemes and morphemes), facial and gestural expressions, and writing.

Thought Process, Content, and Perception　　There are two realms of symptoms that are consistent with psychosis. One of the ways those symptoms are often categorized are as "positive and negative" symptoms of psychosis (Carson, Butcher, & Mineka, 1998). Positive symptoms are symptoms that are present but should not be there. Examples of positive symptoms of psychosis include delusions, hallucinations, illusions, ideas of reference, agitated and bizarre behavior, loose associations, neologisms, blocking, hostility, and affective lability. The second category of symptoms, negative symptoms, are so-called because in psychotic individuals certain key aspects of social and emotional functioning that should be present are deficient or lacking. The negative symptoms of psychosis include blunted or inappropriate affect, apathy, paucity of thought, and inability to engage in abstract conceptualization. Your subjective experience while interviewing an individual with psychotic symptoms will be one of bewilderment, confusion, and possibly intimidation. It can be quite unsettling to converse with someone who is functioning within an elaborate delusional network or who is actively hallucinating.

Cognition, Insight, and Judgment　　Cognition and insight are areas in which you need to give the client specific tasks and evaluate the quality and accuracy of the task solutions. Essentially, what you are assessing is clarity of thought process—the appropriateness of the client's judgment, clarity and logic in flow of thought—and the client's ability to understand abstract concepts. If you are doing an intake session, you may choose not to assess these two areas. However, if you are considering possible referral for hospitalization, or if you believe the client is presenting with serious emotional or mental difficulties, these two categories are diagnostically important. This is especially true if you see deficits in cognitive ability or impaired judgment in a client who had a much higher premorbid level of functioning, the client's ability to perform tasks prior to the onset of symptoms. Clearly, if the client was concrete and demonstrated poor judgment prior to having the current symptoms, those deficits have certain implications for diagnosis and treatment. On the other hand, if a client had a graduate degree and had been successfully employed as a professional, inability to engage in logical thought process would suggest possible disorders that need to be assessed and diagnosed immediately.

Included in the category of cognition are manipulations of well-learned material, abstract reasoning, problem solving, and arithmetic computation. During the interview, when the time arises to assess cognition, preface questions can be prefaced with an explanation to the client that you need to ask some questions that might seem odd. Then you can move from this transitional introduction into some specific cognitive tasks, saying, "Mr. Smith, I'd like you to begin at 100 and count backward by 7s, like this—100, 93, 86, and so on. Okay, go ahead." In this exercise, you are looking here for accuracy, speed, and ability to stay focused on the task.

It is also important to evaluate abstract reasoning. A common method is to give a client a proverb and ask her or him to interpret it. Examples are "What does this saying mean—'People who live in glass houses shouldn't throw stones'?" and "What does the saying 'Still waters run deep' mean?."

Insight is the ability to be aware of internal and external realities to the extent that they can be known. Judgment is the process of consideration and formulation regarding situations that can lead to decisions and action. Social judgment is a complex ability that requires a basic knowledge and understanding of social situations and of what would constitute a socially appropriate response for each situation, as well as the ability to exhibit the appropriate response when one finds oneself in that situation (Strub & Black, 1977). This would obviously be best assessed in an actual situation, because if you present a client with a hypothetical situation and the client reports to you that she or he would make an appropriate response, you do not know that the client would really behave that way in that situation. One way to navigate around this difficulty in the interview is to ask clients to provide a series of examples of ways they have behaved in past situations, such as going to a party when they know only one person there. Another example is asking clients how they behaved the last time they were furious with their relationship partner. Often, if clients have a deficit in insight or judgment, the pattern becomes apparent in the context of how they describe their method of resolving conflicts, behaving in social situations with friends, and so on.

Finally, depending on the client, you may also be asked to perform a Mini-mental State Exam (MMSE). This is a concise way to determine if the client is oriented to person, place, and situation (sometimes referred to as "oriented X3" or "clear sensorium"). Folstein, Folstein, and McHugh (1975) developed the MMSE for assessing cognitive states in patients who may be suffering from psychiatric or neurological disorders. This is only a screening measure and is not to be used to diagnose conditions such as dementia.

SERVICE PROVISION: CRISIS

A man is born gentle and weak. At his death he is hard and stiff. Green plants are tender and filled with sap. At their death they are withered and dry. Therefore the stiff and unbending is the disciple of death. The gentle and yielding is the disciple of life.

Tao Te Ching

The word *crisis* is derived from a Greek root meaning "decision." A crisis is truly a decision point for the person undergoing the crisis. As such, the definition of crisis is specific to the individual, indicating an opportunity for rapid change in either a positive or a negative direction. This has been described mythically by Joseph Campbell (1949) as the point at which the hero (or heroine) is pushed as if to the edge of an abyss. At this point, there is no turning back, and the only choice is to move forward or remain paralyzed at the edge of the abyss. The longer one remains at the edge of the abyss, the more terrifying becomes the inevitable step into it. In Campbell's motif, entering into the mythic crisis and dealing with the situation is an act of faith, an act of saying "yes" to life, no matter how difficult that may be at the time.

A Comparison of Definitions of Crisis

Various authors have taken various approaches to the conceptualization of crisis. We will first consider some alternative definitions of crisis and then will look at the common characteristics and symptoms of a crisis state.

Crisis can develop in response to stressors, such as receiving a medical diagnosis with serious implications (such as kidney disease or HIV-positive status), or in response to behavior by others in one's support network.

Roberts (1991) defines crisis as "a period of psychological disequilibrium, experienced as a result of a hazardous event or situation that constitutes a significant problem that cannot be remedied by using familiar coping strategies" (p. 4). A problem reaches crisis proportions when the problem poses an obstacle to long-term life goals—an obstacle that cannot be surmounted. When you think in those terms, both of the examples in the cartoon at the beginning of this chapter could potentially constitute a crisis. For one person, being unable to graduate at the scheduled time could precipitate a crisis; for another person, having a teenage son wreck the only car, missing a beloved family pet that has run away, and losing her or his job could create a crisis situation.

Crises can arise during transitions from one life stage to another (hence the term *developmental crisis*). People may more typically envision crisis as the result of a natural or nonnatural disaster, such as a tornado or the bombing of the Federal Building in Oklahoma City in 1995.

In contrast, Hoff (1995) defines crisis as "acute emotional upset arising from situational, developmental, or sociocultural sources and resulting in a temporary inability to cope by means of one's usual problem-solving device" (p. 4). Hoff's definition seems to be similar to the second of three interrelated factors Rapoport (1962) identified that create a state of crisis:

- Occurrence of a hazardous event
- Threat to life goals
- Inability to respond with adequate coping mechanisms

When we experience an occurrence, our assessment that the occurrence constitutes a crisis depends on our assessment of our ability to cope with the stress of any situation. When we perceive ourselves as unable to cope, crisis ensues. Contemporary crisis theory, according to Hoff (1995), views crisis as either a destructive event or as a growth opportunity. The outcome of a crisis can be appropriate resolution, which can lead to growth, or it can be emotional or mental illness, addiction, suicide, or violence against others.

Crisis Intervention

In dealing with clients in crises, the counselor's goals are (a) at the very least, to return the person to the level of precrisis functioning; (b) to attempt to help the person reframe the crisis, grow stronger, and become more efficient in solving problems; and (c) to be alert constantly to danger signals so as to ensure client safety. In the last instance, the goal is to decrease the danger and increase the opportunity for growth.

Following are some assumptions offered by Hoff (1995) that counselors might consider when working with people in crisis.

- People in crisis are basically normal.
- People in crisis are social and live in specific cultural communities by necessity.
- People in crisis have the desire and the ability to help themselves.
- Psychological-social-emotional-spiritual growth and development are the ideal outcomes of a crisis.

Crises have a powerful phenomenological component. A crisis for one person may be a minor stressor for someone else. The variables that determine the subjective stress a person feels depend on several factors:

- The number of stressors present at that time
- The sophistication and adequacy of the person's coping strategies

- The quality and extent of the support system
- The person's amount of resilience

As you embark on the crisis intervention interview, these determining variables will be pieces of data you need to assess as part of the interview itself. We will discuss each of these variables as determinants here, and will return to them when we present a model for assessment of crisis state.

The Number of Stressors   If you took an undergraduate psychology course on psychology of adjustment, you may recall learning about some objective inventories used to quantify the extent of stress to which a person has been exposed. The first such scale was developed by Holmes and Rahe (1967) and is a data-based system for assigning point values to the degree of stress caused by a variety of life events that typically involve a change from one's previous life. The ratings are measured in terms of "life change units" (abbreviated LCUs), which range from going on vacation (13 LCUs) to experiencing the death of a spouse (100 LCUs). On this scale, positive stress (eustress) is still stress and requires mental and physical energy to accommodate the changes involved. As the points accumulate, the person's capacity for coping with any one of those events diminishes. For example, the cumulative effect in six months' time of losing one's job, selling one's car, having a child graduate from high school, and placing a parent in a nursing home might put that person at very high risk for developing a physical or mental disorder, even though each of those events alone is not necessarily a significant stressor.

The Sophistication and Adequancy of Coping Strategies   Some people have healthier coping strategies than others. One variable, called cognitive rigidity, refers to how well people can adapt their thoughts and plans to accommodate unanticipated changes. You may know someone who experiences great anxiety if things do not go exactly according to plan. These people may be prone to experience significant distress.

The Quality and Extent of Support System   Selye (1976) presented data, now accepted as common knowledge, that prolonged exposure to stress increases the likelihood of developing a serious physical illness. Monroe and Steiner (1986) found that the effects of stress can be mitigated somewhat by the presence of a support system. Conversely, then, the risk of physical or psychological decompensation is accentuated among people who have little or no support system. Humans are social animals, and, although some people enjoy human contact more than others, a certain amount of contact and support is necessary for survival. People who prefer minimal contact are more vulnerable to the negative effects of stress if they have a limited or nonexistent support system. One of the areas necessary to assess about a client is the adequacy of the person's support system. *Adequacy* means not only the number of people in the support system but also the kind of people they are. For example, substance-abusing friends who are friends mainly while using with the client are not considered ideal supports. Likewise, a best friend can be a great source of support, but, if the best friend is the only friend and that person is unavailable, the client essentially has no support system.

Common Symptoms and Stages of Crisis

When clients are in a state of crisis, they may display the following prominent characteristics:

- Lowered attention span. For people in crisis, the crisis events in the foreground become the focus, while the life events in the background recede further from awareness.
- Introversion. People in crisis often become more withdrawn, focusing their attention inward to make sense of the crisis.
- Emotional reaching out. People in crisis may present as needing a great deal of support and may demonstrate a lessened ability to control their emotions.
- Impulsive and unproductive behavior. People in crisis may engage in such behavior as an attempt to do *something*, as opposed to doing nothing. This may include ineffective and disorganized attempts to pull together resources and information.
- Subjective sense of extreme vulnerability. This perception is due to overwhelming anxiety and helplessness in the face of a life event over which the client perceives little or no control.

Tyhurst (1957) studied individuals who had experienced community crises, such as disasters and migration, and identified three stages people experience as an emotional reaction to crisis:

1. Impact
2. Recoil
3. Posttraumatic recovery

This identification of stages is most applicable to a reaction to crisis when the stressor is a catastrophic experience, such as attack, rape, the death of a child from sudden infant death syndrome, or a diagnosis of terminal disease. Following the progression of impact, recoil, and posttraumatic recovery, there is a continuum of possible outcomes of the crisis (see figure 5.2).

Clearly, as a counselor working with a client in crisis, the most desirable outcome is one incorporating personal growth, if possible. At the least, you will want to help the client return to a previous level of functioning without developing emotional and behavioral problems as a result of the crisis experience.

Some mediating variables that affect how a person will adapt to crisis include the person's belief system and spiritual wellness the person's belief in a religious paradigm that provides a frame for making sense of the occurrence,

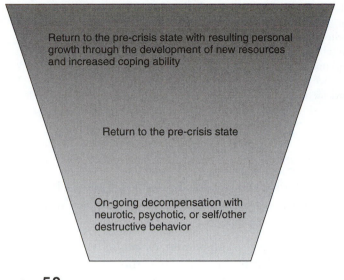

Return to the pre-crisis state with resulting personal growth through the development of new resources and increased coping ability

Return to the pre-crisis state

On-going decompensation with neurotic, psychotic, or self/other destructive behavior

FIGURE **5.2**

Possible personal outcomes of crisis.

and the availability and adequacy of a support system. As you process and work through the crisis with the client, you need to be aware of these things. If you are a crisis intervention worker, you may be responsible for determining what needs to happen to help the client handle the crisis. Sometimes this involves using other community resources, such as a hospital, to ensure that the client is safe. Your immediate goal and overriding concern in assessing a client in crisis are to make an accurate assessment of the danger to the client or others.

The importance of doing a thorough and competent assessment of the client before developing or enacting an action plan cannot be overemphasized. There are critical aspects of the individual, symptoms, and crisis situation that need to be evaluated before developing a strategy for helping the client cope with the crisis. We discussed in chapters 2 and 3 about how nice it is to feel needed. This can be especially seductive in crisis intervention, when many clients openly, ask you to do something to solve their problems. Despite what you will read further on in this section about helping clients take the steps to cope, you must remember that, to help clients maintain a sense of integrity and mastery over their lives, they must be encouraged and supported to do as much for themselves as they can. Client empowerment, assisting them to help themselves, can help them emerge from the crisis with a sense of self-efficacy and possibly increased self-confidence.

> One of my female clients had been suffering physical beatings from her husband for years. After he became increasingly aggressive and threatening toward their daughter, the client left him, appearing at my office in acute distress—fearful

that he would follow her and afraid because she had left him, with no income or money of her own. When the client had decided she was ready to go to the battered women's shelter, I called the shelter and spoke to the intake worker, verifying that there would be beds available for the client and her daughter. Then I put the client on the phone in my office, having her give all the intake information while I sat in the office with her. I also made arrangements for one of our community service workers to transport her to the shelter, so, while supporting her, I gave her tasks to do and steps to take that she could accomplish, even in her terribly upset state.

Assessing a Client in Crisis

Roberts (1991) presented a seven-stage model for assessing and treating clients in crisis, which seems to provide a basic conceptual map for working with clients in acute stages of crisis:

1. *Assess lethality and safety needs.* You need to ascertain the extent of the client's risk of harm to self or others, as well as the risk of harm to the client from others. It is important to ask the client directly, "Are you or your children in any danger right now?" or a similar question. If your assessment of danger informs you that there is impending danger, do not hesitate to contact the police.

> My husband, a psychologist, was out of town at a conference. Although he had made arrangements with a co-worker to cover emergency phone calls, one evening I received a call at our home from one of his clients. The client, a woman with borderline personality disorder, was insistent that I give her the phone number where she could reach my husband. I refused, advising her to call the emergency answering service to contact the clinician who was handling emergencies for my husband. The client informed me she had overdosed on numerous pills and promptly hung up the phone. I immediately called 911 and was able to provide to the police the telephone number from which the client had called (we had caller identification). The police located the client; she had, in fact, overdosed and was transported to the hospital by ambulance.

There is always a possibility that one's assessment of risk is inaccurate. If a situation is the least bit ambiguous, it is better to err on the side of caution, rather than taking a chance and risking a person's life. In the previous example, although the counselor suspected the client was lying about the overdose to get her therapist's phone number, the counselor contacted the police, anyway, because the young woman could have sustained organ damage or died if she had not been taken to the hospital.

2. *Establish rapport and communication; reflect feelings.* The same techniques you will be learning, or have learned, about establishing a relationship apply in crisis counseling. However, you may need to be more active in addition to reflecting the client's feelings, making a conscious effort to let the client tell you her or his story, and interjecting with statements that

communicate empathy and understanding of the client's circumstances. At this stage, it is imperative to establish psychological contact through the reflection of feelings.

3. *Identify the major problem.* In a crisis situation, typically there is a very recent event that created the crisis, or there was a recent development of numerous factors, . . . that pushed the client to what feels like the breaking point. The client's story might involve other individuals besides just her- or himself. You need to help the client stay focused on her or his own feelings, perceptions, and problems. It will be the most fruitful and efficient use of time to get and keep the client focused on the one specific problem that brought the client to you at this time. It is very important to any therapeutic relationship for a client to be able to "tell the story."—to share the details of the experience that the client thinks you need to know to fully understand the client's feelings. As you watch and listen to the client tell the story, your focus should be on both the *content* of the story (which is part of identifying the major problem) and the *affect* associated with it.

4. *Process feelings and provide support.* In this stage, you need to help the client identify and explain the feelings she or he is experiencing. Interns with little previous counseling experience tend to focus inordinately on the content of the story the client is disclosing. For example, a young client might say, "My mom and dad had a big fight over the phone about my going to Dad's house for Easter." Inappropriate focus on content would be to then ask the child, "Well, didn't the judge order where you would spend holidays when your parents went to court?" A more appropriate focus on feelings and on support would be to respond, "That makes you feel really sad to have your parents fighting about you. I wonder if you feel guilty, too, as if it's your fault your dad moved out?"

5. *Explore possible alternatives.* The client will be much better able to look at alternatives with you after the feelings about the crisis situation have been identified and explored. Processing the feelings can help temporarily reduce the client's emotional intensity sufficiently to consider possible courses of action. One technique, common to a number of models of counseling, is to help the client explore successful coping strategies used in the past that, while not fully appropriate in the current situation, might be modified to help cope with the current situation. Another, equally important technique is to help the client become aware of what coping she or he has been attempting to use, which has thus far been unsuccessful. Perhaps in the process of increasing client awareness of the unsuccessful coping attempts, you can help her or him also become aware of how unhealthy coping attempts could actually make the problem worse instead of better. Following is an example of an unhealthy attempt to cope with crisis:

> Harold presents at your agency in acute distress because, four days ago, his wife moved out of their home, leaving him with their two small

children. Since he arrived home from work four days earlier to find her gone, he has been anxious and agitated, unable to sleep or eat. The only thing he has found to soothe his nerves is alcohol, and he has basically been barely functioning for the last four days, running mostly on raw nerves dulled by alcohol. His ability to care for the children is markedly impaired, and he has gone to work every day but is experiencing too much confusion to complete tasks; he is essentially immobilized by anxiety.

Your task in the stage of exploring alternatives is to help Harold articulate precisely what aspects of his wife's leaving are most troublesome for him. Perhaps he is fearful about being solely responsible for the children. If so, one alternative is to enlist the temporary help of grandparents who live nearby or of others in his support system such as extended family and have the children stay with them for a few days until Harold can regain his equilibrium. Another possibility is that he fears for his wife's safety and may wish to consider contacting the police to help him locate her. The point here is that you do not know which aspects of her leaving are most upsetting for him, and you need to do a thorough assessment of what he considers the problem to be, as well as what some of his options are for dealing with it.

6. *Formulate an action plan.* Often, when people are in crisis, it is difficult for them to think clearly enough to identify systematic steps for coping effectively.

> In my eighth month of a difficult pregnancy, I received a phone call that my mother had died. I immediately tried to make plane reservations to go to where she was located to take care of funeral arrangements. Then, my husband reminded me our unborn baby could be in danger by my impulsively flying out of town. My own emotional state was one of shock, and I was completely unable to think clearly. He planned out steps for accomplishing medical clearance and making travel plans that were more logical and safe for both me and the baby.

Sometimes a counselor must be quite active in the process of laying out steps to facilitate coping with the crisis. In order to respect the client, after you and the client have jointly identified the best way to proceed in healthy coping, you might first ask the client what she or he thinks the sequence of steps should be. However, if the client is in shock, it might be difficult for her or him to reason clearly enough to identify a sequence. If it becomes apparent to you that this is the case, either because the client is omitting important steps or because she or he simply cannot figure out where to start, you may need to become directive in identifying the steps. In doing so, you must frequently check to see if the steps you are identifying seem logical to the client and possible to accomplish.

7. *Follow up.* It is also important for you and the client to identify a means and time line in which you will have either a subsequent meeting or phone contact to ascertain whether the plan you both devised is helping address the problem. Depending on the nature of the crisis and whether

or not the client has a regular counselor, she or he may wish to initiate regular contact with a counselor to continue coping with the situation that precipitated the crisis. Of course, if the client already has a therapist, it would be most appropriate for the client to continue with that therapist or terminate with that therapist before initiating counseling with another counselor.

Suicide

Our greatest foes, and whom we must chiefly combat, are within.

Cervantes, *Don Quixote*

Suicide is the eighth leading cause of death in the United States (Barlow & Durand, 1999), not including deaths that may have been suicide but could not be definitively labeled as such (Blumenthal, 1990). Most suicidologists believe that the actual incidence is up to four times higher than the reported statistics (McCarthy & Walsh, 1975). The suicide rate for adolescents has tripled in the past 40 years and has been described as an epidemic in American society (Davis & Sandoval, 1991). In addition, suicide is becoming a rapidly expanding problem among the elderly. As Satlin and Wasserman (1998) wrote, "elderly persons compose 12% of the population, yet they accounted for 20% of all suicides in the United States between 1980 and 1992" (p. 147). Perhaps the most important intervention an agency counselor can make is with clients who are thinking of taking their own lives. If you are interested in pursuing further research and study in the area of suicidology, you may want to contact the American Association of Suicidology in Denver, Colorado (*http://www.suicidology.org/*), which provides leadership for research, education, crisis intervention training, and standards for suicide prevention agencies. It also publishes a professional journal.

Assessing for suicidal intention needs to be part of every intake/mental status exam. The responsibility for assessing clients who may be contemplating killing themselves is among the most awesome in agency work. It is indeed a very heavy responsibility to make the determination of how at-risk an individual is—especially if you have not worked with and do not know the client well. There are some variables that you can assess that help determine the likelihood of self-harm, but ultimately, you must determine risk and then decide what course of action is most prudent. In the case of suicide, the accurate assessment of risk is critical because you might get only one chance to assess the person, if she or he truly intend to complete the suicide plan and the means are lethal. Following is an example of a high-lethality plan:

> A client came to the mental health center, having suffered with symptoms of post-traumatic stress disorder secondary to a rape 10 years prior. She also suffered chronic pain from a back injury at work. When her disability benefits were denied, it was the "straw that broke the camel's back." She came to the agency in a

brief moment of mental clarity when she knew suicide would be a mistake. Her suicide plan was to fill her bathtub with water, get in, and drop a plugged-in toaster into the tub.

When all else fails, you can rely at least partially on one critical piece of information: most clinicians working in the field would tell you that the best predictor of future behavior is past behavior. Therefore, for example, if you have a client in your office who has, in the past, brandished a weapon at her relationship partner, threatening murder and suicide, the chances are increased that she would again demonstrate that behavior under the right set of circumstances. On the other hand, sometimes people who have never before attempted suicide successfully complete a suicide on the first attempt.

In a chapter about treating suicidal children and adolescents, Jobes and Berman (1991) observed that suicidal individuals are typically taken to an agency by a concerned other. Therefore, the concept of clients going for counseling and being active, willing partners in their own treatment is often not accurate when applied to suicidal clients taken in by a second party. In fact, a suicidal client might be quite resistant or downright hostile. Nevertheless, your task of assessing risk is not diminished, even if the client is unwilling, based on the assumption that the reason for the suicidal impulse is temporary and situational.

Establishing a Relationship   A counselor needs to become involved quickly, and the importance of using relationship enhancement counseling techniques cannot be overemphasized. A variety of verbal and nonverbal strategies can be used, including leaning forward in your chair, maintaining eye contact, carefully listening, reflecting, and summarizing content and affect. The suicidal person must feel that she or he is talking with someone who truly cares about her or his welfare (Hipple & Cimbolic, 1979). The best way to increase the probability of this happening is to tune-in to the client's feelings. Most suicidal clients report feelings of helplessness, hopelessness, and despair. Moreover, your being candid and honest is extremely important. One important factor to keep in mind is that a suicidal person typically feels her or his life is out of control. If you say in the counseling session, "I won't let you kill yourself," you are further exacerbating that sense of being out of control. Instead, it is much more conducive to acknowledge that the decision to commit suicide ultimately lies with the client alone and that, if you and the client take steps to prevent it temporarily, the client will still have the prerogative to complete a suicide in the future. Although this may sound harsh, the client will recognize the truth of your statement. It will enhance your relationship in that it empowers the client acknowledging the client's control over her or his own choices and destiny, and it strengthens your relationship because, chances are, no one else to whom the client has spoken has acknowledged this truth. On the other hand, it is also appropriate to inform clients that if they do not feel they can keep themselves safe, you will help keep them safe until the crisis passes. You can also explain briefly to clients that your job is to help them look at alternatives and make decisions about how to handle stressors.

Avoiding Misconceptions   Although people training to be mental health professionals may be advanced in their program of study, they may still entertain misconceptions about suicide and talking to suicidal clients. The following are some of the common pieces of misinformation, as presented on the web site for the American Association of Suicidology:

- *Talking about suicide may actually increase the probability that a client will attempt it.* There is no evidence for this statement. If anything, talking to clients about suicide will only raise the possibility that they are cared for and perhaps not as isolated as they feel.
- *Clients who threaten suicide do not usually do it.* You must always take suicidal ideation seriously. There is a small minority of clients who threaten suicide as an attempt to manipulate their therapists, but this becomes apparent only after extensive work with such clients and calls for behavioral interventions to decrease such threats.
- *Suicide is irrational.* Although many of the thoughts that a suicidal person thinks may be irrational, the act itself seems very rational to the person contemplating it. Such a person usually feels that this is the only way out, the final resort, and that life has come to the point at which the final resort should be used. The suicidal person is often seeking nothing more than a cessation of consciousness, which appears to be a solution to their problems.
- *If a suicidal client seems less depressed, she or he is improving.* Although this may be true in some cases, in others it may be that the person has made a decision to kill her or himself. Many times, once the decision is made, the person experiences a relief from stressors, which may manifest as brighter mood.
- *Suicide is always an impulsive act.* Fortunately, this is not true. Most people who attempt suicide report that they had been thinking about it for some time. In retrospect, those close to such clients can recall hints that they were feeling that way.

In addition to understanding misconceptions about suicide, you should remember that most cases of suicide are preventable. Most clients who feel suicidal do not want to die. If they are in your office, talking to you, that is the first step in the right direction.

Doing a Suicide Assessment Interview   If you are a novice counselor attempting suicide assessment, you might consider asking your supervisor or a seasoned, credentialed colleague to offer a second opinion on your assessment. Some agencies have policies about the credentials of the clinician making the determination of risk, in which case a novice is required to obtain the opinion and decision of a more experienced counselor. When the stakes are so high, a conservative approach to determination is advisable—an observation to which we will return shortly.

There are certain key foci that a good suicide assessment interview needs to incorporate. Your ability to conduct the interview and make the best informed evaluation of risk will be enhanced if you have a solid theoretical framework for treatment, have established a good relationship with the client, and have knowledge and understanding specifically about individuals who are suicidal. One general, stylistic aspect of the interview is the importance of asking your client directly, "*How often* do you think about killing yourself?" The phrase "how often" is in italics to emphasize that you should ask as though you assume the client does think about it. In asking this way, you are implicitly giving the client permission to admit to something that is possibly socially unacceptable. A similar tactic is helpful when assessing for other activities to which people may be disinclined to admit if the question were phrased, "Do you . . ." Examples of topics that probably would be best broached in that manner include masturbation, other sexual activity, and substance abuse. The following three skills are the most notable key foci to which we are referring:

Listening for Cues about Suicidal Ideation   As the client is talking, you need to listen carefully not only to what is said but also to what is not said. A client might say, "My mom screamed, 'I don't know what I'm going to do with you!' Well, she isn't going to have to worry about that anymore." This is a statement in which, rather than focusing on how the client felt hearing his mother scream, the counselor would need to focus on the latter statement, responding, "Tell me more about that. She isn't going to have to worry about what to do with you because. . . ?"

Directly Asking about Suicide   When you hear a client make either a veiled or a direct statement about self-harm, you need to respond by asking direct questions about it. Many counseling students express discomfort and fear about focusing on such an uncomfortable topic as suicide. Some students fear that, by asking a client if she or he has contemplated suicide, they might be giving the client an alternative the client had not previously considered. In actuality, many clients will have already thought about suicide, at least in passing. For those in whom the suicidal thoughts are a more frequent occurrence, it likely will be a relief to discuss these thoughts and feelings with someone who can help them verbalize their inner battle between life and death.

Determining Imminent Risk   This is the aspect of the assessment that might come to mind when you think of a suicide assessment. After you have discussed the suicidal thoughts and desires the client is experiencing, you need to determine whether there is imminent danger of self-harm—the degree of likelihood that the client will soon act on the suicidal ideation. The importance of determining imminent risk is driven by ethical, legal, and diagnostic reasons. Sometimes, suicidal ideation is acute and immediate; for other clients, the ideation has been long-standing. If risk is imminent, hospitalization is indicated.

It can be helpful, in determining imminence, to understand the developmental model as applied to suicide. Several authors have superimposed the concept of developmental level over suicide assessment (Hendren, 1990; Stillion & McDowell, 1996). The suicide trajectory model (Stillion & McDowell, 1996) holds that, within our society are age cohorts, and that among an age cohort is a broad peer personality, which was shaped by the cultural, social, and historical events that occurred during that cohort's coming of age. Therefore, as an example of the age cohort model, the individuals who matured into adulthood in the 1930s have a very different cohort personality than the individuals who matured in the 1970s. Furthermore, the risk factors for a given age cohort are, to some extent, related to the cohort personality. If you will be working frequently assessing suicidality among clients or will be working frequently with a particular age group (such as senior clients) you should consult Stillion and McDowell (1996) or another reference that provides developmental data about risk factors for age cohorts. Having an awareness of the risk factors enables you to make a more accurate assessment of imminence. The authors also provide data about the common aspects of suicide across all developmental ages. The following general risk factors are associated with higher risk for attempting and completing suicide:

- Biological risk factors: depression, genetic factors, male gender, history of substance abuse or dependence
- Psychological risk factors: depression, low self-esteem, helplessness, poor coping strategies, unsuccessful medical treatment for a physical trauma
- Cognitive risk factors: negative self-talk, cognitive rigidity, generalization, selective abstraction, inexact labeling
- Environmental risk factors: negative family experiences, family history of suicide, anniversary date of a traumatic event, loss, presence of firearms

For children, suicidal ideation can begin when there is a family disruption or divorce. Also, if a family member has died and the child receives an explanation of death that makes it seem preferable to life ("Daddy's with God now"), this increases the chance that the child may act on suicidal ideation. In addition, family systems may send messages that a child is unwanted. Some children may respond to such messages by taking them literally and contemplating suicide. Fortunately, suicide among children is still a rare event (Davis & Sandoval, 1991).

In adolescents, things that may increase the risk of suicidal ideation or behavior revolve around the adolescent's developing sense of self. It seems that the risk factors for this age group center around suicide as a response to losing face in some manner, break-ups with boyfriends or girlfriends, family problems, and parents' taking control from them in extreme and inappropriate ways. There is also growing evidence that gay and lesbian teenagers are at greater risk for suicidal ideation and behavior due to psychosocial stressors associated with their sexual orientation. In adults, suicidal ideation or behavior is often associated with job loss or demotion, divorce, the suicide of a relative or friend, and family disruption.

As previously noted, elderly people are committing more suicides than ever before. Risk factors for elderly persons have strong developmental characteristics. Loss of meaning in life and loss of autonomy are among the primary risk factors in elderly suicidal ideation and behavior. Commitment to nursing facilities is correlated with both of these risk factors, and in the United States over 50 percent of all elderly people say they would rather die than live in a nursing home (Nussbaum, 1998). In addition, the loss of friends, the loss of mobility, and chronic pain often figure into the elderly's suicide attempts.

Beyond the age cohort/developmental model and evaluation of development-specific motivations and risk factors, there are some general factors that mental health professionals are typically trained to evaluate as part of the assessment of imminence. The following are variables that are weighed in the evaluation of imminence:

- *Psychological intent.* What is the person hoping to accomplish by committing suicide? Is it revenge or inflicting suffering on someone else or escape from one's own pain? As noted, often it is nothing more than a cessation of consciousness.
- *Suicide plan.* There are several aspects of a client's plan that need to be assessed. First, how well thought out is the plan? Is it a vague idea or a specific scenario the client has worked out? The specificity of the plan is one component of imminence, with a clearer plan suggesting higher imminence. If the plan were to be carried out, what is the likelihood someone would intervene? Does the client plan to go somewhere to make the attempt where no one would find her or him or to attempt where there would be a high likelihood of being discovered before death had occurred? For example, would the client tell people she or he was traveling for several days and then check into a hotel room under an assumed name to complete the suicide, or would the client do it at home at a time the client's spouse might discover her or him?
- *Lethality of means. High-lethality* plans include the use of firearms, prescription sleeping pills or barbiturates, hanging, drowning, carbon monoxide poisoning, high doses of aspirin or acetaminophen (Tylenol), car crash, exposure to extreme cold, and antidepressants (such as Elavil). *Low-lethality* plans include wrist cutting, nonprescription drugs

(excluding aspirin and Tylenol), and tranquilizers (such as Valium and Dalmane).

- *Availability of means.* Does the client have access to the means she or he has identified? If so, imminence is much higher.

A Template for Assessing Suicidality   Following is a template, a 10-step process, that can be used for assessing suicidality in clients. As you interview, you will see how the client's risk for suicide increases each time you have to move to the next step.

> *Step 1:* Know your client's risk factors. A little knowledge in this area goes a long way toward precluding the escalation of suicidal ideation or behavior.
>
> *Step 2:* If you suspect that the client is suicidal, ask her or him directly.
>
> *Step 3:* If the person states that she or he is suicidal, find out if the client has a plan.
>
> *Step 4:* If the person has a plan, does she or he have a specific method in mind?
>
> *Step 5:* If the client has a specific method in mind, does she or he have the means to carry out that method?
>
> *Step 6:* If the client has a plan, a method, and the means, what is the lethality of the means?
>
> *Step 7:* Listen to the client's story. Express your concern for the client, and make certain that you tune in to the client's feelings. Remind clients that they will not feel this badly forever, that suicidal crises are time-limited.
>
> *Step 8:* Ask the client if she or he is willing to sign a life contract. This is a written document that the client agrees to. It affirms that the client intends to stay safe until the next appointment. If things get to the point at which the client feels she or he cannot take care of her- or himself, the life contract of outlines resources and supports the client agrees to use in that event. The client, you, and one witness sign this. The protocol is designed after psychological measures of influence that increase the probability that the client will follow through.
>
> *Step 9:* If the client refuses to sign a life contract and maintains suicidal ideation, arrange for a more restrictive environment.
>
> *Step 10:* At no point in this sequence should you ever leave the client alone.

After the Assessment   In general, treatment strategies for suicidal individuals are contingent on the counseling model to which you subscribe. Nevertheless, bear in mind that some people become suicidal as the result of situational variables and do not necessarily require long-term treatment. Often, though, the person who is suicidal has a long history of emotional difficulties, and the suicidal episodes simply represent points at which the symptoms became extremely acute and exacerbated (Barlow & Durand, 1999). Obviously, the approach you take will hinge somewhat on the client's mental health history. The bottom line in terms of immediate treatment is that you will need to do whatever is necessary to keep the client safe. Sometimes, it is helpful to enlist a family member as a support person for the client. Ideally, this is a family member who agrees to stay with the client around the clock until the next counseling session. Some clients are prescribed psychotropic medications to provide relief from the exacerbated symptoms of mental/emotional disorders. For others, it may be necessary to have them hospitalized, and it is preferable to have a family member or another support person do the involuntary hospitalization procedure on the client. This maintains focus on the support system of concerned persons in the client's environment. It also preserves the chances of maintaining rapport with the client if she or he returns to you for treatment following hospitalization. By the way, in today's world, the client will likely be hospitalized for a few days before being discharged and returned for outpatient treatment. Be prepared for the client to return to you shortly. Some patients have been hospitalized for as little as two days for acute suicidal ideation, with high imminence.

Despite your best efforts, sometimes clients do commit suicide. Humans are unpredictable, and you can never know for certain how someone will behave in the future. Real difficulty emerges when a client denies that she or he has intent to harm her- or himself but intuition tells you she or he might. You need to balance the importance of clients' self-determination and integrity with concern for protecting their best interests if they are too emotionally disturbed to protect themselves from their own suicidal impulses. The inventories and psychological tests that have been developed to identify a person as imminently suicidal are not sufficiently valid and reliable to be of any use to counselors; the inventories typically identify many individuals as suicidal who are not, a Type I statistical error (Jobes & Berman, 1991).

To further complicate the issue, therapeutic professionals must wrestle with the question of whether or not each individual is responsible for her or his own destiny. If an individual, in sound mind, chooses to end her or his life, is it the prerogative of that individual to do so? There is much controversy about this issue, which has been exemplified in the media coverage of Dr. Jack Kevorkian, who has assisted in numerous suicides for patients who are terminally ill. This debate is about "rational suicide," initially advocated by Thomas Szasz (1986). There is not sufficient space in this book to fully cover the debate about rational suicide, but you should read further on this topic. Suggestions for further reading include the Szasz (1986) article and the chapter on rational suicide in Stillion and McDowell (1996). Sometimes when a person has finalized the decision to commit suicide, she or he carries out the plan without discussing it with anyone.

> A psychiatrist, who was greatly loved by his clients and respected by his colleagues, failed to appear for rounds at the hospital one morning. When his wife paged him and he did not respond to the page, a search for him was launched by local police. His body was discovered several hours later; he had checked into a hotel and overdosed on prescription medication and alcohol. No one had had any idea he had been feeling depressed.

If a person is willing to discuss the possibility of suicide, that fact suggests that she or he is experiencing some ambivalent feelings about the suicide, which in turn gives a counselor an opportunity to help the client generate alternatives to such a hopeless and final choice. When you can intervene effectively with suicidal clients, this is perhaps one of the greatest contributions you can make as a professional.

Intervention

Your assessment of the client's condition and prognosis will determine the extent of the intervention that needs to occur. At the risk of being overly simplistic, the broad treatment options are in-patient treatment, out-patient treatment, or no treatment. Since "no treatment" is unlikely to be applicable, we will focus our discussion on the in-patient versus out-patient option.

Involuntary Hospitalization   Each state has its own statutes about involuntary commitment to a treatment facility for a mental health disorder or substance abuse disorder. The criteria typically involve determining that the person is either a danger to someone or a danger to her- or himself. Sometimes, the danger to self can take the form of passive danger, in that the person is so depressed or lethargic that to be left alone would place the person in danger due to lack of responsiveness or inability to prepare food. Each state law has elaborate provisions as to who is able to commit another person and on what grounds the commitment should occur (Welfel, 1998). It is imperative that, when you begin your training in an agency, you are knowledgeable about the commitment laws and criteria in your state. Usually, a commitment is for a circumscribed period of time, such as 48 or 72 hours, in which the patient is assessed and evaluated by hospital staff. At the conclusion of that time, a hearing is held with a judge (sometimes referred to as a "mental hygiene hearing"), the patient, and clinical staff to determine whether the involuntary commitment will be continued or if the patient will be released from the commitment. Occasionally, even after the commitment is lifted, a patient will opt to voluntarily agree to treatment.

When a client is being assessed for danger to self or others, and it is apparent that the client requires inpatient treatment, ideally the prospect of hospitalization is discussed with the client, who agrees to sign in for treatment. In other words, the "involuntary" component should be avoided *if possible.* Unfortunately, though, there are situations in which voluntary admission to a hospital is not an option. Examples of situations in which involuntary commitment is unavoidable include a client who is paranoid, has brandished a weapon against the person he claims is having an affair with his wife, and refuses his medication. Another example is a suicidal adolescent who refuses to talk to anyone but you and has a clearly developed, highly lethal plan for committing suicide. Numerous other clinical situations could also occur in which the involuntary route is the only viable option.

In the cases in which involuntary commitment is the only good option, be aware that the therapeutic relationship between your and the client might be jeopardized in the process of your committing her or him. In an ideal situation, even if the client is initially feeling angry or betrayed, she or he eventually realizes that you took steps for commitment because it was in the client's best interest at the time. However, the real world is not always ideal, and there have been times that a therapeutic relationship has been irreparably damaged by involuntary commitment. As previously noted, family members or other involved people, if willing, should be the ones to initiate the commitment proceedings. Family members and other collaterals can be very helpful in this process and are often grateful that a mental health professional can offer some guidance as to how to best help the client. However, sometimes family members are unavailable or unwilling to take steps toward committing the client.

If you have determined that the client's disorder presents imminent danger to self or others, you have an ethical and legal obligation to initiate the commitment yourself. In the long term, the client's immediate safety must preclude concern about your eventual therapeutic relationship with her or him. Nevertheless, sometimes therapeutic rapport with a client takes a very long time to establish, and involuntarily committing someone can be extremely detrimental to the counseling relationship.

Outpatient Treatment   Presumably you will be considering this option if it appears to be clear that danger or risk to self or others is not immediately imminent. At this point, the goal is to obtain follow-up counseling soon—preferably in the next 48 hours, to provide support and re-assess the client.

If the client has an on-going relationship with another counselor, you should advise him or her to contact that counselor as soon as possible to inform the counselor of the crisis. Additionally, you might suggest that the client sign a Release of Information permitting you to communicate with the client's primary therapist. If the client does not have another therapist, it is your responsibility to put some arrangements in place for imminent follow-up care before the client leaves your office. (Failure to do so might be considered client abandonment, per ACA Ethical Guidelines.) This may entail scheduling the client with yourself or another counselor. Alternatively, it may involve scheduling the client at another agency if your agency cannot provide on-going services. However, a client in crisis really should have a short-term follow up with a mental health professional soon after the crisis intervention contact.

If the scheduled follow-up appointment for the client will not occur within the next few days, initiate a follow-up contact, even if only by phone, within a day or two of the crisis contact.

Modes of Treatment

Counseling can take place with an individual client, a couple, a family, or a group of clients brought together because of a common concern. Although a full discussion of individual versus family versus group counseling is far beyond the scope of this chapter, a chapter on service delivery needs to touch on the levels at which counseling services can be offered.

As discussed in chapter 1, there is a certification counselors can earn when they specialize in marriage and family counseling. Systems theory views each individual existing in a larger social unit—a system (Sharf, 1996). Sometimes, even though an individual has sought counseling services, the counselor decides it is necessary to work also with the client's partner and/or children on some issues.

> A client with whom I worked had severe obsessive-compulsive disorder, in which she insisted that her husband and teenage children participate in the handwashing and other rituals she had devised to "rid the house of contamination." She initiated therapy because, after 20 years of rituals she performed and insisted her immediate family perform, her husband threatened to leave the marriage unless she got help.

As in many cases of emotional difficulty, when one person suffers with symptoms, others in the immediate environment also experience sequelae of the disorder. It can be cathartic, as well as empowering, to the family members to give them an opportunity to express the problem from their own perspectives and to give them an opportunity to express their feelings about the problem.

PREVENTIVE INTERVENTION

Lewis, Lewis, Daniels, and D'Andrea (1998) observed that, to a certain extent, providing individual counseling is not the most efficient or effective means of reducing client suffering. In a broad sense, individual counseling is akin to closing the barn door after the cows have already gotten out. In other words, individual counseling is helpful at the level of the individual but is wholly ineffectual in terms of stemming the increasing tide of new clients presenting with problems. Preventive intervention, by contrast, makes it possible to reach large numbers of people, hopefully giving them skills or raising their awareness, so that behavior change can occur or they can access resources before they actually develop serious problems.

A television advertisement shows a mother driving in the car with her teenage son. The scene lasts for about 20 seconds; then the screen goes black and the narrator states, "Another missed opportunity to talk to your kid about drugs." The narrator then offers a free video and booklet with suggestions about how to discuss drug use with one's children. This particular advertisement is paid for by the National Council for the Prevention of Drug Abuse. You may be able to recall similar billboards and radio or television commercials carrying similar messages intended to raise awareness and offer resources for addressing situations before they become problems.

Federal and state monies were available in the 1970s and early 1980s for preventive programs. Although those funds are no longer as easily obtained, prevention remains an important responsibility of community agencies and mental health practitioners. Another goal of preventive intervention is to target the environmental stressors that put people at risk, or to build people's competencies or life skills. One example of targeting environmental stressors is to participate with a school system in developing a zero-tolerance policy for interstudent harassment of students who are gay, lesbian, or bisexual.

CONSULTATION

Last but certainly not least in the range of services counselors provide is consultation. An agency counselor might be called on to consult with other service providers in serving a particular individual or to consult with another agency, organization, or business. Sometimes, businesses contract with outside service providers to conduct wellness or stress-management programs for their employees. As an agency counselor, you could develop the skills and even expertise to provide programs to consultees requesting your services.

> As part of an employee assistance program our agency had contracted to provide to a local bank, I was called in on short notice to do a critical incident debriefing. Earlier that week, a bank teller at another branch office had been held up and robbed. Many employees were highly distraught by the incident and two had resigned. In a four-hour period at the bank that morning, I spoke with about six employees, two of whom I referred for a full intake at our main agency office.

Although many employers have their own, in-house employee assistance programs, sometimes they contract for employee assistance with a service provider outside the business. This could be considered a form of consultation.

TERMINATION

There are many reasons a counseling relationship might be terminated. Ideally, termination occurs because the treatment goals have been met, and the counselor and client are in agreement that maximal benefit has been attained. Again ideally, clients need to perceive termination as an active step, as another of several steps they have taken to help themselves and grow.

When this "ideal" situation transpires, one strategy is to gradually lengthen the time between appointments. Basch (1980) noted that termination needs to be gradual, so that the client has an opportunity to ensure that she or he is ready and able to apply what was learned in counseling. For example, if the client had been seen weekly, a counselor might first move to sessions every two weeks for several sessions, then every four weeks. This pattern might occur over a duration of about three months.

There are other situations in which termination occurs, either due to the client's choice or due to the counselor's decision or action. Counselor-initiated termination occurs when the counselor is resigning, is absent due to illness, is concluding an internship or another training experience, or is referring the client to another therapist due to lack of expertise in treating a particular type of problem.

Welfel (1998) observed that, in a social relationship, we can choose to discontinue the connection with another person anytime we wish, with essentially no negative consequences. Such is not the case in a counseling relationship. Although a client can spontaneously cut off a relationship with a counselor, under no circumstances should a counselor spontaneously terminate a professional counseling relationship simply because she or he chooses to. A counselor has a clear ethical (and, in some cases, legal) obligation to the client to make certain the client's needs have been met. If you are resigning or completing a training experience (such as an internship), you need to begin discussing your resignation with clients several months before your end date. A student intern should be discussing her or his intern status as part of the initial disclosure with a client, so completion of such training does not come as a surprise to the client. As the termination date approaches, the intern needs to discuss the client's options with her or him—first, whether the client wants to continue counseling with another therapist and, second, whom you recommend. It is important to consider the client's unique characteristics and presenting problems when suggesting another therapist, in the hope of making a referral that will be a good fit. It is also strongly advised that you check with the therapist you are suggesting to verify that she or he is able to accommodate new clients in her or his caseload.

Sometimes, the counselor and client may recognize that the client is not making progress in symptom reduction or is not increasing adaptive, healthy behaviors and feelings. There are a host of reasons that a client may not be benefiting from counseling—some of those could be related to counselor variables (age, gender, ethnicity, theoretical approach). You might refer a client to a different counselor due to the client's lack of progress with you.

> A woman of 24 came to the mental health center referred by her physician for symptoms of anorexia and bulimia. She and I immediately experienced rapport, and I had a strong countertransference reaction to her in that we were very similar in many ways. After about 10 sessions, her symptoms began to worsen, as did her medical condition. It was clear that I lacked the clinical skills to help her with the symptoms. She needed a therapist with more specialized training. We discussed it, and I referred her to a therapist I trusted and respected. Six months later, the client was vastly improved.

As in the previous example, clients place a great deal of trust in you and your clinical judgment. If a client's concerns or symptoms are outside your area of expertise, you must refer the client to a therapist who is qualified in the area in which the client needs help. A good question to keep in mind when making a client referral is "Is this new counselor someone I would send a family member to for help?" If your answer is "no," it might be advisable to refer the client elsewhere. Again, out of consideration for the client, you should contact the mental health professional to whom you are making the referral. Be careful to preserve the client's confidentiality until the client has signed a release of information giving you permission to discuss the case.

After termination has occurred, you need to make a decision about whether you will encourage or initiate continued contact with the client. This is a decision that is based partially on the circumstances of the termination. If the termination has occurred because treatment goals were met, some authors (such as George & Cristiani, 1995) contend that the counselor should maintain contact with the client to see how the client is doing. However, there are some clear disadvantages to maintaining contact. It might inadvertently suggest to the client that you do not believe she or he can function without your intermittent assistance. Also, the client might experience it as somewhat invasive, and the client might feel reluctant to tell you of her or his feelings about your phone calls. If the client is currently working with a different therapist, your ongoing contact could confuse the client and the treatment. When a relationship has had closure, each individual must then go on to other relationships. It is a good idea to have a final session with a client and then encourage the client to re-initiate contact if or when she or he feels the need to do so.

One final situation must be mentioned—the client who stops coming for appointments before treatment goals have been attained. Such a pattern indicates ambivalence about counseling, a decision to seek assistance, or possibly discomfort with the counselor or sessions (all of which, some would argue, are forms of resistance). You may wish to call the client or send a letter. It is preferable to write a letter because it allows more "space" for the client. A typical "no show" letter might say

Dear _____:

    I have missed you at our last scheduled sessions. I would like very much for us to continue our work together, yet the choice about whether to counsel is yours. If you do wish to reschedule, could you please do so in the next 30 days? Otherwise, I will close your chart and assume you are not interested in services at this time.

    Sincerely,

    Mary Counselor

Again, some people might find a phone call too threatening, whereas a letter permits more distance and some anonymity, if they choose it.

SUMMARY

In this chapter, we have taken a long journey. Many important points were raised, including ensuring high-quality services for clients, levels of intervention, crisis intervention and suicide assessment, and other types of services you can provide in your capacity as an agency counselor. Depending on your place of employment, you might do all of these things, or just a few of them. There is enough consistency from mental health agency to agency, though, that chances are high, that if you are employed as a professional counselor, you will be doing at least a few of them. This chapter may have raised your awareness about some of the issues involved in providing these services.

DISCUSSION ITEMS

1. What is your position on suicide? Are there particular instances in which you would make exceptions to your opinion about it?
2. A client might become suicidal or homicidal. Considering your ethical and legal obligation to take action, possibly against the client's wishes, what are some techniques you might use to preserve your therapeutic relationship with the client?
3. Are there aspects of conducting a mental status examination that make you feel uncomfortable? Why?
4. How comfortable would you feel doing crisis intervention work? If you would feel uncomfortable, what would help increase your comfort level?

REFERENCES

American Psychological Association. (1993). *Record keeping guidelines.* Washington, D.C.: Author.

Barlow, D. H., & Durand, V. M. (1999). *Abnormal psychology: An integrative approach.* Pacific Grove, CA: Brooks/Cole.

Basch, M. F. (1980) *Doing Psychotheraphy* New York: Basic Books.

Beis, E. (1984). *Mental health and the law.* Rockville, MD: Free Press.

Blumenthal, S. J. (1990). An overview and synopsis of risk factors, assessment, and treatment of suicidal patients over the life cycle. In S. J. Blumenthal & D. J. Kupfer (Eds.), *Suicide over the life cycle: Risk factors, assessment and treatment of suicidal patients.* Washington, DC: American Psychiatric Press.

Campbell, J. (1949). *The hero with a thousand faces.* New York: Pantheon.

Carson, R. C., Butcher, J. N., & Mineka, S. (1998). *Abnormal psychology and modern life.* New York: Longman.

Cohen, R. (1979). *Malpractice: A guide for mental health professionals.* New York: Free Press.

Davis, J. M., & Sandoval, J. (1991). *Suicidal youth: School-based intervention and prevention.* San Francisco: Jossey-Bass.

Faiver, C. (1986). The mental health status examination: Revised. In P. A. Keller & L.G. Ritt (Eds.), *Innovations in clinical practice: A source book* (Vol. 5, pp. 279–285). Sarasota, FL: Professional Resource Exchange.

Faiver, C. (1988). An initial client contact form. In P. A. Keller & S. R. Heyman (Eds.), *Innovations in clinical practice: A source book* (Vol. 7, pp. 285–288). Sarasota, FL: Professional Resource Exchange.

Folstein, M. F, Folstein, S. E., & McHugh, P. R. (1975). Mini-mental state: A practical method for grading the cognitive states of patients for the clinician. *Journal of Psychiatric Research, 12,* 189–198.

George, R. L., & Cristiani, T. S. (1995). *Counseling: Theory and practice (2nd ed.).* Boston: Allyn & Bacon.

Hendren, R. L. (1990). Stress in adoleslence. In L.E. Arnold (Ed.), *Childhood Stress* (pp. 248–264). New York: Willey & Sons.

Hipple, J., & Cimbolic, P. (1979). *The counselor and suicidal crisis.* Springfield, IL: Charles C Thomas.

Hoff, L. A. (1995). *People in crisis: Understanding and helping.* San Francisco: Jossey-Bass.

Holmes, T. H., & Rahe, R. H. (1967). The social readjustment rating scale. *Journal of Psychosomatic Research, 11*(2), 213–218.

Jobes, D. A., & Berman, A. L. (1991). Crisis intervention and brief treatment for suicidal youth. In A. R. Roberts (Ed.), *Contemporary Perspectives on Crisis Intervention and Prevention.* Englewood Cliffs, NJ: Prentice Hall.

Lazarus, A. A. (1989). *The practice of multimodal therapy: Systematic, comprehensive, and effective psychotherapy.* Baltimore, MD: The Johns Hopkins University Press.

Lewis, J. A., Lewis, M. D., Daniels, J. A., & D'Andrea, M. J. (1998). *Community counseling: Empowerment strategies for a diverse society (4th ed.).* Pacific Grove, CA: Brooks/Cole.

McCarthy, P. D., & Walsh, D. (1975) Suicide in Dublin: The under-reporting of suicide and the consequences for material statistics. *British Journal of Psychiatry, 126,* 301–308.

Monroe, S. M., & Steiner, S. C. (1986). Social support and psychopathology: Interrelations with preexisting disorder, stress, and personality. *Journal of Abnormal Psychology, 95,* 29–39.

Nussbaum, P. D. (1998). *Aging of the brain, aging of the mind: A seminar for health professionals.* Akron, OH.

Piazza, N. J., & Baruth, N. E. (1990). Client record guidelines. *Journal of Counseling and Development, 68,* 313–316.

Rapoport, L. (1962). The state of crisis: Some theoretical considerations. *Social Service Review, 36,* 211–217.

Roberts, A. R. (1991). Conceptualizing crisis theory and the crisis intervention model. In A. R. Roberts (Ed.), *Contemporary perspectives on crisis intervention and prevention.* Englewood Cliffs, NJ: Prentice Hall.

Satlin, A., & Wasserman, C. (1998). Overview of geriatric psychopharmacology. In S. L. McElroy (Ed.), *Psychopharmacology across the lifespan.* Washington, DC: American Psychiatric Press.

Selye, H. (1976). *Stress in health and disease.* Woburn, MA: Butterworth.

Sharf, R.S. (1996). *Theories of psychotherapy and counseling: Concepts and cases.* Pacific Grove CA: Brooks/Cole.

Shutz, B. (1982). *Legal liability in psychotherapy.* San Francisco: Jossey-Bass.

Snider, P. D. (1987). Client records: Inexpensive liability protection for mental health counselors. *Journal of Mental Health Counseling, 9*(3), 134–141.

Stillion, J. M.: McDowell, E. E. (1996). *Suicide across the life span: Premature exits.* (2nd Ed.) Washington, D.C.: Taylor & Francis.

Strub, R. L., & Black, F. W. (1998). The bedside mental status examination. In F. Boller & J. Grafman (Eds.), Handbook of Neuropsychology, Vol. 1 (pp. 24–46). Amsterdam, Netherlands. Elsevier.

Szasz, T. (1986). The case against suicide prevention. *American Psychologist, 41,* 806–812.

Trzepacz, P. T., & Baker, R. W. (1993). *The psychiatric mental status examination.* New York: Oxford University Press.

Tuthill, A. R. (1997). Record Keeping-New rules make it more important than ever. *California Chiropractic Association Journal, 62,* 29–32.

Tyhurst, J. S. (1957). The role of transition states—including disasters—in mental illness. In *Symposium on Social and Preventive Psychiatry.* Washington, DC: Walter Reed Army Institute of Research.

Weiner, I. B. (1995). How to anticipate ethical and legal challenges in personality assessments. In J. N. Butcher (Ed.), *Clinical personality assessment: Practical applications.* (pp. 95–103) New York: Oxford University Press.

Welfel, E. R. (1998). *Ethics in counseling and psychotherapy: Standards, research, and emerging issues.* Pacific Grove, CA: Brooks/Cole.

Zimmerman, M. (1994). *Interview guide for evaluating DSM-IV psychiatric disorders and the mental status examination.* East Greenwich, RI: Psych Products Press.

CHAPTER

6

ADVOCACY AND RESEARCH

If you want to raise a [person] from mud and filth, do not think it is enough to keep standing on top and reaching down to lend a helping hand. You must go all the way down yourself, down into the mud and filth. You must not hesitate to get yourself dirty.

The Baal Shem Tov

Cora realizes that, in her eagerness to participate in the rally, she'd neglected to first research the theme.

In this chapter of external, professional exploration, we will look at two areas that lie at the basis of much of what we do as therapeutic professionals. Although the two topics of research and advocacy do not seem, at first, to be closely related, in some respects they are interdependent. Research is often funded by external sources such as private foundations or state and federal governments. Projects are funded partly on the basis of those issues and concerns that are presented as pressing or relevant to consumers. Researchers and practitioners decide if an issue is "pressing." They are, in effect, advocating for their causes.

Conversely, for an advocate to make a compelling case, it is very helpful to have data to support statements she or he is making. Advocates might be making claims about clients, issues, or the profession. For example, if a counselor is providing expert testimony or making a statement at an open legislative hearing about funding programs for chronically mentally ill people, she will be able to make a more compelling case for funding if she can provide favorable data about the effectiveness of existing programs for those clients. Regardless, advocates depend on data generated by research to present a persuasive argument for positions.

In this chapter, we will talk first about advocacy and then look at research issues. The discussion of advocacy is divided into sections on advocating for clients and for the profession. Remember that this division is artificial—it is like differentiating between baking muffins and baking cupcakes—the goal is the same and the behaviors are largely the same—the difference has mainly to do with specific details. We will also look specifically at one of the highly significant ways research has created the knowledge base from which counselors now are trained and practice: therapy process and outcome research. The chapter concludes with the transtheoretical approach presented by Prochaska and Di Clemente, which prescribes particular techniques for stages of client readiness for change.

THE CONCEPT OF ADVOCACY

The need to advocate can really be summed up in one word that implies much complexity—*politics*. Among the therapeutic professions, social work probably has the longest history of political involvement as an integral component of its professional history. Social workers have great strength in their lobbying ability when state laws about licensability and reimbursability are being modified and enacted. Their political strength originates in the philosophical origins of the discipline of social work, and in their recognition that change and helping an individual involves systems intervention at the social and political levels. Thus, political activity and involvement is a central component of a social worker's identity from the outset of her or his professional training.

In contrast, the field of counseling has historically been oriented more toward change at the individual level, or perhaps at the level of marriage or family systems. In comparison with the field of social work, counseling has been slower to act on the importance of political activity for the survival of the profession. It seems that the expansion and dominance of the managed health care industry have pushed the counseling profession to more political activity regarding laws that have an impact on reimbursability from third-party payors.

Nevertheless, Osborne, Collison, House, Gray, Firth, and Lou (1998) noted that critical social issues demand that counselors become involved in meeting their social responsibility to forge changes. These changes must be driven by counselors' awareness of inequities, and their intent must be to move humanity toward an "enlightened world society" (Lee & Sirch, 1994). "Enlightened world society" suggests a society in which no one is oppressed for any reason, regardless of individual differences, although there are numerous definitions of "enlightened world society." Table 6.1 provides examples of a brief summary of the purposes of advocacy and some actions that illustrate each purpose. This summary serves the dual purpose of providing concrete descriptions of advocacy activities and suggesting possible actions to take when considering avenues through which to advocate for a client or a cause.

Advocating to Promote Societal Equity

Alper, Schloss, and Schloss (1995) defined an advocate as a person who acts on someone else's behalf. Much of the available literature about client advocacy focuses on advocating for individuals with developmental disabilities. Mental retardation seems to carry somewhat less of a social stigma than mental illness, and the family members of people who are mentally retarded have been extremely active in advocating for their rights. The Americans with Disabilities Act, enacted in 1990, paved the way for people with a variety of disabilities to be recognized as contributing members of society, with equal rights

TABLE 6.1   PURPOSES OF ADVOCACY

Purpose	Example Activities
Promoting equity for clients	Teaching clients assertiveness skills Coaching clients on writing letters to newspapers and politicians Intervening with clients on their own behalf with members of the community (such as employers and landlords)
Gaining recognition among the general public for the profession of counseling	Doing public service messages for the local newspaper Speaking at local PTA meetings
Gaining recognition of counseling as a discipline among other therapeutic professionals	Becoming involved in professional organizations to develop standards of care Attempting to exert influence over who is assigned to state board for counselors

for housing, employment, and other critical aspects of human dignity. Advocacy can be done by an individual on her or his own behalf, or it can be done by another concerned person in a consumer's life, such as a family member, case manager, counselor, or neighbor. Advocacy activities range from those as simple as making a phone call on someone's behalf to taking legal steps to ensure that someone's rights are not violated. For example, perhaps you have a client that comes for counseling every week, who usually uses his lunch hour to attend a session with you. Perhaps the client's supervisor does not believe that he is truly in need of counseling and is pressuring him to work overtime, through his lunch hour. An example of advocacy on your part is to first obtain the client's permission and a release of information and then to intervene on the client's behalf, such as calling the supervisor to attempt to find a mutually agreeable solution.

Another example of an applied situation is that of helping clients to have a voice in their own treatment plans. One survey, conducted by Brown, Belz, Corsi, and Wenig (1993), focused on residents with developmental disabilities and the staff at a day treatment center. When the staff members were surveyed as to the reasons the residents were not given more options about treatment and/or living arrangements, their responses included their perceptions of residents as unable to make choices due to poor communication and lack of initiative, their fears that the residents might make inappropriate choices, and their feelings that the program structure did not allow for individual choice. Wolfe, Olfiesh, and Boone (1996) noted that research has found that individuals with disabilities tend to have fewer opportunities to make choices, to express their preferences, and to exert control. They also are more likely to be presented with a narrower range of choices when they *do* get choices.

Cunconan-Lahr and Brotherson (1996) conducted a survey of advocacy activities to shed more light on the form that advocacy activities take and who is doing them. Their respondents consisted of both consumers and parents of children with a disability. The participants' responses seemed organized around three prominent themes, the first of which was "empowering voices." Activities in which consumers and parents engaged, within the empowering voices theme, included: persuading, negotiating, and compromising on critical issues; educating people in the community about the consumer's disabling condition and his or her subsequent needs; educating community members about what the consumer has to offer the community; and raising public awareness about basic human rights. The self-reported advocacy activities included publishing letters and articles, serving on a committee or commission, testifying at a public hearing, presenting at a parent or consumer group, and making television or radio appearances. The second theme centered around "networking" with others, defined as communicating effectively and often with local lawmakers and policymakers, as well as with other community members. Finally, the third theme centered around attitudes of courage and leadership. Certain personal characteristics were identified as important to the advocacy effort. These included personal skills and resources that could be of value, such as self-reliance, courage, passion, self-esteem, self-confidence, and the willingness to take risks.

To have a realistic portrayal of advocacy, we not only need to acknowledge the value of it but also must discuss the barriers that tend to impede the advocacy process. A number of impediments have been identified, and forewarned is forearmed. Perhaps one of the most commonly encountered barriers to client advocacy is individuals' perceptions of their job descriptions. We noted in chapter 1 how the mental health professions have been artificially divided by training ideologies that do not necessarily translate into the workplace. One such training ideology is "Client advocacy is to be done by case managers; that is their job. Providing therapeutic services is my job." Although generally such a division of labor may be accurate, in reality counselors often find themselves needing to advocate for their clients.

Cunconan-Lahr and Brotherson (1996) identified time, expense, and emotions as obstacles to advocacy. Advocating could be a full-time job, and one needs to have a realistic idea about how much *time* one is willing or able to invest in the advocacy process. Often, advocating is an unpaid activity, volunteer work that can be done only after other responsibilities are met. In addition, there can be hidden *expenses*. For example, testimony at a state hearing involves traveling to the state capitol and possibly lodging. Long-distance phone calls, duplicating costs, and missed work might also be involved. Obviously, the expenses can add up quickly. In regard to *emotions*, telling your story can be a supportive, cathartic experience. However, if, as an advocate, you are harboring anger and resentment, these emotions can undermine your ability to be an effective leader. You can become so impassioned as to lose your ability to think rationally and clearly about the most effective course of action to achieve a goal. On the other hand, anger can be an energizing, productive emotion when channeled constructively. Even so, your advocacy efforts might be met with anger, which can be challenging and intimidating.

Although advocating for clients is something all therapeutic professionals probably do at some point, it is even *more* important to teach clients how to advocate appropriately on their own behalf than it is to advocate for them. This is related to the discussion in chapter 3 about the power differential between counselor and client and falls within the realm of empowerment. There is an ancient fable, the essence of which is that, when a man is hungry, you can catch him a fish to feed his family, but, if you teach *him* how to fish, he can feed the whole village. It cannot be emphasized strongly enough that clients need to be empowered in the process of their own affairs, to the greatest extent they are capable of participating.

> I worked with a gentleman who had schizophrenia and was being evicted from his apartment for unhygienic living conditions. I assisted the client in obtaining legal aid and met with the client, his attorney, and his landlord over several appointments to remedy the problem and avoid his eviction. At each meeting, I coached the client ahead of time on what to say and how to say it. The client had the experience of resolving his own difficulty, rather than "having other people fight the battles," as the client so aptly put it.

Clients need to perceive themselves as the persons primarily responsible for their recovery or improvement. It is tempting to inflate your self-evaluation, when a client says, "I couldn't have done it without you," to think, "I *did* do a good job, didn't I?" However, such an approach is detrimental to the client's sense of mastery over her or his difficulty—and the bottom line is that mastery over the problem is the result of the *client's* work, in making use of tools that you taught her or him how to use. It may seem a minor point, but it is actually a very important one. The whole point of counseling is to help the client acquire sufficient coping skills and resources to not need you. The same principle applies to advocacy efforts. Although it may be helpful in some instances for you to "go to bat" for a client, you will not always be around for her or him, and your efforts will be better spent teaching the client how to advocate on her or his own behalf.

When you do begin teaching clients how to advocate, there are developmental phases that, according to Kieffer (1983), you can expect the clients to progress through. Actually, these stages are applicable regardless of whether the advocate is the client or the counselor. First is the "entry" phase, when the person first begins getting involved in and becoming aware of the need for advocacy efforts. Second is "advancement," in which a person becomes increasingly involved in organizational activity, perhaps developing a mentoring relationship with another person already in the organization. Third, the "incorporation" phase occurs when the person develops a sense of mastery over and competence in the advocacy activities. Finally, in the "commitment" phase the person develops a further sense of mastery and participatory competence. It may be in the incorporation or commitment phase that an individual mentors another individual who is in an earlier stage of development. The point has been made (Balcazar, Keys, Bertram, & Rizzo, 1996) that empowerment in and of itself is necessary but not sufficient for advocacy to be successful. The real outcome measure of effectiveness must result in concrete actions and outcomes for the advocacy effort to have truly been successful.

One of the best known and remarkable stories of a consumer who became an advocate was that of Helen Keller, a woman who was both visually and hearing impaired. Her activities as an advocate made a tremendous impact on the public's awareness of people with disabilities, as well as people who were victims of economic exploitation, gender bias, and other forms of oppression. Smith (1997) observed, "Helen Keller is an outstanding example of a person with severe disabilities but magnificent achievements who was, therefore, able to eclipse the prevailing attitudes about people with those disabilities" (p. 138). Ms. Keller graduated from Radcliffe College, and she espoused a philosophy of radical socialism. She helped found the Civil Liberties Union to advocate free speech, was a member of the Industrial Workers of the World (the union persecuted by the Wilson administration), and framed her work for the American Foundation for the Blind as social advocacy, since blindness was concentrated more in the lower class (Loewen, 1995). When you think about the personality characteristics that lend themselves to successful advocacy, Ms. Keller demonstrated many of them. She clearly had great strength of character and willingness to take major risks in public speaking. She also was impassioned about her cause but was able to communicate effectively, without expressing anger or resentment about her own disability. Being able to advocate for herself allowed so much more personal dignity than she would have had if the advocating and public speaking had all been done by her teacher, Annie Sullivan, and her parents. Although Ms. Keller had sensory disabilities, rather than a mental health disability, she is one of the greatest examples of successful advocacy.

The principles of advocacy remain the same, regardless of the specifics of a person's disability or limitations. The very act of raising the public's consciousness about the plight of people with a given problem can have a healing effect. If communicating about it can help generate funds for additional research on the condition, or if it can help ameliorate the suffering of others with similar conditions, it can help people give meaning to their own suffering. A poster seen in some mental health centers lists famous individuals who have had some type of mental illness, including Sylvia Plath, Abraham Lincoln, Albert Einstein, Michelangelo, Ernest Hemingway, and Patty Duke; the point of such a list is to advocate for the awareness of emotional disability to reduce its associated stigma and to illustrate that having a disability does not preclude a person from making valuable contributions to society. Other commonly known examples of people advocating for a cause include Magic Johnson, having contracted HIV, advocating for safe sex, and Christopher Reeve, advocating for additional research on spinal cord injury and treatment. Obviously, people other than celebrities advocate for issues. The National Alliance for the Mentally Ill was established by consumers and families of consumers. Mothers Against Drunk Driving, MADD, was established by the mother of a child killed by a drunk driver.

The issue of advocacy is of great importance to everyone involved in the field of mental health counseling because state laws and legislation have tremendous impact on the daily lives of professional counselors. They also have great impact on many aspects of client care, such as whom a client can see for mental health counseling, what type of treatment the client can receive, and what other community services (such as housing and transportation) are available, in the forms of funding for programs and contracts with businesses that provide those services.

Of course, advocacy can have a draining effect, as well as a healing one. The draining effect comes about when challenging the status quo. Calling certain rules and regulations into question can be interpreted as an attack by people who feel they represent those rules and regulations. Often, they counterattack the challenger (Osborne et al., 1998). This is the aspect of advocacy that requires the courage mentioned earlier.

Advocating for Recognition of the Profession

We also need to address how you as a counselor can advocate for the profession. In chapter 1, we talked about membership in professional organizations. Membership in national and state counseling associations is one of the best ways to promote the recognition and acknowledgment of the profession. Membership dues go, in part, to employing lobbyists to speak to members of Congress. This is obviously a necessary part of making counselors' voices heard.

Before a state law is passed, there are usually several opportunities for public hearing, in which concerned individuals can appear and testify, supporting either passage or denial of the proposed law. A good state counseling association keeps its members apprised of relevant pending legislature, so that members can then do their part by writing or calling their senators and by testifying at the open hearings if it is feasible for them to do so. Later in this chapter, we will talk about counseling research and all the reasons it is such a critical component of the profession. One of those reasons is that empirical data lends credence to statements you make and positions you take with your local lawmakers.

It is also important to remember, as noted in chapter 1, that, throughout the history of counseling, professional advocacy was necessary to ensure that trained counseling professionals were not blocked by other therapeutic professionals from doing the work they were trained to do. There are several instances in which other therapeutic professionals attempted to block counselors from ethical and appropriate practice (for example, *Weldon vs. The Virginia State Board of Psychologist Examiners* and *City of Cleveland vs. Cook,* cited in Hosie, 1991).

In addition to being involved in state and federal law enactment, advocating for the profession means trying to maintain a visible profile in your local community. Possibilities include volunteering to speak at PTA meetings and other local interest groups. Try to find an area of specialty or expertise about which you can do some public speaking. By taking a visible role in your locale, you increase people's awareness of mental health issues. Another benefit of taking an active community role is that you then can attempt intervention at the primary level—the prevention of emotional problems.

It may seem that chapter 1 minimized the differences among therapeutic professionals and that, in this chapter, you are being asked to think more categorically (for instance, counselors in one category and psychologists in another). In a sense, you are. The artificial divisions of therapeutic professions are most evident in professional advocacy, and this is typically a polemic experience. You should entertain a Zen, or paradoxical, understanding of professional identity. In Zen, the process of enlightenment is approached with great faith and great doubt. The faith is that there is a way to experience reality, and the doubt is that you will never fully capture that experience. In professional identity, great faith should be placed in your commitment to the ethical practice of your profession, whereas great doubt should be exercised in accepting politically motivated definitions of your profession as mutually exclusive.

As we move to the topic of research in counseling, consider the relationship between advocacy and research. Although the two topics are not typically discussed in the context of one another, there is a mutual dependence that warrants a closer look. Research in counseling focuses on numerous aspects of counseling, which will be discussed further in the next section. For now, we can observe that, in general, the purpose of counseling research is to maximize the benefit and minimize the harm for clients and others who are receiving counseling services. To some extent, advocacy for clients has a parallel goal of maximizing benefit and removing barriers to that benefit. Research in counseling lends credence and a scientific platform from which practitioners can know that their efforts to help their clients will be both safe and effective. Research in counseling also lends credence to the aspect of advocating for the profession. This occurs because outcome research that demonstrates positive change in clients can become a justification for continued funding and support from tax monies, and it helps earn the respect and acknowledgement of other professional groups, such as physicians.

RESEARCH IN COUNSELING

One who deceives will always find those who allow themselves to be deceived.

Niccolo di Bernardo dei Machiavelli

If you think about the typical interest profile of a person entering the human service professions, you probably envision someone who enjoys human contact, feels comfortable interacting verbally, and likes to be helpful to others. Although the idea of scientific research does not necessarily fit neatly into this typical profile, reviewing and using research results is a vital part of being a good counselor. It is important to spend time perusing professional journals on a regular basis to keep abreast of new knowledge about areas that have a direct impact on client treatment. Examples include the development of new treatment procedures for a particular disorder, new information about a disorder, and emerging trends and developments in your specialty area.

Although your master's program will likely require a research course, this section offers a preview of the issues inherent in the topic of research in counseling. Regardless of whether or not you actually conduct research yourself, you have a responsibility to your clients to be aware of new knowledge about clients and treatments—knowledge that is emerging from contemporary research. Further, you need to know about research design to be able to evaluate whether a study is designed appropriately for the researchers to justify their conclusions.

Included in this discussion of research is a brief overview of the debated issues in the field, as well as a little bit of what is known about treatment based on the most up-to-date research evidence. Some of the topics we will touch on in this section include information about client and counselor variables related to counseling outcome and the ways in which research is used related to professional resources, such as the *DSM-IV.*

The Role of Research

McLeod (1994) observed that many practitioners of psychological therapies do not read research articles and do not consider research articles to be relevant to their work. This is a value judgment on the part of the practitioners—a manifestation of the belief that practice should inform research, rather than vice versa. It may be based on the idea that conditions and outcomes in controlled research studies do not readily generalize to conditions and outcomes in applied situations with "real" therapists and "real" clients. It is important to recognize that neither position—practice informing science or science informing practice—is inherently good or bad; both are merely values and beliefs from which a therapist operates.

Being a good consumer of research allows you to have an empirical basis for the treatment strategies you select to use in your work with certain clients. It also enables your personal and professional development. Growth as a professional does not end with a graduate degree. New knowledge and skill acquisition should continue throughout your career. The fact that licensure boards require people to earn continuing education credits to maintain their licenses is evidence that professional learning needs to be a lifelong process. Part of the reason for continuing education requirements is that new developments are always occurring in the field, some of which have great relevance to client treatment.

Bergin and Garfield (1994) noted that therapists are increasingly being asked to demonstrate that treatment results in positive outcome. As will be discussed in chapter 8, managed care has intensified this trend. Because of increased demands for accountability, much of the research in the counseling field over the past 40 years has focused on treatment outcome. Although the term *treatment outcome* seems straightforward, there is lack of agreement among researchers as to what constitutes "outcome," which in turn affects the utility of the results that are generated. In general, Kazdin (1994) identified the goals of psychotherapy research as being (1) understanding the alternative forms of treatment for a particular disorder, (2) understanding the mechanisms and processes through which treatment operates, and (3) understanding the impact of treatment and other moderating influences on adaptive and maladaptive behavior.

Kuhn (1962) and McLeod (1994) offered perspectives on the emergence and evolution of professional disciplines that lend themselves to our discussion. McLeod observed that, in other branches of science, the typical progression is that a theory emerges from research that adequately explains phenomena that are commonly observed. After most scientists can prove the theory, the researchers then form a "scientific community," which links them together through the shared paradigm (acceptance of the theory as probable fact). Kuhn defined *paradigm* as accepted scientific practices, including theories, laws, applications, and instrumentation. McLeod further defined *paradigm* as a web of knowledge used by the members of a scientific community. This knowledge is communicated to community members through accepted theories and concepts, educational experiences that are common to all community members, and the readership of key books and journals. A period of immersion in a particular paradigm is a period of "normal science." When more questions are raised than the paradigm can address, a new paradigm sprouts to fill the gap. This is a period of revolutionary science. In the therapeutic professions, the growth of cognitive therapy is an example of a paradigm shift. When psychodynamic and behavioral therapies failed to provide answers to certain problems, the cognitive therapies began formulating their own approach to answer some of those questions.

The problem in the fields of counseling and psychotherapy is that no theory of counseling has been rejected on the basis of research evidence, and there are *many* theories. Various authors have estimated that between 200 (Prochaska & Di Clemente, 1982) and 400 (Bergin & Garfield, 1994) theories of therapy currently exist. This high number suggests that the therapeutic professions are far away from arriving at a unifying paradigm of therapy.

Inherent Problems in Conducting Research

Research can be defined as a systematic process of critical inquiry that leads to valid propositions and conclusions, which are communicated to interested others (McLeod, 1994). The field of counseling research falls into the category of soft science as opposed to the hard sciences, such as biology and chemistry. One readily apparent difference is that, in a chemistry experiment, all possible variables can be controlled. This allows for the clear illustration of cause-and-effect relationships among variables. However, the types of variables associated with mental health are rarely concrete, observable, or measurable. It is one thing to note that a client expresses an appropriate range of positive emotions and reports emotional well-being. It is quite another thing to understand what that actually means to the client. The client in question may be mourning the death of a loved one and feel "blocked" from the experience of sadness and loss normal in such a situation. The point is that all of the constructs referred to as "emotionally healthy" require dialogue with the client and cannot be monologically observed and measured. When dealing with variables related to human behavior, it is not possible to control every variable. Serious ethical problems are created when controlling variables that might result in deprivation or other negative outcomes for the people participating in research. Because of the research limitations imposed by ethical concerns, social scientists are not always able to conclude, with the same scientific certainty as "hard" scientists, that given variables cause particular outcomes. In addition, some of the topics about which researchers are trying to get information are very sensitive topics.

Sieber and Stanley (1988) defined socially sensitive research as studies in which there are potentially negative consequences for the people who are participating in the research. The negative consequences might take the form of guilt, shame, embarrassment, or negative social outcomes, such as being harassed or socially ostracized. Further, a sensitive topic according to Renzetti and Lee (1993), is one that ". . . potentially poses for those involved a substantial threat, the emergence of which renders problematic for the researcher and/or the researched the collection, holding and/or dissemination of research data" (p. 5). Research that is possibly threatening to participants includes studies that intrude into a deeply personal experience, studies that focus on some aspect of deviance or control, studies that impinge on the vested interests of people in positions of power, and studies that deal with things sacred to the people who are being studied. Participants' disclosure of information, or even the fact that they are identified as participants in a particular study, could put them in a position of experiencing negative consequences. There is clearly latitude here for individual perceptions of "negative consequences" and "deeply personal." A topic that might be sensitive to one study participant might not be the least bit sensitive to another.

One researcher of a sensitive topic, Etherington (1996), shared some of the difficulties she encountered researching adult male survivors of childhood sexual abuse. One of the most uncomfortable difficulties for her was the duality of roles, in that she was the principal researcher but was a therapist by profession. As a researcher, she had to maintain objectivity in order to gather information that would be valid and replicable for other researchers. If Etherington had established a therapeutic relationship with her participants, it would have departed from research and become a treatment. This created great discomfort for her while she was interviewing participants. She also encountered information which created great conflict for her, in that she became aware of individuals in the community who had allegedly sexually abused children. She was torn between her commitment to honor the confidentiality of the participants who were cooperating with her interviews and her moral outrage at the fact that there were sexual predators who remained in the community, possibly continuing to abuse children.

The Etherington (1996) study was conducted in Britain. An additional difficulty could have been posed if she had done her research in the United States. In some states, receiving disclosure about sexual offenses from research participants may have made her a mandatory reporter, meaning that she would have been required by law to report the disclosure to the proper authorities. As in the case of Etherington (1996), there are many reasons people choose to keep secrets. When a person, either as a researcher or as a therapist, becomes privy to those secrets, it can be with a cost.

Good Consumers of Research Results

You may have heard a claim on a television advertisement that "four out of five dentists surveyed preferred Sparkle for their patients that use toothpaste," or a similar statement. The piece of information the advertisers neglect to mention is which dentists were surveyed. It may have been that the dentists surveyed were only those who had previously agreed to give all their patients free sample tubes of Sparkle toothpaste. Obviously, an extensive discussion of population sampling theory is beyond the scope of this text. Nevertheless, there are some basic principles of research consumerism, such as sampling technique, as illustrated in the Sparkle example, that are important to discuss.

McLeod (1994) identified some general criteria that can be applied in evaluating research results. Different criteria need to be applied to qualitative, as opposed to quantitative, studies. Qualitative research can be broadly defined as ". . . the studied use and collection of a variety of empirical materials—case study, personal experience, introspective, life story, interview, observational, historical, interactional, and visual texts—that describe routine and problematic moments and meanings in individuals' lives" (Denzin & Lincoln, 1994, p. 2). Qualitative research techniques typically include in-depth interviews or observations and then the analysis of prominent themes that emerge from the recorded information. Quantitative research, in contrast, is research methodology designed specifically to examine quantitative differences between individuals on some key variable(s) as the result of controlled experimental manipulation. It can generally be said that, although there is some excellent qualitative research, the quantitative approach is by far the dominant one, as far as studies that appear in the professional literature and studies that are awarded most research monies. In evaluating quantitative studies, you must consider

- How generalizable the results are
- Whether the results could be replicated by another, uninvolved researcher
- Whether the key variables have been clearly operationally defined
- Whether there are ways to explain the results
- How much the studies contribute to the body of knowledge about theory and practice

In the qualitative realm, a consumer of research needs to examine

- How clear the research procedures were
- Whether the study succeeds in generating knowledge that is specific to a particular time and place
- Whether the research helps develop theory and interpretive frameworks for organizing knowledge

Furthermore, a good qualitative study should systematically address competing interpretations of the data, the credibility of the primary researcher, and the replicability of the results.

The Diagnosis of Pathology

We would be remiss is discussing the relevance of research in general without talking about the *DSM-IV* and the integral role research has played in its development and ongoing revision. The *DSM-IV* may be the most commonly used reference book across all the disciplines in the therapeutic professions. It is a tool that enables clear communication among helping professionals because it offers clear parameters for defining many types of mental disorders. This structure thus allows for a common vocabulary in research, clinical, and educational settings. What is most relevant about the *DSM-IV* in this discussion of research is the way in which the *DSM-IV* was developed and how it has been updated over the years.

The initial impetus for developing a standard nomenclature was the need to collect statistical information. The first official attempt to get information about mental illness in the United States was made in 1840, by adding one item to the census, in which a person could check off "idiocy/insanity" on the census form (American Psychiatric Association, 1994). Research technology has progressed considerably since that time.

The most recent *DSM* was developed by creating task forces of researchers, clinicians, and academicians, each with its own categories of diagnoses and mental disorders. These task forces engaged in several activities to incorporate the most recent and sophisticated information available about the disorders they were studying. The activities included comprehensive and systematic reviews of the literature, using electronic databases; reanalyzing already existing data sets; and conducting extensive issue-focused field trials to determine the utility of the diagnostic criteria that were under consideration. The resultant diagnostic criteria that are used by so many mental health professionals are based on the most extensive, comprehensive review of the research data to date.

The diagnostic criteria identified for a given disorder begin with the most commonly endorsed symptoms of the disorder and descend through symptoms that are less common but still indicative of the disorder. The *DSM-IV* carries much controversy related to human rights issues, such as the inappropriateness of reducing people with emotional difficulties to diagnostic labels. One classic example of how politics are implicated in the use of the *DSM* is the progression of homosexuality from a diagnosable mental disorder in the second edition of the *DSM* (the *DSM-II*). Due to the diligent efforts of people who advocated for gays, lesbians, and bisexuals, the diagnosis of homosexuality was dropped from the *DSM* list of mental and emotional disorders (Bayer, 1981). Despite the admittedly controversial nature of the *DSM* and diagnosis, in the context of our discussion about the relevance of research to your ability to help people in need, the *DSM* has played an important role in providing operational criteria for certain groups of participants in research studies.

The Problem of Theoretical Relativity

Many counseling techniques are embedded in particular theoretical approaches. For example, the concept of unconditional positive regard, which today is such an integral part of a beginning counseling student's learning, originated in Carl Rogers' person-centered therapy. Because there are so many theories and approaches to therapy, some theorists (such as Prochaska and Orlinsky) have begun moving toward a generic model of therapy that is transtheoretical, i.e., a model that incorporates factors common across many counseling models. The idea is to identify treatment techniques and strategies that are effective in helping clients with symptom reduction, then to systematically dismantle the technique to isolate the specific aspects of the treatment that are most helpful.

Does counseling work? That is a million-dollar question, because it has been quite difficult to investigate. There are methodological problems with the outcome research, which has made it difficult to reach definitive conclusions about the meaning of the results.

The answer to the question "Does counseling work?" actually depends the definition of *work*. Herein lies the essence of the research problem in the therapeutic disciplines. The definition of *favorable outcome* is embedded in the theoretical orientation toward the helping process. A client-centered therapist states that therapy has worked if the client has experienced positive personal growth and movement toward increased genuineness and authenticity. A behavioral therapist states that therapy can be said to have worked only if the client has demonstrated a consistent increase in frequency or duration of desired positive behaviors or a decrease in undesirable behaviors. This discrepancy among definitions is called theoretical relativity.

With the understanding of theoretical relativity as a given, two basic terms we need to review are *validity* and *reliability*. Validity is the ability of the research design to enable the investigator to answer the questions the study was intended to answer; reliability is the likelihood that, if the study were repeated, the same results would be obtained. When a study has problems with validity or reliability, it is unlikely that the information it generated is accurate or of use to others.

McLeod identified a number of threats to internal and external validity that can render results questionable. One of the threats to internal validity is statistical regression, which is the tendency for extreme scores to move toward the mean on retesting. Another threat is selection bias, which has to do with the assignment of participants to control or treatment groups, which could introduce systematic bias to the study. There also can be differential attrition rates, meaning that participants drop out of either the treatment or the control group at different rates, making comparison difficult. There also could be external events in participants' lives that intervene and have direct effects on the outcome. For example, if, in the course of the treatment study, a participant experiences a highly upsetting event, such as death of a family member, it can confound the results. Conversely, if a participant experiences a significant positive event, such as winning a million dollars in the state lottery, that, too, can confound the results. In either case, such an event could invalidate any conclusion that the outcome was attributable to the treatment in question.

There are a number of external threats to validity as well, which could similarly compromise the accuracy of the results. One example is test reactivity, in which the very act of administering a test to a person at one time affects his or her performance on the same test at a later date. Another, related threat, is reactivity of experimental arrangements, in which the act of participating in the study influences the participant's behavior. Due to the parameters of a study, research findings might be limited to a particular setting. There might also be an interaction effect between history and treatment, which, if unaccounted for in the research design, could create a confounding variable.

Outcome Measures

A variety of outcome measures have been used in treatment research (McLeod, 1994). These include (1) self-report inventories; (2) client satisfaction questionnaires; (3) ratings of target symptoms, either by the client or by a clinician; (4) behavioral measures; (5) structured interviews by expert clinicians; (6) ratings by significant others; (7) ratings by therapists; and (8) cost-benefit analysis.

McLeod (1994) arrived at the conclusion that there are three recurring broad issues that are often debated and never resolved with regard to counseling research. First, what kind of knowledge is considered valid—data based on precise measurements or knowledge based on people's stories and experiences? If both, how can they be integrated? Second, what is the relationship of research to practice—what is the role of research in an applied discipline? Third, what is the place of theory in applied practice? To put it another way, is the purpose of research to inform practice, or is the purpose of practice to inform research? As we noted in chapter 1, the psychology profession has long used the Boulder model in training psychologists. Although the Boulder model advocates training scientist-practitioners, research indicates that most people are either scientists or practitioners. The scientists want research to inform practice, and the practitioners want practice to inform research.

There needs to be a healthy balance of both perspectives. As a practicing therapist, you might find particular techniques that seem to work especially well with a certain type of client. Based on that clinical experience, you might generate hypotheses that seem valid. However, you would not know for a fact that the hypothesis is accurate until you have investigated it in a systematic way, controlling for other variables that might be contributing to the outcome.

This issue will be clearer if we look at an applied example. You are a therapist working in a community mental health agency, and in your practice you see many women who report that they were sexually abused as children. You have noted that there seems to be a pattern in which the women enter therapy complaining of depression and relationship problems. Often, after several months of counseling, the clients come to realize that their current sexual problems in relationships are connected to their uncomfortable feelings about their abuse. You have found that, when this pattern becomes apparent, what helps the clients with their relationship problems is a combination of counseling sessions that include the relationship partner empty chair work with her abuser. (The empty chair technique is an experiential technique that arises from the Gestalt work of Fritz Perls. An empty chair is placed in front of the client, who then imagines that the key figure [in this case, the abuser] is sitting in that chair. This enables the client to express, in the present moment, thoughts and feelings about the perpetrator.) In your experience of using this combined couples and individual work, your clients seem to have a lessening of their depressive symptoms within a few months, in most cases. You have had an ongoing, friendly disagreement with one of the other therapists in the agency, who works with sexually abused clients by targeting their inappropriate and distorted self-talk about their abuse. The other therapist insists that his cognitive approach is more effective and produces longer-lasting results than your couples/experiential approach.

At this point, you have one of several options. The first thing you need to do, which you probably should have done in the first place, is consult the existing professional literature about what technique researchers have found works best with people who are victims of sexual abuse. You might look to see whether there have been any studies specifically comparing the effectiveness of cognitive therapy versus experiential therapy, especially for clients with a history of sexual abuse. If there are no such studies to be found, you might then consider either doing some research to further investigate those two approaches or contacting someone who has done other research about treatment for people who have been sexually abused, to see if that researcher is interested in collaborating on some research.

Let us continue with this hypothetical scenario. By using one of the electronic databases, such as PsychInfo, at your local library, you notice that one author has done a lot of writing and research about the types of relationship problems often experienced by people who have been sexually abused. You send an e-mail to her, asking if she is interested in looking at a comparison of treatment techniques for those clients. She e-mails back to you that she is, and a collaborative research relationship is thus established. You meet and discuss how you would like to design the study.

The study design includes decisions, such as how your client population will be identified, what its diagnosis will be, what types of clients will specifically be excluded from the research and why you need to exclude them, how many participant groups there will be, how the treatment groups will differ, who will actually do the treatment, who your comparison (control) group will be, what the outcome measure will be, and how the group differences will be analyzed. These are the questions that need to be addressed in designing and implementing a sound research project. You need to design your research in such a way that differences observed between groups at the conclusion of the research can definitely be attributed to the treatment you manipulated in the research project. Also, these are the types of questions you need to keep in mind when you are reviewing research someone else has done.

Since you are interested in comparing the effectiveness of cognitive versus experiential/relational therapy, you decide to have two groups of clients. The participants who will receive cognitive therapy will undergo treatment with your colleague, who did extensive postgraduate training in cognitive therapy. The participants who will receive experiential/relational therapy will undergo therapy with you. The pre- and posttreatment measures will be the client's self-report on a structured interview and the client's profile on the SCL-90-R, the Symptom CheckList-90-Revised (Derogatis, Rickels, & Rock, 1976). You will be interested in comparing the two groups before treatment, when there should be no difference between the groups, and after treatment, when there should be group differences if one treatment approach is more effective than the other. After obtaining approval from your board of directors to conduct this research, you implement the study until both you and your colleague have treated a predetermined number of clients, who continue their therapy until each respective researcher and client determine that maximum benefit has been reached. After comparing the outcome data from both groups, it appears that the clients in the experiential/relational group are reporting slightly more reduction of disturbing symptoms than the clients in the cognitive group.

Despite what appears to be an adequate research design, it has multiple problems in terms of variables that were not specifically identified and controlled, which may have confounded the research results. One obvious variable is the therapist administering the treatment. Perhaps you are a more highly skilled therapist than your colleague, despite his advanced clinical training in cognitive therapy. It is possible that your clients would respond more favorably to treatment, regardless of your treatment technique. Another potential confounding variable is the cultural backgrounds of the therapists administering the treatment and of the clients receiving the treatment—that is, there may be differential effects of the treatment approach, depending on the gender of the client and the therapist, the sexual orientation of the client and the therapist, and so on. Another problem is, that in your group, you actually were using two techniques—the empty chair technique and the therapy sessions including the client's relationship partner. Without controlling each of those, it is not possible to determine which is causing the treatment effect—the interaction of the two might be the curative mechanism. Also, despite the fact that the clients were randomly assigned to the two treatment groups, it is necessary to analyze the data on a number of participant variables, such as level of education, ethnicity, and age. There are additional client variables that could have strong implications for treatment, such as age at the time of the abuse, number of abusive incidents, and number of perpetrators of abuse. It is possible that, just by random chance, the two treatment groups were really not comparable on these variables and that such variables have a significant effect on how a client responds to treatment. For example, perhaps with fewer abusive incidents, cognitive therapy is more effective, whereas, with more extensive or severe abuse, experiential therapy has better treatment effects.

Even in a relatively simple and straightforward example like this one, you can see that proving definitive treatment results can be a complex and overwhelming task. When you try to do research that involves human beings, you are trying to control a virtually infinite number of combinations of personality and situational variables. It quickly becomes apparent why counseling and psychology are referred to as soft sciences. To conduct research, strictly, controlling all relevant variables to demonstrate a clear 1:1 causal relationship between life events and subsequent emotional or psychological symptoms, you would probably need to create conditions that could be damaging to the participants or that were otherwise unethical.

One way that researchers and consumers of research navigate around this problem is to do meta-analysis, which looks not just at one study but, instead, at large groups of studies, to illuminate general trends in the data. Meta-analysis is a technique that has emerged in the past 15 years (Kazdin, 1994). The technique involves summarizing a large number of studies, determining the effect size demonstrated in individual studies. There is a fairly simple equation for calculating effect size, which enables researchers doing meta-analysis to have a common unit of measurement to quantify treatment effects across many studies that used many different units of measurement as dependent variables.

Meta-analysis is very helpful for several reasons. First, there may be many studies that support a hypothesis about treatment, but, because the sample sizes of the studies are small, the actual effect size of the treatment is also smaller. Usually the smaller the sample size (number of participants in the study), the less powerful are the results of a finding of significant effect. In other words, if a study uses a large number of participants, it is more likely that the results will be generalizable to other people and situations. If the sample size is small, it cannot be said with certainty that the observed treatment effects due to the treatment, not to chance. Therefore, trends that are found in the process of meta-analysis are even more compelling than the results of individual studies because meta-analysis trends indicate that many studies have replicated and found similar results when investigating similar variables. Meta-analysis represents what probably is a closer approximation of truth, or accurate observation of cause-and-effect.

To go back to our original applied example, imagine that you were able to locate 75 studies published in professional journals that compared the effectiveness of therapy techniques for clients who have a history of sexual abuse. When you look at all of those studies, you notice that most of those studies compared directive, behavioral techniques with nondirective, client-centered techniques. You notice further that the studies used mostly client self-reported behavioral changes as the main outcome measure. Some knowledge is yielded by the meta-analysis, but there also are more questions. You can analyze average treatment effect, comparing behavioral with client-centered techniques. You need to investigate further whether there are other changes observed in clients' lives that occur concomitantly with the clients' self-reports of feeling better as a result of the treatment.

One recent example of a discrepancy between practice and controlled settings is the emergence in the behavioral literature of a treatment technique for post-traumatic stress disorder (PTSD). The technique is called eye movement desensitization reprocessing (EMDR), developed by Francine Shapiro (1989). When Shapiro initially published the results of her pilot study on EMDR, she reported virtually miraculous outcomes, with Vietnam veterans who had suffered from PTSD symptoms for many years having a total remission of symptoms after a few treatment sessions using EMDR. Such an efficacious treatment for PTSD, up until that point, was unheard of. Shapiro did another study, got similarly positive results, and began offering training sessions for mental health practitioners (psychologists, counselors, social workers), so they could learn to use EMDR with their clients. Shapiro was strongly criticized for offering training before her treatment approach had become better established through research by other investigators who were not affiliated with her.

Many case study articles began to appear in the professional journals, written by clinicians who had undergone the EMDR training and then used EMDR on a client with great results. Gradually, more studies began to be published, that compared EMDR with other treatment techniques that had been recognized as efficacious for PTSD. What emerged was a consensus that EMDR is, in fact, an effective treatment technique for PTSD. However, it does not necessarily exceed other treatment approaches, such as exposure, in magnitude of treatment effect.

During the time of the debate, a series of correspondence between Shapiro and some critics of her work appeared in some of the professional literature. The gist of the controversy was that Shapiro's critics stated it was unethical of her to be conducting training sessions, for which she was charging large fees, to train clinicians in a technique not yet established as safe and effective. What she was especially criticized for was that she had not published the specific treatment protocol to conduct an EMDR session, so no other researchers could attempt to replicate her results, unless they attended her training seminar. Shapiro retorted that she had not published the treatment protocol because she wanted to be able to control access to the protocol because the treatment was so powerful. If an untrained person learned to administer the technique, it would be akin to a child playing with matches. She was reportedly screening applicants to her workshops very carefully and granting admittance only to licensed or certified mental health professionals. Furthermore, Shapiro made the point that, although EMDR was still in experimental stages, if clients had failed to respond to more established techniques for treatment of PTSD, why not use another approach if there was a chance it could help? This is the same argument that often occurs between the Food and Drug Administration and victims of a particular medical condition who wish to try experimental drugs. The parameters are also the same—a practitioner needs to balance the potential benefits of an unresearched treatment with the potential risks. Ultimately, the decision should rest with the patient or client.

The EMDR controversy has since resolved somewhat, in that Shapiro published a book with the treatment protocol clearly spelled out (Shapiro, 1995). Quite a number of controlled studies have now been published, and EMDR has been formally recognized by the American Psychological Association Division 12 (Division 12 is the Society of Clinical Psychology) Task Force as "probably efficacious."

Ways in Which Research Enables Science to Inform Practice

If we look at science informing practice as one of the main functions of research, we see a good reason to use some of the documents that exist for treatment selection. This issue is of sufficient importance that the American Psychological Association Division 12, the Society of Clinical Psychology, developed a task force specifically to identify empirically validated therapies. The task force then published a report of its findings (Chambless et al., 1998). The authors differentiate between effectiveness and efficacy. *Efficacy* means demonstrating that a particular treatment approach is helpful to clients in a tightly controlled treatment study. Effectiveness, on the other hand, refers to how an efficacious treatment can be transferred from the laboratory to applied clinical settings. The results of the meta-analyses done by the task force, although appearing in clinical psychology literature, also have implications for other therapeutic professionals, such as counselors, who may be seeing clients with anxiety disorders, mood disorders, eating disorders, and the other disorders that were researched.

The task force has established stringent criteria for defining techniques that are "well established" and "probably efficacious." To move from the probably efficacious category to well established, there must be at least two group studies in which the treatment approach in question is significantly superior to a placebo or another treatment, or the treatment must have been found to be equivalent in effectiveness to another treatment that has already been established as effective.

When a client comes to see you about a particular problem, and you determine the diagnosis, you then need to make a decision about how to best treat the client. One way to go about making that decision is to do so based on your theoretical orientation. Although a complete discussion of counseling theory is beyond the scope of this book, suffice it to say that, if you are client-centered, your counseling sessions will unfold somewhat differently than if you are cognitive-behavioral. In fact, your sessions from the very first contact will be different. In past years, a therapist's choice of how to proceed with a client might have been mainly on the basis of theoretical orientation. However, with the advent of managed care, there is increasing emphasis on making every session count—that is, on achieving the maximum therapeutic gain in the least possible amount of time, despite the fact that therapeutic gain is almost impossible to operationalize. Although that does not necessarily translate into brief, solution-focused treatment every time, it does mean that the selection of a treatment strategy may need to be based more on what has been proven in the research than on a particular theoretical orientation.

The controlled research on treatment outcome is almost always behavioral or cognitive-behavioral. The reason is partially because other theoretical approaches do not as readily lend themselves to the operational definition of disturbance or symptom improvement. The other "reason," which is controversial in and of itself, is that behavioral and cognitive-behavioral approaches have been demonstrated to be more helpful than other approaches for some disorders. However, if you were to ask therapists in the field the question about whether behavioral approaches are the most effective, you would get a wide range of responses, largely dependent on each practitioner's training and value system. Behaviorists believe that the only true measure of change is that which can be readily observed objectively. A client-centered or humanistic therapist believes that the main measure of change is what the client experiences subjectively: congruence and genuineness, with an ability to be fully in the moment. This is not a concept that readily translates into observable behavior—moreover, a client-centered therapist does not believe translating into observable behavior is necessarily important.

Carl Rogers, the founder of client-centered therapy, looked at the *process* of therapy rather than the outcome (Rogers, 1958). Process is how change takes place in the course of therapy. Although nondirective, client-centered treatment approaches have great value and appeal, the harsh reality is that political and economic factors contribute to the type and nature of treatment clients can get. For clients who have insurance coverage to see a therapeutic professional, the insurance company will have some control over the services for which the professional will be reimbursed. Insurance companies allow the fewest number of sessions possible to treat a client with a given disorder. If it has been demonstrated in the professional literature that a client with a simple phobia can be treated in six sessions using systematic desensitization, then insurance providers may authorize six sessions for you to treat such a client. If you do not treat the phobia in six sessions, and cannot provide a good reason for needing more sessions, the insurance company will deny authorization. The client may still have the phobia but will have used up some of her or his benefits, not a good situation. This brings us to an alternative model for treatment-selection strategy.

Your other alternative, which will better arm you to interact effectively with insurance companies, is to be well versed in the treatment strategies that are indicated for particular disorders. Being able to cite references that justify your treatment approach places you in a position of power with the insurance companies. Furthermore, it increases the likelihood that you will be providing the best treatment you possibly can. There are a number of publications you can consult to obtain such information. One is the previously mentioned articles on empirically validate therapies published periodically by the American Psychological Association Division 12 Task Force. They are published every few years in the professional psychology journals. These articles differentiate diagnostic categories based roughly on *DSM-IV* groupings. Another option is the treatment guidelines published by the American Psychiatric Association.

Some books offer counselors a synopsis of outcome research. Examples of these include *Challenges in Clinical Practice* (Pollack, Otto, & Rosenbaum, 1996), *What Works for Whom?* (Roth & Fonagy, 1996), and *Integrating Outcome Research into Counseling Practice and Training* (Sexton, Whiston, Bleuer, & Walz, 1997).

Another source is a book by Linda Seligman (1990) called *Selecting Effective Treatments.* One helpful component of Seligman's book is that she talks not only about what is known about a particular disorder but also what the research says about the personality style and approach of the practitioner most likely to be effective in working with a client who has that disorder. An effective personality style and approach for dealing with clients who are abusing alcohol and street drugs is very different from the style for dealing with clients who have social phobia or avoidant personality disorder. For example, according to Seligman, a client who presents with an anxiety disorder will tend to be worried, apprehensive, and tentative about situations or events related to the focus of the anxiety. Seligman suggests that, to be most helpful, the therapist develop a positive working relationship that includes encouragement, instruction, and suggestion. In contrast, a client who presents with substance abuse issues might present with depression, low self-esteem, poor coping mechanisms, and interpersonal difficulties. A therapist working with a substance abusing client also needs to be optimistic and encouraging but additionally must be prepared to confront the client and set firm limits. An example of limit setting is to conduct a breathalyzer test at the beginning of each counseling session and rescheduling the meeting if the test indicates alcohol consumption.

Standards of Care   A recurrent theme in the research section of this chapter was the relative value of empirical evidence versus clinical or intuitive knowledge about what works with clients. However, there is an artistic, creative component to counseling that often is not captured in the quantitative research. Sometimes, counselors are faced with a client in a particular situation, and based on their gut level reaction, use a particular technique that is quite effective in helping the client. The difficulty with allowing counselors to follow their intuition about what works rather than perusing the professional journals for empirical studies is that doing so makes the critical assumption that the counselor has a good, accurate sense of clinical intuition. An apt analogy is to pull into a gas station to ask the attendant for directions to a good restaurant. You are making the critical assumption that the attendant has taste in food that is similar to yours knows how to get there, and will give you accurate, followable directions. It is a hit-or-miss proposition. In the case of client care, however, the stakes are quite a bit higher than in getting directions to a restaurant. Clients' lives are at stake, and, they go to a counselor in good faith, assuming that the counselor will given them help that meets a minimum level of competence.

An article by Granello and Witmer (1998) in the *Journal of Counseling and Development* spoke to the issue of clients' receiving the best possible treatment. The concern raised in the article was that the field of counseling has been slow to act on developing clear standards of care. The concept of standard of care has legal and ethical implications and is directly related to the topics we have been discussing in the context of research and the application of new information generated by research. A straightforward definition of *standard of care* is professional conduct practiced by reasonable and prudent professionals. Standard of care is the measuring stick against which a therapist's treatment is measured when others are trying to determine whether a client was treated in a manner that other reasonable, prudent therapists would have treated the client. When a counselor is being sued for malpractice, the most likely basis for malpractice is negligence, meaning that the therapist failed to meet the standards of care.

There are clear standards of care spelled out in the medical profession. In counseling, however, there are not, so, when a client goes to court, claiming that a counselor was negligent in treating the client, the court must rely on expert testimony to try to figure out what the most prudent course of action *should have been* for that therapist, client, and situation. This puts counselors at a huge disadvantage for two reasons. First, if a client and her or his attorney have enough money, they can find a credentialed professional willing to testify about reasonable prudent action (Hagan, 1997). Second, even if under ideal circumstances the plaintiff obtains expert testimony that is honest and ethical, the expert testifying has the benefit of hindsight that the acting counselor did not have at the time the alleged negligence occurred. The bottom line, according to Granello and Witmer, is that it would benefit the profession of counseling to determine its own standards of care proactively rather than reactively and that it would further benefit counselors and clients for counselors to adhere to standards of care in their practice. When standards of care are developed for the counseling profession, they will very likely be based on knowledge that has been acquired through standard, controlled means, either qualitatively or more probably quantitatively.

The decision about whether to consider meta-analysis as the most definitive source of information, compared with other forms of information, is a value judgment made by the counselor. Some academicians and clinicians would argue that decisions based on empirical data are the most sound. But laws of probability say that, although unusual, there are always "out-liers" and exceptions to the rule. Thus, despite your best-informed guess about what approach will work best with a given client, previous studies do not provide a guarantee that your treatment approach will be the most effective for that particular person.

We will not go into the detail needed to address fully all the types of disorders, treatment approaches, and therapist attributes for dealing with every type of disorder. One of the things that makes this such a difficult topic to address adequately is the sheer complexity of human beings. However, it might be interesting to discuss a little about what research has taught about client and counselor variables in general. We also will explore what is now known about the process of therapy in general and the movement toward a generic model of therapy process that transcends theory. As a final caveat, although certain therapeutic strategies such as counterconditioning, stimulus control, and reinforcement management are intrinsically embedded in behavior theory, they have been empirically demonstrated to be real phenomena, which have a place in a more generic, transcendent therapy approach.

Client and Counselor Variables   There are some discrepancies in the professional literature with regard to the variables that have an impact on treatment outcome. Some variables that are demographic have been found, in some instances, to be related to treatment outcome. For example, Mogul (1982) found that the gender of the therapist is the most critical when the treatment is brief. Berman and Norton (1985) further found that matching a therapist and client in age can contribute to effectiveness. Therapists with Ph.D.s, as well as therapists who themselves had participated in treatment, tend to have fewer clients who terminate therapy prematurely (Greenspan & Kulish, 1985).

Some individual studies, most conducted in the 1980s, support what would seem to be commonsense assumptions about the therapist attributes and behaviors that correlate with effectiveness in counseling. Examples of the therapist behaviors that correlate with positive outcome include acceptance of the client's values and beliefs and interventions that communicate that acceptance (Beutler, Crago, & Arizmendi, 1986); the communication of accurate empathy (Lambert, 1982; Shapiro & Shapiro, 1982); and the communication of the expectation that the client will assume responsibility and take steps to make positive change (Shapiro & Shapiro, 1982).

In an investigation about therapist and client variables, Beutler, Machado, and Neufeldt (1994) conducted a meta-analysis of more recent research. Similarity in age, gender, and ethnicity facilitates retention in therapy, but there is no definitive evidence that it affects treatment outcome. However, there is evidence that justifies transtheoretical approaches to treatment, integrating techniques and treatment models based on critical aspects of the client's presentation. Much more knowledge is needed about how to enhance the development of a therapeutic relationship among groups of clients that generally do not respond to treatment. Interestingly, despite the citations in the preceding paragraph about individual studies on therapist attributes that contribute to effective therapy, the meta-analysis indicated that there are no apparent global personality dimensions of counselors that correlate with effective treatment. There are so many variables at so many levels of the counseling process, beginning with the circumstances that led the client to counseling initially, that a variable that, is influential in determining therapy effectiveness with one client may be immaterial with a different client.

THE PROCESS AND OUTCOME OF THERAPY

The process and outcome of therapy are being incorporated in this chapter because much of what is now known about process and outcome is the direct result of empirical work that cuts across many forms of therapy. The information you will gain in this section is the direct result of an accumulation of a huge amount of data amassed by the concerted efforts of many researchers.

The term *process* as used in this context refers to the mechanisms and conditions under which clients make emotional, behavioral, and cognitive changes through the course of therapy. *Outcome* refers to what happens at the conclusion of treatment and includes not only clients who successfully address the concerns with which they initially presented but also clients who drop out of counseling prematurely or decide, with their counselors, that counseling is not appropriately meeting their needs.

Seligman (1990) noted many methodological problems that present themselves when one is trying to study the process of therapy:

1. A large number of client variables that can potentially influence outcome
2. Variability in level of therapist expertise
3. Variability in severity of the disorders being treated

4. Participant and observer bias
5. Questionable ethics of establishing true treatment and placebo groups
6. Difficulty in assessing how much progress has been made

In the past two decades, some authors have turned their attention to differential treatment selection based on clients' key characteristics. This movement is probably one outcome of the proliferation of therapy approaches that have evolved, as noted earlier in this chapter. Perry, Frances, and Clarkin (1985) noted that frequently a client presenting for therapy receives the therapy best known or practiced by the first person the client consults, rather than the therapy best indicated for the client's particular disorder. This is in stark contrast to medical treatment, in which the symptoms and diagnosis usually illuminate the best course of treatment for a practitioner to follow. We would be in big trouble if the physician we went to treated patients only in the one method in which she or he had been trained, such as antibiotic treatments or surgery!

The works of Seligman (1990), Perry et al. (1985), Prochaska and Di Clemente (1982), Prochaska, Di Clemente, and Norcross (1992), and Orlinsky, Grawe, and Parks (1994) support a generic model of assessment and treatment that cuts across the vast number of specific theoretical approaches to treatment and identifies the key elements of the therapy process common to all approaches. Earlier we noted, in the context of therapeutic professionals' developing a unifying body of empirically based knowledge, that a profession or discipline truly evolves when all members of the discipline accept certain observations and conclusions as universal truths. Some authors see this evolution as critical for the continued growth of the collective therapeutic professions.

It is exciting that, in recent years, researchers have begun to look toward the common denominators across the multitude of theories. Perry, Francis, and Clarkin (1985) reviewed and analyzed the literature and generated the following synopsis of therapeutic elements common to all therapeutic approaches.

1. Establishing and maintaining a therapeutic relationship; unconditional positive regard in which the individuals have the best interest of the client as their primary goal
2. Providing support by reality testing, suggestions, confirmation, and acceptance
3. Providing education and information
4. Decreasing or eliminating painful feelings, especially anxiety and depression
5. Decreasing or eliminating maladaptive behaviors
6. Modifying specific misperceptions of stimuli
7. Helping clients put concerns in meaningful context to make sense of them
8. Expanding emotional awareness
9. Enhancing interpersonal effectiveness

Orlinsky, Grawe, and Parks (1994) approach this unifying model somewhat differently, identifying aspects of the system of psychotherapy that are found in all forms of therapy. These aspects of the therapy process are therapeutic contract, therapeutic operations, therapeutic bond, self-relatedness, in-session impact, and sequential flow. Following are brief descriptions of these aspects and the information the researchers' meta-analysis yielded about the six aspects.

The *therapeutic contract* is the understanding, either implicit or explicit, about the client and couselor's goals and the conditions under which the two people are working together as a client and counselor. The ACA Code of Ethics stipulates developing and communicating a clear contract with all clients. The counselor's level of skill and the client's suitability for the treatment conditions are important factors in the therapy outcome. Determining patient suitability and educating the client about the client role helps the client form accurate expectations about treatment. Another notable aspect of the contract that has implications for treatment is the stability of the treatment arrangements. Having an established meeting place, keeping prompt appointments and clear time parameters in session, and not rescheduling all contribute to a sense of stability.

Therapeutic operations are the specific, technical, clinical procedures that counselors and clients perform within the parameters of the therapeutic contract. This includes what clients are discussing as their presenting problems (that is, problems in living, here-and-now in session behaviors, and relationship problems), the therapist's expert understanding, therapist interventions, patient cooperation, the therapeutic bond, personal role investment (patient motivation and therapist engagement versus detachment), interactive coordination, communicative contact, and mutual affect. It involves the interpersonal relationship that transpires between counselor and client; the therapeutic bond can be either positive or negative. This is one of the most studied aspects of the therapeutic process. Therapist affirmation of the client is an important factor in treatment outcome. One aspect of the bond that has not been investigated systematically is the client's affirmation of the therapist. Although it would seem that reciprocal affirmation is a circular process, it has not been specifically studied.

Self-relatedness is the manner in which counselor and client respond to internal experiencing. This includes, among other things, experiencing emotional arousal, perceiving and interpreting their own wishes and intentions, self-monitoring and controlling their own verbalizations, and experiencing feelings such as guilt, shame, and incompetence. It seems that self-relatedness is like self-awareness, and higher levels of it suggest greater emotional health if one can maintain the self-awareness without moving too far into narcissism. Clients' self-relatedness is associated with counseling outcome. It appears that this occurs because the characteristics of self-relatedness are conducive to benefiting from treatment.

In-session impact is the client's experience during the session, as a result of the interaction of the therapeutic bond, operations, and self-relatedness. In-session impact can also be positive or negative. Examples of positive in-session impact include moments of insight, emotional catharsis, the resolution of negative feelings, and the development of alternative perceptions; examples of negative in-session impact include anxiety and anger. Therapeutic realization is positively correlated with treatment outcome. In-session impact, however, does not correlate perfectly with treatment outcome.

Sequential flow is the temporal sequence of counseling, both within sessions and across the whole process. More research attention is beginning to be paid to the sequence of counseling and how it develops in predictable stages. In general, clients who stay in treatment longer tend to get better than clients who do not. Of course, there are exceptions to this, such as clients with chronic mental illness who will continue in therapy indefinitely for symptom management.

The Client Readiness Model   A totally different perspective is the model of Client Readiness, originated by Prochaska and Di Clemente (1982). The authors noted the need for a counseling approach that integrates directive and nondirective techniques. In their view, exclusive focus on either the internal (insight-oriented therapies) or the external (behavioral therapies) is unbalanced, omitting half of the essential equation. They advocated a combination of the two approaches, yielding "a more balanced view that moves along the continuous dimensions of inner to outer control, subjective to objective functioning and self to environmentally induced changes" (p. 281). Prochaska and Di Clemente conducted a meta-analysis of the treatment and outcome literature and identified stages in the process of change. A further feature of this model is the premise that the selection of a treatment strategy should be based on the stage of readiness for change that the client is in. This is a provocative approach because it stands in contrast to other approaches previously discussed—for example, selecting a strategy based on the client's primary diagnosis or selecting a strategy based on a number of empirical or qualitative studies.

In his later work, Prochaska, Di Clemente, and Norcross (1992) focused on people with addictive disorders to generate a model of how change occurs. His work focused on the cycle of change that occurs in people with addictive disorders. This population was of interest because many people make multiple attempts to quit before they can abstain successfully from the addictive behavior. Some people, however, are able to quit the first time they try, either with or without seeing a counselor or getting other outside help. Although Prochaska's seminal work focused on clients making therapeutic changes of behaviors that had implications for their physical health, at least some of these stages of change are probably applicable to the process of change for other types of concerns as well, such as depression and anxiety. This model of change takes into account not only people who feel better as the result of being in therapy but also people who are able to address their problems independently, without the intervention of a therapeutic professional.

The concept of readiness for change appears to transcend addictive disorders to encompass an array of emotional disorders. If you have had experience with clients, you may be familiar with the frustrating experience of having a client who says she or he wants to work on an issue, only to find after several sessions that the problem has magically resolved itself. What may be happening in some of those instances is that, when the client begins to examine the issues, she or he decides that making the changes necessary to alleviate the problem will be more trouble than it's worth and prematurely terminates counseling.

> I can clearly remember three clients with whom I worked, all of whom dropped out of counseling after a few sessions. I felt frustrated with all three cases because the clients came to the agency complaining of specific concerns, yet, when I gave them behavioral assignments to gather baseline information, they did not follow through. In retrospect, their premature termination was probably due to my own lack of experience and inability to recognize that they were feeling ambivalent about the extent of their problems and even more ambivalent about committing the time and effort to make real behavioral, cognitive, and emotional changes.

In *precontemplation,* the individual is generally unaware or is underaware that a problem exists, or perhaps the individual knows that people around her or him have a problem with the individual's behavior. Despite this knowledge, the individual does not personally perceive the problem or symptoms as generating enough discomfort to warrant focusing on it. There is no intention to change the behavior at any point in the foreseeable future. As an example, consider the individual who is actively consuming alcohol during the workday and perceives herself to be fully capable of meeting her job responsibilities while inebriated. In contrast, her supervisor and co-workers perceive her to be more labile, less efficient, and disorganized in the afternoon, after she has had several drinks on her lunch hour. Her co-workers perceive her to have a problem, and her supervisor informs her that she must attend counseling to keep her job. She goes to counseling to meet the expectations of others in her social environment but does not personally believe her drinking to be a problem. As a result of this perception, she is "humoring" her supervisor but, deep down inside, has no intention of changing her behavior. At this point, the payoff she gets for drinking far exceeds the cost of drinking.

The next stage of treatment readiness after precontemplation is *contemplation*. In the contemplation stage, the person is beginning to be aware that there is a problem, but there is minimal commitment to take action to change it. If you were to have the client honestly list the pros and cons that occur as a result of the behavior, the pros would still outweigh the cons. The woman in the previous example would believe that the relaxation and socialization op-

portunities that come from her going to a bar on her lunch hour are more important than the cost of the drinking behavior—in this case, the disapproval of
her co-workers and the supervisor. Characteristic statements a client might
make in this stage are "Yeah, I really need to cut down. I'll start tomorrow, so,
for today, I'll take another margarita. In fact, since I'm quitting tomorrow,
make it a double!" Although the idea of change is getting lip service, there is
not yet any notable degree of commitment to do the behaviors that need to
accompany the change.

The stage that follows contemplation is *preparation*. At this point, the
person has come to the decision that the cons of maintaining the behavior
outweigh the pros. She or he is intending to make the behavior changes within
the next month and has unsuccessfully taken action in the past year. The intention that developed in the contemplation stage is now being paired with
thoughts about the behavioral criteria the person will use to monitor change.
Now, the client in the example is thinking seriously about how her behavior
will be different if she does not go to the bar during her lunch hour. She is
making clear plans about how she will spend her time, and what she might
plan for afternoons and evenings to reinforce herself for not drinking. She is
also investigating Alcoholics Anonymous meetings that meet during the lunch
hour as an alternative to her previous activities.

Following preparation is the *action* stage, in which the individual modi-
fies her or his behavior, experiences, or environment for the purpose of overcoming her or his problems. This is the stage that most people probably think
of when envisioning "quitting drinking"—there are behavioral changes that
signify both to the person and to others in the environment the changes in
thought process and values that have occurred. The woman in the example is
now completely abstaining from alcohol, has joined a health club, and attends
an AA meeting three days a week. Her supervisor and co-workers are noticing
more emotional stability and punctuality for afternoon meetings. Her productivity seems to be improving.

In the final stage, *maintenance,* the person works to maintain the behavioral changes achieved in the action stage. This involves identifying the stimulus situations in which a relapse would be most likely, developing an awareness
of the warning signs that might emerge before a full relapse. Most important,
the person develops a relapse plan, which consists of actions she or he will
take if events occur that put the person at high risk for relapse.

In the context of addictions work, Prochaska observed that many professionals may design excellent action-oriented treatment plans, but, if the client
is not in the action stage, the treatment plan is likely to fail because the client
has not yet developed the motivation to engage in the behavioral steps necessary to initiate the change. You may already be well aware that particular theoretical models of counseling have treatment techniques and strategies that
are embedded in the theoretical approach. In their research on readiness,

Prochaska and Di Clemente (1982) identified helping strategies that were common across numerous models of counseling. By examining the frequency with which clinicians implement various strategies, they were able to conclude that there are particular techniques that are used more often than other techniques for certain presenting problems. Following is a summary of the helping strategies that transcend theory:

1. Consciousness raising—developing an awareness of the problem and how it affects oneself; observations, interpretations, bibliotherapy
2. Self-reevaluation—assessing one's feelings and thoughts about oneself in the context of the problem; value clarification, imagery, corrective emotional experience
3. Self-liberation—accepting responsibility for making changes; decision-making therapy, New Year's resolutions, logotherapy techniques, commitment enhancing techniques
4. Counterconditioning—replacing maladaptive behaviors with adaptive ones; relaxation, desensitization, assertiveness training
5. Stimulus control—removing or avoiding stimuli that stimulate maladaptive behaviors; removing alcohol or fattening foods, avoiding high-risk cues, fading techniques
6. Reinforcement management—rewarding oneself or having others administer a reward for making and sustaining changes; contingency contracts, overt and covert reinforcement
7. Helping relationships—developing a warm, supportive interpersonal relationship; therapeutic alliance, social support, self-help groups
8. Dramatic relief—experiencing and expressing feelings about one's problems and solutions; psychodrama, grieving losses, role-playing
9. Environmental reevaluation—evaluating how one's problem has an impact on the physical environment; empathy training, documentaries
10. Social liberation—developing alternatives for the exhibition of socially acceptable, healthy behaviors; advocacy for the rights of the oppressed, empowerment, policy intervention

Within the model of readiness for change, the selection of a treatment strategy is based not on theoretical orientation but, instead, on the client's stage of readiness. See table 6.2 for a representation of the model. In the precontemplation to contemplation stages, the work needs to be more insight-oriented, exploring issues such as positive and negative short- and long-term consequences of the behavior, the motivations for engaging in the behavior, and the impact of the behavior on others in the client's environment.

As the client moves from contemplation to action and maintenance, the treatment strategies become more structured and directive, focusing on behavioral and cognitive strategies for the identification of stimuli that will enable the sustenance of the new, more adaptive behaviors. As stated previously,

Source: "In search of how people change" by J.D. Prochaska, C.C. DiClemente, and J. C. Norcross in *American Psychologist* 47, pp. 1102–1114. © 1992. Used with permission.

TABLE 6.2	THE STAGES OF CHANGE MODEL FOR TREATMENT STRATEGY SELECTION			
Precontemplation	**Contemplation**	**Preparation**	**Action**	**Maintenance**
Consciousness raising				
Dramatic relief				
Environmental reevaluation				
	Self-reevaluation			
		Self-liberation		
			Reinforcement management	
			Helping relationships	
			Counterconditioning	
			Stimulus control	

although this model has been demonstrated empirically primarily in the context of addictions work, it also seems to apply to clients with other types of problems. This is an area in which more research is needed to ascertain the degree to which the readiness model can be generalized to disorders besides addictions.

SUMMARY

We covered much ground in this chapter—ground that often lies unturned in an introductory agency counseling course. Nonetheless, the issues of advocacy and the use of research are central to the delivery of competent services to the individuals being served. We discussed the importance of teaching clients to advocate for themselves and looked at the potential benefits of advocating for yourself as a mental health professional.

Knowing how to identify efficacious and effective treatment techniques will be a desirable skill for new counselors entering the job market. In order for a counselor to survive in the world of third-party reimbursement, she or he will need to be aware of treatments of choice for given disorders and be able to justify the selection of alternative treatment approaches if not using the treatment of choice. Regardless of treatment strategies selected by a counselor, she or he will also need to be able to cite relevant data that support the course of action chosen. The information in this chapter should provide a starting point from which you can further hone your skills and knowledge in this realm.

DISCUSSION ITEMS

1. In your opinion, to what extent should a counselor base treatment decisions on the knowledge acquired by sound empirical research?
2. Identify a problem you would like to address in your work as a therapeutic professional. How would you go about investigating the extent of the problem? How would you investigate a treatment for the problem? How would you know if you were successful?
3. What populations do you have a difficult time imagining yourself advocating for? Discuss the situation in small groups, sharing as much related material as feels safe.
4. In your opinion, to what extent are people are responsible for their own problems? How does this belief relate to your role as an advocate for your clients?

REFERENCES

Alper, S., Schloss, P. J., & Schloss, C. A. (1995). Families of children with disabilities in elementary and middle school: Advocacy models and strategies. *Exceptional Children, 62,* 261–270.

American Psychiatric Association. (1994). *Diagnostic and statistical manual of mental disorders (4th ed.).* Washington, DC: Author.

Balcazar, F. E., Keys, C. B., Bertram, J. F., & Rizzo, T. (1996). Advocate development in the field of developmental disabilities: A data-based conceptual model. *Mental Retardation, 34,* 341–351.

Bayer, R. (1981). *Homosexuality and American psychiatry: The politics of diagnosis.* New York: Basic Books.

Bergin, A. E., & Garfield, S. L. (Eds.). (1994). *Handbook of psychotherapy and behavior change.* New York: John Wiley & Sons.

Berman, J. S., & Norton, N. C. (1985). Does professional training make a therapist more effective? *Psychological Bulletin, 98,* 401–407.

Beutler, L. E., Crago, M., & Arizmendi, T. G. (1986). Therapist variables in psychotherapy process. In A. E. Bergin & S. L. Garfield (Eds.), *Handbook of psychotherapy and behavior change* (3rd ed., pp. 257–310). New York: John Wiley & Sons.

Beutler, L. E., Machado, P. P., & Neufeldt, S. A. (1994). Therapist variables. In A. E. Bergin & S. L. Garfield (Eds.), *Handbook of psychotherapy and behavior change* (4th ed., pp. 229–269). New York: John Wiley & Sons.

Brown, F., Belz, P., Corsi, L., & Wenig, B. (1993). Choice diversity for people with severe disabilities. *Educational and Training in Mental Retardation, 28,* 318–326.

Chambless, D. L., Baker, M. J., Baucomb, D. H., Beutler, L. E., Calhoun, K. S., Crits-Cristoph, P., Daiuto, A., DeRubeis, R., Detweiler, J., Haaga, D. A., Bennett Johnson, S., McCurry, S., Mueser, K. T., Pope, K. S., Sanderson, W. C., Shoham, V., Stickle, T., Williams, D. A., & Woody, S. R. (1998). Update on empirically validated therapies II. *The Clinical Psychologist, 51.* 3–16.

Cunconan-Lahr, R., & Brotherson, M. J. (1996). Advocacy in disability policy: Parents and consumers as advocates. *Mental Retardation, 34,* 352–358.

Denzin, N. K., & Lincoln, Y. S. (1994). *Handbook of qualitative research.* Thousand, Oaks CA: Sage.

Derogatis, L. R., Rickels, K., & Rock, A. F. (1976). The SCL-90-R and the MMPI: A step in the validation of a new self-report scale. *British Journal of Psychiatry, 128,* 280–289.

Etherington, K. (1996). The counselor as researcher: Boundary issues and critical dilemmas. *British Journal of Guidance and Counselling, 24,* 339–346.

Granello, P. F., & Witmer, J. M. (1998). Standards of care: Potential implications for the counseling profession. *Journal of Counseling and Development, 76,* 371–380.

Greenspan, M., & Kulish, N. M. (1985). Factors in premature termination in long-term psychotherapy. *Psychotherapy: Theory, Research and Practice, 22,* 75–82.

Hagan, M. A. (1997). *Whores of the court: The fraud of psychiatric testimony and the rape of American justice.* New York: Regan Books.

Hosie, T. W. (1991). *Historical antecedents and current status of counselor licensure.* In F. O. Bradley (Ed.), etc., pp 23–52.

Kazdin, A. E. (1994). Methodology, design, and evaluation in psychotherapy research. In A. E. Bergin & S. L. Garfield (Eds.), *Handbook of psychotherapy and behavior change* (4th ed., pp. 19–71). New York: John Wiley & Sons.

Kieffer, C. H. (1983). Citizen empowerment: A developmental perspective. *Prevention and Human Services 3,* 9–36.

Kuhn, T. S. (1962). *The structure of scientific revolutions.* Chicago: The University of Chicago Press.

Lambert, M. J. (1982). *The effects of psychotherapy.* New York: Human Sciences Press.

Lee, C. C., & Sirch, M. L. (1994). Counseling in an enlightened society: Values for a new millennium. *Counseling and Values, 38,* 90–97.

Loewen, J. L. (1995). *Lies my teacher told me: Everything your American history book got wrong.* New York: New Press.

McLeod, J. (1994). *Doing counseling research.* London: Sage.

Mogul, K. M. (1982). Overview: The sex of the therapist. *American Journal of Psychiatry, 139,* 1–11.

Orlinsky, D. E., Grawe, K., & Parks, B. K. (1994). Process and outcome in psychotherapy—noch einmal. In A. E. Bergin & S. L. Garfield (Eds.), *Handbook of psychotherapy and behavior change* (4th ed., pp. 270–376). New York: John Wiley & Sons.

Osborne, J. L., Collison, B. B., House, R. M., Gray, L. A., Firth, J., & Lou, M. (1998). Developing a social advocacy model for counselor education. *Counselor Education and Supervision, 37,* 190–202.

Perry, S., Frances, A., & Clarkin, J. (1985). *A DSM-III casebook of differential therapeutics.* New York: Brunner/Mazel.

Pollack, M. H., Otto, M. W., & Rosenbaum, J. F. (Eds.). (1996). *Challenges in clinical practice: Pharmacologic and psychosocial strategies.* New York: Guilford Press.

Prochaska, J. O., & Di Clemente, C. C. (1982). Transtheoretical therapy: Toward a more integrative model of change. *Psychotherapy: Theory, Research and Practice, 19,* 276–288.

Prochaska, J. O., Di Clemente, C. C., & Norcross, J. C. (1992). In search of how people change. *American Psychologist, 47,* 1102–1114.

Renzetti, C. M., & Lee, R. M. (Eds.). (1993). *Researching sensitive topics.* London: Sage.

Rogers, C. R. (1958). A process conception of psychotherapy. *American Psychologist, 13,* 142–149.

Roth, A., & Fonagy, P. (1996). *What works for whom? A critical review of psychotherapy research.* New York: Guilford Press.

Seligman, L. (1990). *Selecting effective treatments.* San Francisco: Jossey-Bass.

Sexton, T. L., Whiston, S. C., Bleuer, J. C., & Walz, G. (1997). *Integrating outcome research into counseling practice and training.* Alexandria, VA: American Counseling Association.

Shapiro, D. A., & Shapiro, D. (1982). Meta-analysis of comparative therapy outcome research: A critical appraisal. *Behavioral Psychotherapy, 10,* 4–25.

Shapiro, F. (1989). Eye movement desensitization: A new treatment for post-traumatic stress disorder. *Journal of Behavior Therapy and Experimental Psychiatry, 20,* 211–217.

Shapiro, F. (1995). *Eye movement desensitization and reprocessing: Basic principles, protocols, and procedures.* New York: Guilford Press.

Sieber, J. E., & Stanley, B. (1988). Ethical and professional dimensions of socially sensitive research. *American Psychologist, 43,* 49–55.

Smith, J. D., (1997, April). The challenge of advocacy: The different voices of Helen Keller and Burton Blatt. *Mental Retardation,* 138–140.

Wolfe, P. S., Olfiesh, N. S., & Boone, R. B. (1996). Self-advocacy preparation of consumers with disabilities: A national perspective of ADA training efforts. *Journal of the Association for Persons with Severe Handicaps, 21,* 81–87.

FUNDING AND POLITICS IN AGENCY COUNSELING

Government involvement in providing mental health services is so heavy that caring for the mentally ill . . . is primarily a socialized undertaking.

Robert Connery

A unique era [in mental health care] is ending, and the intellectual and financial resources that have driven reform in community mental health for the previous three decades appear to be exhausted.

William Vega and John Murphy

Although well intended, Hank and Issac's funding strategy for a new mental health center proved ineffective.

> I remember a quote attributed to Winston Churchill that went something like
> this: "A younger person who is not somewhat liberal has no heart. An older per-
> son who is not somewhat conservative has no brain." This seems to represent my
> own development as I approach midlife. I remember my politics being quite lib-
> eral as a younger person. My political philosophy was certainly never what you
> would call socialist, but I did believe, perhaps simplistically, that government in-
> tervention could cure social ills. This philosophy was complemented by a reli-
> gious worldview that equally emphasized compassion as social action. This period
> of my life paralleled my entry into community agency counseling work. Some of
> the things that I discovered in my work experience were that not all people who
> seemed to need help wanted it, many who wanted it didn't want to put forth much
> effort to make it work, and others who wanted and needed it but never got it
> managed to do okay on their own. One dynamic that was readily apparent in my
> work was that, given equally decent therapeutic relationships, clients who had to
> pay for their counseling showed far more motivation than those who did not.

Clearly, the past and the future of community agency counseling are tied directly to mental health funding policies in the United States. Funding policy
hinges on numerous human variables, including political battles based in economic philosophy that seeks to answer the questions "Who is responsible for
caring for mentally ill citizen?" and "Who has the authority to do so?" (Harper,
1994). The notion of mental health has been politicized since the end of the
Second World War (Torrey, 1997), and mental health funding has always been
somewhat political (Grob, 1983). As such, the funding and reform debate is as
much about effective treatment as it is about who pays for that treatment.
One important dynamic that emerges from a history of mental health funding
is the cyclical nature of funding strategies, correlating with whether a conservative or a liberal political party is in power (Rocheforte, 1989). The cycle of
funding is like the flow of ocean tides. Over the past 300 years, there has been

an ebb and flow of funding strategies tied to the politico-economic trends of the age, as well as the predominant philosophy of the ruling political party.

Here we return to questions asked in chapter 4, on ethics. Are we truly "our brother's keeper," or must people be primarily responsible for themselves and their families? Should government collect vast resources from taxpayers to care for those at varying levels of need, or should each person be allowed to keep as much of her or his income to do with as she or he pleases? If the government is going to pay, should the money come from local, state, federal, or all three levels of government? Perhaps most important, is there a moral imperative underlying these positions? These questions are not ones we can fully answer, which is why they reemerge throughout the history of mental health funding. The questions will certainly resurface over and over again throughout this chapter.

As previously noted, treatment is always tied to funding. Professionals do not (nor should they) work for free. In chapter 1, we examined the various training models and philosophies of the therapeutic professions and noted that the medical model had ascended to the dominant position in human services. Vega and Murphy (1990) claim that the medical model does not meet the needs of people with mental illnesses (especially culturally different people with those illnesses). They believe that social models that view environmental ills as contributors to mental illness need more emphasis for treatment to be effective.

Bell (1989) tied many funding problems to the imprecise and ever-changing terms used in mental health treatment. This has been a constant criticism of the mental health fields (Sykes, 1992). The effort at cataloging diagnoses in the *DSM-IV*, which is a primary component of the medical model, has brought about a common vocabulary that lends a sense of (if not an illusion of) consistency to treatment issues. Despite this, many practitioners argue that the *DSM*, and the medical model on which it is based, neglects too many other crucial variables in the treatment of mental and emotional disorders. Vega and Murphy noted that the consistency in individual treatment possible with the *DSM's* clear diagnostic nosology neglects crucial psychological and social dynamics. They emphasized that the lessons of the past 30 years support social models of health, but, as Kleinman (1988) noted, the narrow disease model of mental illness is easier to quantify and less burdensome to fund.

Added to the difficulties is the fact that, although most mental health professionals agree that an ounce of prevention is worth a pound of treatment, funding strategies seem to favor the "pound of cure." This is why most therapeutic professions, including psychiatry, begin by emphasizing wellness and, in the end, focus on treating pathology. In this chapter, we will review the funding history of community mental health and examine current changes in funding dynamics that led into the era of managed care. Managed care will then be treated more extensively in chapter 8.

IMPORTANT FUNDING TERMS

Throughout this chapter, we will examine three federal funding strategies, which were outlined by Rocheforte and Logan (1989): categorical grants, general revenue sharing, and block grants. All three have been used in the United States to fund mental health and other programs. A categorical grant is one that is controlled at the federal level. It is money stipulated for specific programs that are delivered at the local level but are overseen at the federal level. The National Institute of Mental Health (NIMH) has overseen many categorical grants in the history of mental health funding in this country. General revenue sharing is a strategy in which federal funds are delivered to states and local agencies with very few stipulations, allowing the state or agency almost total control of the money. Block grants fall midway between these two strategies. Block grants are monies directed to certain populations in need identified at the federal level. However, each state receiving money decides which activities best meet the defined needs. This funding strategy seems to balance federal and state influences.

A HISTORY OF MENTAL HEALTH FUNDING

Most authors writing on the history of mental health funding and mental health policy note that World War II had a profound effect on heightening the awareness of the American public of the prevalence of mental and emotional disorders. During the war, a large number of men drafted and enlisting (12 percent) were rejected for military service because of a mental or an emotional disorder (Cameron, 1989). At the same time, a large number of military personnel were discharged for psychiatric reasons or treated for "battle fatigue," a condition now labeled posttraumatic stress disorder (Manus, 1999). The treatments pioneered at this time reinforced the notion that mental illness has environmental precipitants and can be treated by helping the client adapt to the environment (Cameron, 1989; Grinker & Speigel, 1945). This notion was not new. It was articulated in part by Adolph Meyer in his psychobiological theory of mental and emotional disorders (Barlow & Durand, 1995). Meyer believed that mental and emotional disorders are the individual's personality reacting to biological, psychological, and social factors. This viewpoint was the basis for the first *DSM,* compiled in 1952, but was discarded 16 years later for the *DSM-II.* This theory of environmental etiology in mental illness reached its peak in the social activism of the 1960s but quickly lost momentum in the 1990s, the "decade of the brain" and biological psychiatry.

During World War II, the shortage of personnel trained to deal with mental and emotional disorders and the large numbers of psychiatric casualties prompted unprecedented involvement by the federal government. Prior to this, mental health programs were run at the state level, typically through state mental institutions (Dorwart & Epstein, 1993). Also prior to this, psychiatrists were the only people licensed to offer direct interventions to those with mental and emotional disorders. The shortage of personnel was one factor contributing to the licensing of psychologists and, subsequently, other nonmedical therapeutic professionals. Another factor was the growing concern in the patriarchal ranks of psychiatry that their professional power was increasingly being challenged by the female-dominated American Association of Psychiatric Social Workers and the American Occupational Therapy Association (Grob, 1983). As noted in chapter 1, also on the horizon were the eager-to-be-licensed psychologists.

The Postwar Years

The end of the war marked the emergence of the Group for the Advancement of Psychiatry (GAP), led by William Menninger, who headed the Menninger Foundation, which led the infusion of psychoanalysis into the U.S. culture. Menninger was also the U.S. army's chief psychiatrist during the war. The GAP was a strong advocate for more community-based psychiatric practice. Menninger's group was the new guard leading a movement away from the psychiatrist as hospital administrator to the psychiatrist as active, community-based therapist. Encouraged by the success of military psychiatry, by the lobbying efforts of groups such as GAP, and by the abysmal conditions of postwar inpatient units, the federal government in 1946 established the National Institute of Mental Health (NIMH) (Cameron, 1989). The NIMH was established to dispense new funds for training, research, and community support. It was funded through the national Mental Health Act of the same year (Public Law 79-487). This law authorized the surgeon general to improve the mental health of U.S. citizens through research into the etiology, diagnosis, and treatment of mental/emotional disorders. It assisted states in the prevention, diagnosis, and treatment of mental/emotional disorders.

The Mental Health Act of 1946 and the establishment of the NIMH marked the beginning of a large federal role in funding the country's mental health services. The role was characterized by an increasing commitment to community-based care for people with chronic mental and emotional disorders. This raised awareness of remedial and preventive services as well. As noted in chapter 1, preventive services almost always take a backseat to remedial services in the mental health system. The 1946 premises of these preventive services went far beyond the traditional individual services thought of as counseling or psychotherapy to far-ranging community interventions designed to address social problems that had an impact on the mental and emotional well-being of citizens.

This was clearly an expensive undertaking. It was also an undertaking that would become a political watershed. Torrey (1997) noted that the increasing emphasis on mental health in the postwar United States made conservatives uneasy. Torrey wrote about how conservatives were particularly uneasy with psychiatrists proclaiming a prominent role for themselves in this new movement and, by association, in the affairs of the country. Conservatives at the time seemed to feel that the psychiatrists were talking about values, not science, and thus began the politicization of mental health. Torrey did a good job of illustrating how, once a topic becomes politicized, it is easily led by human emotion rather than reason. Conservatives in the late 1940s and early 1950s branded the mental health movement a "Marxist weapon," "a communist plot," and "out-and-out brainwashing" (Torrey, 1997, pp. 172–173).

Conservative mistrust of mental health movements continues to this day. Over the past 50 years, it seems that the mental health movement has been associated with liberal politics in the public eye, and this association is not undeserved. Torrey (1997) chronicled the association of the mental health movement with sexual liberation, the Students for a Democratic Society (SDS), the antiwar movement, the more extreme versions of self-actualization (such as nude encounter groups), and Karl Menninger's (1969) notions that criminals ought to be considered victims of bad childrearing and that prisons really ought to be treatment centers. Menninger's thesis has been reinvented over the years and has been used by certain groups to avoid personal responsibility (Sykes, 1992). "Reality is complex and complexity is our friend." There is really no way to tease out all of the influences on a single life and make a pronouncement of "victim" or "author."

Deinstitutionalization

One of my first jobs in the field of mental health was in 1985 at an agency that had been contacted by a mental health advocacy group. The group had initiated a class action suit against the state for deplorable conditions in the state hospitals. Our job was to evaluate patients who had been institutionalized for many years and to determine which patients were functioning highly enough to adjust to a community-based group home rather than the hospital. When I went to the first state hospital for the first time, I saw naked patients running around a ward that had rooms marked off only by chain link walls. The three staff members on duty were sitting in another chain link "office" in the middle of the ward, smoking cigarettes, drinking coffee, and watching television. There were bars on the windows of the ward. These were conditions unfit for animals, let alone people with mental illness and developmental disabilities.

Before to World War II, attitudes favored the institutionalization of the mentally ill. Reformers such as Dorothea Dix promoted the building of state psychiatric hospitals as a humane and moral approach to caring for those with severe mental illness. Grob (1983) noted that the change in sentiment about deinstitutionalization, the movement of a population of people suffering from mental illnesses from inpatient psychiatric hospitals to community settings, has nineteenth-century roots in the evolution of psychiatry as a specialty, changes in the patient population, and changing political dynamics. Grob noted that, as psychiatry became more associated with medical practice, psychiatrists moved away from their role as state mental hospital superintendents and administrators and toward research and practice in nonhospital settings. Also, the type of patient housed in mental institutions changed to include elderly patients who, 20 years earlier, were cared for in almshouses, as well as patients suffering physical disorders such as syphilis and who had severe behavioral symptoms. Finally, the political dynamics related to funding increased the population of state mental hospitals at the turn of the twentieth century. The local funders for facilities such as almshouses to care for the indigent elderly found that, by presenting senility as a psychiatric condition, these people could be transferred to state hospitals. Not only was the care better, but the responsibility for financial support shifted from local to state sources. Thus began the politicization of mental health care funding. By the midtwentieth century, the tide shifted again, and the steady trend toward inpatient admissions gave way to the rising trend of deinstitutionalization.

Deinstitutionalization developed over a period of 50 years. By the 1950s, the trend of deinstitutionalization was gaining momentum. The label is associated with the philosophy that people suffering from mental illness should live in the least restrictive environment, and the process has led to large numbers of people suffering from mental illness leaving inpatient settings and returning to the community. This movement was multiply determined, but there are three clear contributors to it. One often cited factor is the introduction of chlorpromazine (brand name Thorazine) in 1954 as a drug treatment for severe mental and emotional disorders. The most significant effect of drug treatment was a decrease in the inpatient population, as it was discovered that the drugs modify patients' behavior, so that they can more easily live in the community. The use of Thorazine was pioneered by French neurosurgeon Henri Laborit, who believed it inhibited the release of histamine during surgery and calmed his patients the evening before surgery. It was the calming effect that prompted him to recommend its use to his colleagues in psychiatry for highly agitated patients.

Two of those colleagues, Jean Delay and Pierre Deniker, then did the preliminary work characterizing Thorazine as an antipsychotic agent. Their work spread to the United States, where Thorazine was routinely administered to highly agitated patients who, before the introduction of the drug, had been treated with variations of shock therapy (including electroconvulsive therapy) and prefrontal lobotomy (Kalinowsky & Hoch, 1962). It should be noted that treatment with Thorazine had the most impact on younger patients. Older patients were made more manageable with the drug but were discharged into the community at a far lower rate and, more often, were simply transferred into nursing home facilities. This dawning event in psychopharmacology was not without its critics. Many psychotherapists claimed that the new treatment simply sedated patients and erroneously equated quieter wards with improved conditions in the patients (Bell, 1989).

A second, more politically fueled trend that paved the way for deinstitutionalization and funding of community mental health was a growing concern over the practice of involuntary restriction, as well as the general conditions of inpatient facilities. Psychiatric facilities had been deteriorating throughout the Great Depression and the war years. At midcentury, inpatient treatment was for the most severe and most chronic patients, whose average psychiatric hospital stay lasted 7 to 10 years (Levy, 1969). In addition, indigent and senile elderly people were transferred from local almshouses (which were slowly dying out) to the state hospitals. Finally, there were increases in the number of patients suffering from chronic and terminal disorders ranging from Huntington's Chorea to brain tumors. This added to overcrowding.

After the war, significant efforts were made to change life on wards. Interpersonal training emphasizing the work of Harry Stack Sullivan became more common for staff, as well as improved the physical conditions of the wards. Many improvements were made, including a decrease in punitive measures and an increase in patient governance. Due to a lack of controlled studies at that time, it is impossible to say whether improved social conditions in the units, the introduction of Thorazine, or a combination of various efforts accounted for the improvements. Despite these improvements, only a minority of inpatient units made dramatic changes.

A third (and dominant) contributor to deinstitutionalization was the establishment in 1965 of Medicaid and Medicare. Medicaid (Title XIX of the Social Security Act) has been referred to as the country's largest mental health program (Keisler, 1980). When Torrey analyzed the deinstitutionalization statistics following the introduction of Thorazine, he found that the inpatient hospital population decreased 4 percent between 1955 and 1960. However, the census decreased an additional 11 percent between 1960 and 1965. Had this discharge rate, correlated with the introduction of Thorazine, continued up to 1994 (keeping pace with population increases), the number of inpatients should have been around 350,000 instead of 72,000.

The largest increase in deinstitutionalization occurred after the enactment of Medicaid and Medicare. The state psychiatric hospital population decreased 29 percent between 1965 and 1970, 43 percent between 1970 and 1975, and 32 percent between 1975 and 1980. The benefit is that, when a patient is in a state-run psychiatric hospital, the state assumes 100 percent of the costs for that patient. When the patient is discharged from the state hospital, she or he is eligible for Medicaid, Supplemental Security Income (SSI), food stamps, and benefits from other federal programs, providing huge cost relief to states. This is the same cost-shifting strategy that transferred patients from almshouses to state hospitals in the early twentieth century (Grob, 1983; Torrey, 1997). We will discuss more about federal programs such as Medicaid later in this chapter.

Funding and Community Mental Health Centers

In 1955, the Mental Health Study Act created a Joint Commission of Mental Illness and Health, which spent five years studying the nation's mental health services. In 1961, it released its report "Action for Mental Health," in which it criticized most of the nation's inpatient institutions and recommended the establishment of outpatient, community treatment centers and legislation restricting involuntary practices. Psychiatry generally supported the outpatient mental health movement, although there were some voices of dissent. Despite these, in 1963 the Kennedy administration passed the Community Mental Health Centers Act. Torrey (1997) claimed that it was Kennedy who "permanently bonded the mental health professions to the Democratic Party" (p. 178). Kennedy had a younger sister who was born mentally retarded and then suffered from mental illness as a young adult. She received a lobotomy, which only worsened her condition. The last act that Kennedy signed before his assassination was the Community Mental Health Centers Act of 1963 (Public Law 88-164).

The Community Menthal Health Centers Act provided federally matched funds for the state construction of community mental health centers, which would then offer a comprehensive range of services. The funds would be provided state-by-state, based on population and need. The budget also included provisions for staff salaries, which drew the fire of the American Medical Association, which claimed that they were an effort at socialized medicine, and the staffing provisions were eventually dropped before the act was signed into law. Each state was to submit a comprehensive plan to divide the state into service, or "catchment," areas encompassing 75,000 to 200,000 people. The NIMH staff was charged with interpreting the law regarding the services to be offered. They decided on five key services: inpatient, outpatient, emergency, partial hospitalization, and community services, such as education).

By 1964, it seemed that the plan was a failure. Few states had the start-up funds, and only a handful had submitted plans. As Cameron (1989) noted, both the Johnson administration and the Congress were anxious to fulfill the social programs inherited from the Kennedy administration. Given this, the way was paved in 1965 for the NIMH to draft amendments to the Mental Health Centers Act of 1963, giving the NIMH full control of the program. Cameron noted that the only lobby that could have effectively opposed these amendments, the American Medical Association, had depleted its resources and reputation in opposing Medicare and Medicaid legislation earlier in 1965. The amendments passed easily and were signed into law by President Johnson in 1965.

The amendments reinstated staffing provisions and increased the federal funding from 50 percent to 75 percent. The plan used the concept of seed money and intended that the 75 percent federal funding would decrease by 15 percent each year until it reached 30 percent. At the 30 percent mark funding would stop and, ideally, be replaced by state and local sources. The amendments also bypassed states through giving full control of the funding to the NIMH, making the monies categorical grants. Cameron (1989) noted that this reflected a basic political strategy of the Democratic Party. The party strategy assumed that state governments had little incentive to create programs to address the needs of the poor and underserved. The funds for social programs were assumed to reach the poor more rapidly under the control of federal leaders committed to the programs meant to bring about social change. This was a theme in federal spending during the 1960s. In fact, health and human resource programs increased from 13 percent to 40 percent of total federal aid under the Johnson administration.

The first years of the 1965 amendments were proclaimed a success, and the Mental Health Amendments Act of 1967 (Public Law 90-31) extended federal support for another three years. Under the Johnson administration, Congress reacted to growing public concern over drug use by enacting the Alcoholic and Narcotic Addict Rehabilitation Act of 1968 (Public Law 90-574). This was followed by the Comprehensive Drug Abuse Prevention and Control Act of 1970 (Public Law 91-513). Federal funding for these programs was dovetailed into the community mental health centers legislation, further expanding the federally funded program. This began a process of identifying specialized populations and then adding services to the growing federally funded mental health services.

The Community Mental Health Centers Amendments of 1970 (Public Law 91-211) further extended federal funding for yet another three-year period in addition to identifying children as a population in need of mental health programs. Cameron noted that, by 1970, it was clear that communities were having trouble finding nonfederal sources of funding to replace what was intended to be federal seed money. A primary assumption was that comprehensive CMHCs would serve numerous clients, who would be able to pay for services out-of-pocket, in addition to those who would have some insurance benefits. These assumptions were seriously flawed, contributing to the increased competition for decreased funding (Ray & Finley, 1994).

Inability to replace federal seed money was just one problem with the expanding federal programs. Categorical grants were becoming associated with ineffective, top-heavy bureaucracies. States and local agencies were becoming too dependent on the federal monies and having trouble generating plans to replace them. In addition, tension was growing in many sectors over the federal control over the states. The practice of issuing federal categorical grants was seen by many as an infringement of the federal government in state and local matters. Rocheforte and Logan (1989) noted that, by 1978, the federal dollars states were receiving equaled almost 40 percent of the revenue from their own resources. This was close to double what it had been 30 years earlier. In addition, the more specialized the services became, the more fragmented the services became. This was further confounded by the situation of federal control over state programs, which resulted in poor communication and subsequent administrative difficulties.

As Rocheforte and Logan pointed out, these problems increased the public perception that the programs were wasteful and inefficient. Foley and Sharfstein (1983) pointed out the difficulties when local agencies, heavily dependent on NIMH monies, interacted directly with their federal connections but did not interact at all with state mental health systems. Further, the problem of inpatient versus outpatient dollars, a problem since the beginning of deinstitutionalization, persisted. Throughout the past five decades, there has been an increased emphasis on outpatient treatment, while most dollars go to inpatient settings (Rocheforte, 1989; Rubin, 1990).

It should be noted that there had also been the expectation that the CMHC programs would "mainstream mental health with other health care services" (Ray & Finley, 1994, p. 285). At the time, Congress had plans to make grant money available to hospitals and to encourage conjoint locations that realigned mental health with general health care. It was erroneously thought that the collaboration of physicians and psychiatrists would fuel this goal. Apparently, professional parochialism triumphed over the more ideal goal of well-integrated health-care delivery.

During the 1970s, the Republican administrations recommended less federal influence in mental health and funding. One state that consistently opposed federal mental health funding was California, where Richard Nixon was a senator in 1956. As president, Nixon consistently opposed extensions of federal funding but was ignored by the Democratic Congress. This continued for six years through the Ford administration. Each time the monies hit the deadline to be phased out, this was supported by the White House, only to be ignored by Congress. In 1973, President Nixon tried to impound funds appropriated by Congress for the CMHCs. That battle ended in a federal court ordering the administration to release the funds. In August 1974, when Nixon resigned, Congress reauthorized CMHC funding. It was immediately vetoed by then-President Gerald Ford, and Congress responded by overriding the veto. It should be noted that Presidents Nixon, Ford, and Carter all attempted some forms of revenue sharing, but it never accounted for more than a small part of the federal funding.

The election of President Carter in 1976 marked the beginning of another administration supportive of federal funding for mental health. In 1977, First

Lady Rosalyn Carter led the push for community mental health, and in that year the Presidential Commission on Mental Health was established. In 1978, the commission recommended the following:

- Greater attention to underserved populations
- Greater support for research
- Continued support for clinical training
- Greater flexibility in developing services to meet the needs of the communities
- Need for better third-party reimbursement for mental health care
- Increased attention to epidemiology (the study of the cause, prevalence, and incidence of a disease) and prevention
- Commitment to the problems of the chronically mentally ill
- Commitment to deinstitutionalization
- Links between mental health and general health

Despite these developments, it seemed that, by 1978, Congress was realizing that the CMHCs would never reach the level of development hoped for in the initial legislation. Sharfstein (1978) noted that, of 675 fully funded CMHCs, only 60 were not receiving any federal support, and there were still over 800 unfunded catchment areas.

In July 1980, the Mental Health Systems Act was passed and signed into law by President Carter. It was designed to meet many of the recommendations in the Joint Commissions report. Four months later, the Reagan administration led the movement to roll-back federal funding of community agencies and leave funding in the hands of the states. In 1981, the Omnibus Budget Reconciliation Act of 1981 (OBRA) (Public Law 97-35) dispensed with the federal funding of mental health services and instead offered block grants to be used by states as they saw fit. There were provisions that certain monies be used for mental health. The Reagan policies further challenged the use of social security support for the chronically mentally ill and the Department of Housing and Urban Development's (HUD) efforts to create federally funded housing for the mentally ill. NIMH suggestions for evaluating this change of direction were rejected by the administration.

As previously noted, throughout all of these changes, the inpatient money did not follow the patients into the outpatient world of the CMHC. This is referred to as the situation in which the money did not follow the clients. This may have been due to the power of the AMA lobby. Current hierarchies in mental health, as well as current trends in research, suggest that the medical model will continue to enjoy prestige in the treatment of mental illness.

As Torrey (1997) noted, President Reagan was also a product of the California antimental health region. Reagan's election in 1980 marked the beginning of more difficult times for mental health agencies dependent on federal funding. The Reagan administration also implemented stricter reviews of people receiving Social Security Disability Income (SSDI) and Supplemental Security Income to trim federal expenditures for mental health. These stricter reviews resulted in the cutting off of 300,000 people from the benefits, many of which suffered from mental or emotional disorders. Torrey concluded that the debates over SSI and SSDI "further solidified the association of mental health with Democrats and anti-mental-health sentiment with Republicans" (p. 181).

It should be noted that block grants are is not exclusively a Republican strategy for mental health funding. Lyndon Johnson initiated the first block grants as part of his administration's "Great Society" program. Those grants were for health and crime prevention but constituted a small percentage, compared with the level of categorical grant funding. As such, control still rested heavily at the federal level. Transferring the control of many federal programs to the states was a high priority for the Reagan administration. The block grant is a mechanism used to bring this about. The basic idea is to take funding from several programs, each with its own regulations, and deliver it in one "block" of money to the state. The state then has greater administrative flexibility in using the money, as opposed to a categorical grant, in which full control rests at the federal level. Once again we see the ebb and flow pattern. The categorical grants were designed to wrest control away from states because advocates at the time believed the states to be wed to an outdated model of inpatient mental health services. The categorical grants created what Rocheforte and Logan (1989) called a federally controlled alternate mental health system. The states, nevertheless, eventually regained greater control with the shift from categorical grants to block grants.

In the OBRA, 57 federal aid programs were grouped into 9 block grants, which covered preventive health; maternal and child health services; primary care; social services; community services; low-income energy assistance; community development; and alcohol, drug abuse, and mental health services. The alcohol, drug abuse, and mental health block grant (ADAMHA) was one of the largest of the 9. It included 10 previous categorical grant programs, which had been funded on a project or state formula basis (Rocheforte & Logan, 1989). The states had to apply each year for these grants and report on the uses of the money at the end of each fiscal year. The states had minimum requirements for spending the money but greater flexibility in dividing the money between mental health and substance abuse programs.

In the process of dividing the funds between substance abuse treatment and mental health treatment, an artificial categorization was created, which resulted in a specific group of clients—clients with a dual diagnosis—being eliminated from eligibility for either service. The phrase "dual diagnosis" refers to an individual carrying both a substance abuse and mental health diagnosis. In a study by the National Institute of Drug Abuse (NIDA), it was concluded that over 50 percent of all clients being seen for substance abuse in federally funded programs also had a mental or emotional disorder (Reiger et al., 1988).

Depending on the state policy regarding access to treatment programs, many such clients were turned away on both fronts because they did not fit exclusively into one category. In analyses of ADAMHA-block grants, Rocheforte and Logan noted that the states ended up paying most (about 75 percent) of the costs. Under block grants, states seem to have made up for the federal retrenchment. These authors also noted that the Reagan administration was actually able to cut the federal budget and "weaken organized private interests by dispersing their influence across a decentralized policymaking environment" (Rocheforte & Logan, 1989, p. 157).

The impact of block grants on CMHCs was variable. If a state passed along the block grant money to existing centers, the decrease in funding and disruption in services was nominal. If, on the other hand, a state government exercised its right to redefine the best way to accomplish the goals for which the monies were intended, funding could shift in such a way as to put agencies in fierce competition, in which one agency gained at the expense of another. If, in addition, the state was not willing to make up the lost money, services could suffer severely.

Block grants, although still in existence, have failed to keep up with inflation. For example, from 1982 to 1994, the annual grant amount decreased in purchasing power by over $80 million (Ray & Finley, 1994). Rocheforte and Logan noted that, by the late 1980s, as CMHCs became less dependent on the federal government for block grant money, their dependence on Medicaid money escalated rapidly.

MEDICARE AND MEDICAID FUNDING FOR MENTAL HEALTH

Private health insurance emerged in the United States in the 1930s. This made it possible for more people to get needed care and caused an expansion of the health-care industry. In the Second World War, health benefits became institutionalized when they were substituted for wage increases due to economic factors. The first insurers were nonprofit and regulated by the states. The insurers charged an average rate, which included all age groups; however, as the number of private, "for-profit" insurers entered the market, they changed from an average rate to "experience rated" policies. These were based on the health-care needs of more limited age groups, which were usually younger and healthier and did not incur the health costs that the elderly typically did. It was partly this shift that set in motion the forces leading to Medicare and Medicaid (Dowart & Epstein, 1993).

Medicare

Medicare is available to persons over age 65 in the United States who are eligible for social security and some people under age 65 with specified disabilities. The under-65 age group uses far more mental health services than the over-65 group. Co-payments are required for outpatient mental health services for elderly Medicare recipients. It is estimated that about 12 percent of all elderly Americans suffer from a diagnosable mental or emotional disorder but that they are far less likely to seek treatment than young or middle-aged adults. The co-payment is certainly not an added incentive. The total Medicare costs for outpatient mental health services are considerably low (less than .1 percent), leading some authors to conclude that Medicare recipients underuse the benefits for outpatient services. Whereas 7 to 18 percent of private health insurance monies are used for drug and alcohol treatment, only about 3 percent of Medicare monies are used for mental health treatments (Dowart & Epstein, 1993). This figure increases to 4 percent when inpatient services are included. Clearly, inpatient mental health services are the primary mental health expenditure paid for by Medicare.

Medicaid

Unlike Medicare, Medicaid is the primary source of funding for the indigent mentally ill. Although the amount spent on Medicaid has steadily increased since its inception, the amount nearly doubled between 1988 and 1994, from about $51 billion to $135 billion, which, as Torrey (1997) pointed out, made a substantial contribution to the federal deficit. In 1994, 15 percent of Medicaid funds ($11.7 billion) were spent on people with mental illnesses. Although a significant percentage, it has remained at 15 percent since 1988 (Koyanagi, 1988).

In many states, Medicaid supports a substantial number of mental health programs and was one of the few new government sources of mental health money in the 1990s (Torrey, 1997). Although states must match funds they receive from the federal Medicaid program, there are usually savings. Medicaid must provide benefits to people receiving Aid for Dependent Children (AFDC), to low-income persons over age 65 who are not covered by Medicare, and to people with physical disabilities. These funds cannot be used for the care of those between ages 21 and 65 in psychiatric institutions or psychiatric skilled nursing homes. However, this does not rule out nonpsychiatric nursing homes, in which about 23 percent of the total population suffers from a mental disorder. Of these, 37 percent of those under age 65 and 27 percent of those over age 65 receive Medicaid as their primary source of payment (Dowart & Epstein, 1993). Nonpsychiatric nursing homes constitute an increasingly lucrative market for therapeutic professionals to deliver much needed treatment.

Medicaid recipients suffering from mental illness use far more Medicaid dollars than do nonmentally ill Medicaid recipients (Dobson & Scharff-Corder, 1983). It is noteworthy that people living in poverty who are receiving Medicaid benefits are far more likely to use outpatient mental health services than those who do not received Medicaid. This may seem like common sense but is important when considering the stressors correlated with poverty, the incidence of mental health problems associated with those stressors, and thus the need for access to mental health services in those populations. It should be noted that deinstitutionalization continued to escalate through the 1980s, and the average CMHC increased services to clients suffering from serious mental or emotional disorders from approximately 9 percent in 1981 to nearly 50 percent in 1987 (Ray & Finley, 1994).

THE 1990S

The decade of the 1990s was proclaimed by President George Bush to be "the decade of the brain" psychiatry (decade of the brain web site is *http://www.loc.gov/loc/brain/activity.html*). Scientists received increased recognition, being honored for such things as the introduction of lithium, the study of hemisphericity in the brain, and the use of PET, CAT, and MRI scanners to study the brain. The technological advances further increased the power of the medical model, as scientists became able to peer inside the brains of people suffering from mental and emotional disorders. The rapid increase in funds for biologically based research furthered the ascendancy of the medical model and the funding crisis. The costs of technology contributed to the health-care "crunch," which includes mental health care.

As far as CMHCs go, the 1990s saw the culmination of some legislative trends begun in the State Mental Health Planning Act of 1986 (Public Law 99-660). This act began a series of amendments to Medicare and Medicaid, making those funds more accessible to CMHCs. These amendments included establishing case management as a benefit paid by Medicaid, expanded services to homeless people suffering from mental illness, and prohibiting using nursing homes as a "dumping ground" for patients with severe mental/emotional disorders. By 1990, 46% of clients at the average CMHC suffered from severe mental/emotional disorders (Ray & Finley, 1994).

The Clinton Administration

It is difficult to assess the impact of the Clinton administration on mental health funding. As Torrey (1997) noted, when Clinton was first elected to office in 1992, advocates of federal mental health funding were optimistic. Vice President Al Gore's wife, Tipper Gore, had earned a master's degree in psychology and seemed to have taken on the cause of federally funded mental health care and the idea that insurance should cover mental illness at full parity with physical illness. Any optimism regarding these plans disappeared in 1994 with the election of a Republican majority in Congress. Torrey noted that the episode not only was one more "skirmish in the ongoing mental health war between liberals and conservatives" (p. 181) but also failed to distinguish psychologically based disorders from brain disorders, thus further muddying the waters for the general public.

The Clinton administration's fiscal year (FY) 1998 and 1999 budgets both sought to increase NIMH funding while holding steady or decreasing monies going to CMHCs. In particular, the principle sources of state mental health funding had not received any increases since 1994. The FY 1998 budget proposed some monies for mental health but limited the use of those monies to substance abuse treatment. The FY 1999 budget proposals may have potentially trimmed the amount of Medicaid monies available to people disabled by mental illness. Clinton also sought repeal of the Boren Amendment, which required Medicaid to pay providers at rates comparable to those of private practice. Also in the FY 1999 budget, the Clinton administration proposed a (theoretically) temporary expansion of Social Security called the "Ticket to Independence Program." The program would allow people collecting SSI and SSDI benefits to use a "ticket" with any public or private rehabilitation or employment provider participating in the program to wean off public support as they integrate into the world of work. This could potentially affect many mentally disabled persons collecting SSI and SSDI (National Alliance for the Mentally Ill, 1999). Where these policies will land us in the beginning of the twenty-first century is still unknown.

The 1990s and Beyond: Consequences and Possibilities

It is indeed difficult to sort out the end result of all the policy and funding shifts in the past 40 years. Most agree that, although states make up a great deal of the funding lost under the Reagan and Bush administrations and although the use of Medicaid and Medicare funding expanded, there was still a significant decrease in services throughout the 1990s. Between the decreases in funding and the continued deinstitutionalization of inpatient populations, the severely mentally ill suffered substantially. One unintended consequence of these policies is a drastic increase in the number of mentally ill people in jails and prisons (Harper, 1994; Torrey, 1997). This trend began again in the 1970s after it had not been reported since the nineteenth century (Lamb & Weinberger, 1998). Lamb and Weinberger noted that this trend fulfills a hypothesis by Penrose (1939), which states, in any industrial society, a generally stable number of people are confined and, if one form of confinement is phased out, another form will increase its numbers to make up the difference. Penrose noted that this seemed to be the relationship between mental health facilities and prisons.

Torrey (1995) quoted a San Diego sheriff, who stated that the prison system was rapidly becoming a primary mental health care provider. Often, people with severe mental disorders are detained for up to five days in jails before they get a psychiatric examination. Soloman, Draine, and Meyerson (1994) noted that mentally ill forensic clients in their study had a six-month recidivism rate of 32 percent. They blamed a lack of community-based services for the high rates of reincarceration. Steadman, Barbera, and Dennis (1994) studied the prevalence of mental health diversion programs in jails and prisons. In their sample of more than 1,000 prisons, 685 returned the surveys. Of those 685, only 52 had formal mental health diversion programs. French (1987) noted that the increased and often unnecessary incarceration is one of many risks the mentally ill are exposed to in the absence of adequate inpatient or community-based facilities. He claimed that, because mental health care is costly, the mentally ill are often living in poverty "on the lowest rung of American society and vulnerable to the hostility of mainstream society" (p. 502).

One of the challenges of mental health services funding in the twenty-first century is addressing the problems faced by the severely mentally ill. Certainly, there needs to be more coordination between the criminal justice systems and the mental health delivery systems, but the resources have to be in place for this to be effective. Torrey (1997) made the compelling point that mental disorders with clear physiological etiologies need to be considered brain disorders and addressed as such. He believes that this will at least decrease the politicization that occurs around the diagnosis and, thus, around the funding targeted toward interventions.

CMHCs were designed to provide a broad range of community care, particularly to those with severe mental illness. Since the 1970s, this population has consistently fallen through the cracks as services have been geared toward higher-functioning clients with more ability to pay for services. There is concern that, unless the current crisis is resolved, the conditions for many people suffering severe mental or emotional disorders could worsen to the levels of centuries past.

THE ISSUES OF AUTHORITY AND RESPONSIBILITY

Robert Harper (1994) made the compelling point that, of the numerous problems facing community agency counseling centers, the root problem is ambiguity regarding who (organizations, structures, branch of government) has the authority and responsibility to provide treatment and coordinate treatment settings. This is certainly one template that can consistently be laid over the decades of funding debates, cost shifting, and polemic regarding the delivery of community-based services. Harper noted that, historically, the government's primary responsibility was providing for the public safety. This includes protecting the public from particular individuals, protecting particular individuals from themselves, and, paradoxically, protecting individuals from the government when necessary and possible.

Issues of public and individual safety historically were addressed in the use of almshouses and state psychiatric hospitals. With the introduction of antipsychotic medications, cost shifting could more readily be accomplished via deinstitutionalization, since the new medications significantly increased certain patients' ability to live in the community, as well as decreased their potential danger to themselves or others. It was within this environment that mental health providers at the state and federal levels began advocating for the least restrictive treatment environment. All these dynamics contributed to the federal government's taking responsibility and claiming authority for the treatment of people suffering from mental illness. Harper noted that within this third role fell the notion of "asylum" for people suffering mental illness but cautioned that "there was and is no clearly articulated political theory and structure that defines and obligates the state to provide treatment" (p. 320).

Harper also pointed out that an additional function of the government has developed—"the obligation to remove barriers and obstacles that discriminate against individuals and various classes of individuals" (p. 320). He concluded that this could provide the basis for a rationale for treatment and rehabilitation of people suffering from mental or emotional disorders.

Although treatment and rehabilitation were the charge of the CMHCs, their effectiveness has been compromised through both funding battles and inefficiency related to the various shifts in funding. The current issue is still how to deliver and pay for the treatment and rehabilitation. Harper noted a Robert Wood Johnson project that demonstrated that, until the question of responsibility for treatment is settled, research on treatment and rehabilitation will not be put to efficient use. Indeed, the competition for funding has only increased, as CMHCs are now competing with privatized and managed care organizations. Because of this, more and more the issue of responsibility is being addressed through service contracts, not the political process. Those service contracts will likely exclude increasingly more people suffering from serious mental and emotional disorders.

AGENCY COUNSELING IN THE TWENTY-FIRST CENTURY

Sheila Baler (1994) wrote that agency counseling (and community mental health in particular) has been dealt a "triple blow." The three aspects of this blow are association with a government that fewer people trust, health care that most people find too expensive, and a population of people whom society would rather forget. Despite much of the rhetoric in the 1990s about diversity (including disabilities), a study by Yankelovich (1990) supports the notion that people value living with others more like themselves than those suffering mental or emotional disorders. This is one reason that the original CMHC mission of heterogeneous communities has failed.

Another point that cannot be ignored is the position that mental health professionals and the programs they are trained in neglect the issues of people suffering from chronic mental and emotional disorders. Castanuela (1994) noted that, across the therapeutic professions, service providers are increasingly choosing private practice over community settings in which the chronically mentally ill clients are most likely to be seen. Certainly, funding dynamics and market forces contribute to this decision, but Castanuela's point is important. In addition, Castanuela noted that surveys indicate that the academic programs in which therapeutic professionals are trained underemphasize the issues of treating people with chronic mental illness. Finally, Castanuela pointed out that typically what is happening in this country is that people suffering from chronic mental or emotional disorders are often cared for by lay-professionals with no formal training. These issues have persisted, even when mental health funding for community based programs was plentiful. There are some future directions for agency counseling centers that integrate components for indigent, chronically mentally ill clients.

Several authors Baler (1994); Dyer and Williams (1994) outlined several options for community agency counseling. Baler noted that CMHCs could benefit through collaboration with the general health-care system, particularly with adult and elderly people who suffer from mental or emotional disorders that seem to have a strong biological component. This harkens back to the collaborative ideal first articulated in the 1963 CMHC initiative. Although most mental or emotional disorders are multiply determined, many show far more prominent biological features than others. These cases could be more efficiently treated through this collaborative model. Baler admitted that, given the difficulty in ferreting out the biological component, a more probable scenario is the collaboration between mental health and rehabilitation agencies. Even in cases in which the biological components are fairly prominent, rehabilitation is essential. Baler also noted that agencies need to develop long-range plans for their organizations. This is as difficult as it is essential in an era of decreasing funds. Long-range plans need to include the consideration of practice guidelines, standards of care for particular diagnoses, attention to economic and quality-of-client-life variables, and client improvement and level of satisfaction with services.

Dyer and Williams (1994) used the Quinco Behavioral Health System in Indiana as a case study. Quinco had been a comprehensive CMHC for over a decade and typically served 1 percent of its catchment population yearly with a budget of $2 million. Initially, Quinco's board of directors wanted to increase the number of people using services and wanted more distance from government monies, which they perceived as having too many "strings attached." Their approach drew on accepted business practices using a mission statement, measurable goals, specific values, a menu of services, a flow chart identifying responsibilities within the organization, and a plan for implementation. Other business practices included ensuring internal and external accountability, increasing staff credentials, identifying target populations, and, when appropriate, marketing services to those target populations.

The notion of internal and external accountability meant that not only were employees evaluated on the work done to further the agency mission but also all employees were held accountable to the customers who defined "quality of treatment." The customers included consumers, third-party payors, and community gatekeepers. For consumers, quality had to include accessibility to services and convenience. Cost considerations were subsumed under accessibility, which included reasonable sliding fees. For third-party payors, services had to be packaged in a way that they would encourage their constituents to use. Community gatekeepers had to be lobbied to understand the benefits of using the agency. Part of accountability inevitably led to more time-limited offerings and fewer programs that involved personality reconstruction. A component of external accountability included focusing the business plan on external criteria. This means that trends in the health-care industry had to be considered and not just trends in mental health systems still largely dependent on government monies. In order to decrease dependence on government funding, the target populations had to include people with the ability to pay or third-party payors. One way to do this was to increase the visibility and range of services, as well as the credentials of the staff. Clinicians without the ability to be licensed were not hired.

In terms of employee recognition, Quinco used a team approach in which individual specialization was tied into the team concept. The teams were "mission-focused" and shared in the consequences of their work activities. Pubic and peer recognition was seen as a necessary complement to financial incentives. Financial incentives were based on rewarding revenue generation and consumer results, rather than just "being busy." The financial incentives required increasing their revenue expectations to more closely approximate the fiscal patterns seen in private practices. Given the goals of Quinco, comparison with agencies still dependent on government funds were inappropriate. In the Quinco case study, these efforts were fiscally successful (Dyer and Williams provide no data on staff reaction). The annual budget grew 225 percent within seven years, and most of that growth was accomplished with nongovernment funds. During the same period, the number of indigent people treated tripled. This resulted in better public relations in the community and an easier time hiring well-qualified professionals.

SUMMARY

You may find the interweaving complexity of mental health funding a challenge for your abstract thinking and your attention span! There are no simple summaries or formulae for either the history of mental health funding or useful future directions. Harper's (1994) point about settling the issues of responsibility and authority is an important one, yet, in a constitutional republic, these issues can never be decided without a system of checks and balances to protect the rights of the individual. Certainly, the underlying philosophy must be addressed as well. Are we truly our "brother's keeper"? Is there any way to integrate government and private monies into an efficient treatment delivery system that is not ruled by temporary political climates? It seems certain that if therapeutic professionals abdicate wrestling with these difficult questions, the decisions will be made by those with the most economic power. This is, in fact, occurring, and in the next chapter we will consider the development, impact, and potential of privatization and managed care in agency counseling.

DISCUSSION ITEMS

1. In your opinion, to what extent is the "funding crisis" a crisis of politics versus a crisis of finances? In small groups, members argue both positions.
2. If your income as an agency counselor is so dependent on funding sources, what do you see as your role in lobbying, educating, and dialoguing with those sources?
3. Debate the merits of federal, state and local funding for counseling agencies. What are the pros and cons of each system of funding?
4. How do your aspirations to be a therapeutic professional relate to your political philosophy? Who should pay for the treatment of indigent persons suffering from mental or emotional disorders?
5. What are your thoughts on the corporate model used in the overhaul of the Quinco Behavioral Health System, described at the end of this chapter?

REFERENCES

Baler, S. G. (1994). Community mental health in the year 2001: Is there a place for CMHCs? *Administration and Policy in Mental Health, 21,* 325–333.

Barlow, D. H., & Durand, V. M. (1995). *Abnormal psychology: An integrative approach.* New York: Thompson International.

Bell, L. V. (1989). From the asylum to the community in U.S. mental health care: A historical overview. In D. A. Rocheforte (Ed.), *Handbook on mental health policy in the United States.* New York: Greenwood Press.

Cameron, J. M. (1989). A national community mental health program: Policy initiation and progress. In D. A. Rocheforte (Ed.), *Handbook on mental health policy in the United States.* New York: Greenwood Press.

Castanuela, M. H. (1994). Have mental health professionals abandoned the chronically mentally ill? Yes. In S. A. Kirk & S. D. Einbinder (Eds.), *Controversial issues in mental health.* Boston: Allyn & Bacon.

Dobson, A., & Scharff-Corder, L. (1983). Six months of Medicaid data. *Health Care Financing Review, 4,* 115–121.

Dorwart, R. S., & Epstein, S. S. (1993). *Privitization and mental health care: A fragile balance.* Westport, CN: Auburn House.

Dyer, R. L., & Williams, R. (1994). CMHC survival: Adapting to the community mission. *Administration and Policy in Mental Health, 21,* 309–317.

Foley, H. A., & Sharfstein, S. S. (1983). *Madness and government: Who cares for the mentally ill?* Washington DC: American Psychiatric Press.

French, L. (1987). Victimization of the mentally ill: An unintended consequence of deinstitutionalization. *Social Work, 32,* 502–505.

Grinker, R. R., & Speigel, J. P. (1945). *Men under stress.* New York: Blakiston.

Grob, G. N. (1983). *Historical origins of deinstitutionalization. New directions for mental health services: Deinstitutionalization,* No. 17. San Francisco: Jossey-Bass.

Harper, R. J. (1994). The future of CMHCs: The role of the state. *Administration and Policy in Mental Health, 21,* 319–324.

Kalinowsky, O. B., & Hoch, P. H. (1962). *Shock treatments, psychosurgery, and other somatic treatments in psychiatry.* New York: Grune & Stratton.

Keisler, C. A. (1980). Mental health policy as a field of inquiry for psychology. *American Psychologist, 35,* 1066–1080.

Kleinman, A. (1988). *Rethinking psychiatry.* New York: Free Press.

Koyanagi, C. (1988). *Operation help: A mental health advocate's guide to Medicaid.* Alexandria, VA: National Mental Health Association.

Lamb, H. R., & Weinberger, L. E. (1998). Persons with severe mental illness in jails and prisons: A review. *Psychiatric Services, 49,* 483–492.

Levy, L. (1969). Financing, organization, and control: The problem of implementing comprehensive community mental health services. *American Journal of Public Health, 59,* 40–47.

Manus, M. (1999, March 5). *Treating post-traumatic stress disorder: A spiritual approach.* Unpublished lecture at Cuyahoga Community College, Cleveland, OH.

Menninger, K. (1969). *The crime of punishment.* New York: Viking Press.

National Alliance for the Mentally Ill. (1999). *Clinton administration releases its FY 1999 budget proposal.* [On-line] http://www.nami.org/update/990113.html

Penrose, L. (1939). Mental disease and crime: Outline of a comparative study of European statistics. *British Journal of Medical Psychology, 18,* 1–15.

Ray, C. G., & Finley, J. K. (1994). Did CMHCs fail or succeed? Analysis of the expectations and outcomes of the community mental health movement. *Administration and Policy in Mental Health, 21,* 283–294.

Reiger, D. A., et al. (1988). One month prevalence of psychiatric disorders in the U.S.— Based on five epidemiologic catchment area sites. *Archives of General Psychiatry, 45,* 977–986.

Rocheforte, D. A. (Ed.). (1989). *Handbook on mental health policy in the United States.* New York: Greenwood Press.

Rocheforte, D. A., & Logan, B. M. (1989). The alcohol, drug abuse, and mental health block grant: Origins, design, and impact. In D. A. Rocheforte (Ed.), *Handbook on mental health policy in the United States.* New York: Greenwood Press.

Rubin, J. (1990). Economic barriers to implementing innovative mental health care in the United States. In I. Marks & R. Scott (Eds.), *Mental health care delivery: Innovations, impediments, and implementation.* Cambridge, MA: Cambridge University Press.

Sharfstein, S. (1978). Will community mental health survive the 80s? *American Journal of Psychiatry, 134,* 133–148.

Soloman, P., Draine, J., & Meyerson, A. (1994). Jail recidivism and receipt of community mental health services. *Hospital and Community Psychiatry, 45,* 793–797.

Steadman, H. J., Barbera, S. S., & Dennis, D. L. (1994). A national survey of jail diversion programs for mentally ill detainees. *Hospital and Community Psychiatry, 45,* 1109–1113.

Sykes, C. J. (1992). *A nation of victims: The decay of the American character.* New York: St. Martin's Press.

Torrey, E. F. (1995). Editorial: Jails and prisons—America's new mental hospitals. *American Journal of Public Health, 85,* 1611–1613.

Torrey, E. F. (1997). *Out of the shadows: Confronting America's mental illness crisis.* New York: John Wiley & Sons.

Vega, W. A., & Murphy, J. W. (1990). *Culture and the restructuring of community mental health.* New York: Greenwood Press.

Yankelovich, D. (1990). *Public attitudes towards people with chronic mental illness.* Report prepared for the Robert Wood Johnson Foundation program on chronic mental illness.

MANAGED MENTAL HEALTH CARE

You can lead a horse's ass to wisdom but you cannot make him think.

Robert Anton Wilson

Ultimately, the buck drives treatment.

Larry Hill

Reviewing the advertisement for the upcoming lecture, Ned's hopes for a fair presentation of managed care are dashed.

This final chapter devoted to "outer explorations" represents a dramatic shift in mental health care. The delivery of services and the financial reimbursement for services have changed drastically through managed mental health care. In this chapter, we will explore the dynamics, mechanisms, and history of managed mental health care and the implications for people currently training to enter the field. Despite the fact that many students of the therapeutic professions have come of age in an era of managed care, studies indicate that many counselor education (and other) training programs are not up to speed with the current market situation (Cummings, Budman, & Thomas, 1998; Lawless, Ginter, & Kelly, 1999). With that in mind, in this chapter we will examine the complexity of the phenomenon, noting both the advantages and disadvantages.

INTRODUCTION TO THE PROBLEM OF HEALTH CARE COVERAGE

Before the 1950s, mental health and substance abuse coverage was not included routinely in health insurance. Interestingly, before the Great Depression there was very little health insurance, and health insurance plans were instituted to keep a steady flow of cash going to hospitals and essential health-care personnel (Dugger, McCarthy, & Burroughs, 1996). Since that time, health-care costs, including those for mental health care, have spiraled out of control. Health-care costs accounted for 26 percent of corporate net earnings in 1989 and increased to 45 percent in 1990 (Foster Higgins & Co., 1992). Overall, health-care costs account for more of the Gross National Product (GNP) in the United States than in any other industrialized country (Schreiber Poullier, & Greenwald, 1991). In the 1990s, costs for substance abuse treatment and mental health care grew more rapidly than other types of medical care (Frank, Salkever, & Sharfstein, 1991), increasing by an average of 50 percent between 1986 and 1990 (Iglehart, 1996). Foos, Ottens, and Hill (1991) noted four factors that contributed to spiraling costs, including the increase in the number and specializations of mental health practitioners and hospitals trying to make up for shorter surgical stays with psychiatric hospitalizations. In addition, they noted an increased reliance on inpatient treatment in the 1970s and 1980s and increasing numbers of employees in need of mental health and substance abuse services. To these four factors, we add an increased practice and awareness of insurance fraud. Of all these dynamics, the last three require more elaboration.

Reliance on Inpatient Treatment

For many years, insurance companies reimbursed more consistently for inpatient treatment than for outpatient treatment. This did not go unnoticed by treatment providers, who, when the political time was right, capitalized on this bias in the treatments offered for minors. This relates to a little noticed U.S. Supreme Court decision in 1979 (*Parham vs. J.R.*). In this decision, the Court determined that the states do not need to adopt measures to regulate the confinement of minors in psychiatric facilities. The Court noted that parental judgment and the judgment of the admitting staff were adequate to protect minors' constitutional interests. As Holtz (1995) noted, "legal protections that apply to adults in attempts to commit them to psychiatric hospitals no longer pertained to minors" (p. 89). In 1971, there were approximately 6,500 minors in inpatient psychiatric facilities. That number increased exponentially to almost 200,000 by 1989 (Hewlett, 1994). According to data compiled in the mid-1980s by the House Select Committee on Children, Youth and Families, in 40 percent of cases in the early '80s, adolescent psychiatric confinements were later found to be unnecessary (Gelman, 1986). A past president of the American Psychiatric Association commented that "sophisticated marketing campaigns targeting adolescents and substance abusers [resulted] in many unjustified and even harmful hospitalizations as well as sharply increased costs" (England, 1993). In addition, other studies have concluded that, in nonmanaged care environments, there are many cases of unnecessary hospitalization (Strumwasser, Paranjpe, & Udow, 1991).

Throughout this discussion, we will need to rely on a fairly obvious point. Whenever someone receives mental health services from a provider, that provider needs to be paid. The money for those services must come from somewhere. Where the money comes from is the primary topic of mental health funding, private insurance, and managed care. For our purposes we need to reflect on the fact that most of these adolescent hospitalizations in the decade of the '80s were covered under what have been referred to as indemnity insurance plans. These are plans, paid for by employers, in which cash benefits were paid to the insured individual following the submission of a claim. At that time, health insurance providers were more willing to pay for inpatient treatment because of the perception that it denoted more serious problems. By 1986, 13 states had mandated that insurance plans provide this type of coverage. The costs for employers were rising rapidly.

From an insurance company's perspective, it was unfair for legislators to mandate the type of coverage they had to supply. Insurance companies, by and large, dealt with the dilemma by passing the extra cost on to the employer and through the use of carve-out companies described below. The employer's perspective was that this cost cut into the profit margin (this among a widespread belief that mental health and substance abuse treatments do not really work [Dugger et al., 1996]). Typically, insurance companies and managed care organizations (MCOs) were uncomfortable paying out for mental health services because of the poorly defined nature of mental and emotional disorders. The MCOs dealt with this through the carve-out method. This is a method whereby MCOs separate out mental health benefits and subcontract them to a specialty behavioral health-care MCO. These companies were able to greatly curtail the costs of mental health care primarily by reducing reimbursement for inpatient treatment. As in any area of business in a free market economy, the carve-out companies ranged from very good to out-and-out unethical. Whether good or bad, these mental health managed care organizations have basically dictated the treatment of mental and emotional disorders in the United States by setting their own parameters for utilization review and treatment necessity.

IBM was one of the first U.S. corporations to contract with an MCO for its mental health benefits. In the 1980s, IBM's costs for mental health and substance abuse services rose at a far faster rate than its costs for general medical services. IBM carved out its (Mental Health/Substance Abuse) benefits in 1990, and its mental health expenditures decreased from $97.9 million in 1992 to $59.2 million in 1993 (Battaglia, 1994). Other companies, such as Xerox, Chevron, Dupont, Federal Express, and Pacific Bell, also reported reductions of 30 to 50 percent for mental health benefits after adopting managed care mechanisms.

The rise of MCOs specializing in behavioral health care has also had an impact on MCOs providing general care. The competition has forced the general MCOs to improve their behavioral health care benefits, so they can compete with the specialty MCOs to whom the general MCOs previously passed on the carved-out benefits. Between 1993 and 1997, the California-based Kaiser Permanente Medical Care Program invested $100 million to improve its behavioral health care. Kaiser customers such as Wells Fargo and the Teamster's Union, criticized Kaiser's behavioral health care as inadequate. Because these customers then paid a specialty MCO for behavioral health care, they were paying twice, once for the MH/SA benefits they wanted, and once for the MH/SA benefits they were not using. This led them to demand a premium reduction from Kaiser, which in turn prompted Kaiser to improve its MH/SA services (Iglehart, 1996).

Increased Need and Rising Costs

The number of employees using mental health services has grown at a rapid pace in recent decades. In the 1980s, costs for mental health and substance abuse treatment increased at four times the rate of the overall consumer price. General inpatient admissions for mental health and substance abuse–related disorders increased 85 percent from 1982 to 1989, while adolescent inpatient psychiatric admissions more than tripled (Barge & Carlson, 1993). Although the costs of treating employee mental health issues has increased in the past 20 years, the complexities of managing employee claims and benefits has also increased. In an effort to organize and manage claims, the National Council on Compensation Insurance (NCCI) (1985) summarized the three categories into which stress-related claims now fall:

1. Mental-physical: a mental cause produces a physical health problem, such as when a stock broker develops an ulcer from stress
2. Physical-mental: a physical cause produces a mental health problem such as a person who suffers a workplace injury, which has since healed, develops anxiety about the tasks related to the earlier injury
3. Mental-mental: a mental cause produces a mental health problem, such as a person who was sexually harassed who develops depression

Most states recognize variations on the first two claims but differ significantly on the third. The NCCI maintains that the mental-mental claims are growing considerably nationwide, as well as state to state. In California mental-mental claims increased from 4,000 in 1979 to 30,000 in 1987, which resulted in legislative action in 1989 and again in 1991 to curb the growth of such claims (Barge & Carlson, 1993).

It is important that employers understand the unique mental health risks that their employees may face. Stress claims fall under occupational disease. Occupational disease is defined by the lack of any kind of single identifiable traumatic event and includes cumulative trauma (carpal tunnel) and mental illness. Totaling direct and indirect costs for stress claims alone, the New York Business Group on Health estimated that about 25 percent of workers in the United States suffer some kind of stress-related health problem, at an estimated cost of $150 billion per year.

As companies move to provide services, they are met with higher and higher costs. Mental health and substance abuse benefits continue to be more limited than medical/surgical benefits in terms of number of inpatient days and total coverage. Whereas a company might currently have a generous medical-surgical benefit of $1 million or unlimited lifetime benefit, the same company may limit MH/SA benefits to a lifetime maximum of $10,000–$50,000 with other restrictions and a co-pay. In addition, the rate of inflation for mental health and substance abuse benefits has been significantly greater than the inflation for medical-surgical benefits. MH/SA benefit costs per employee increased 27 percent in 1987, then 18 percent in 1989. Also alarming to companies paying for these benefits was that, in an average year (late 1980s), 7 percent of their employee population receiving MH/SA benefits used up to 33 percent of the total benefit dollars. A parallel trend in society was an increase in particularly cocaine and opiate use in the 1980s and a further destabilization of families, necessitating more treatment, but aggressive marketing including scare tactics, was also a major force. From the corporate perspective, in 1983, 24 percent of after-tax profits went to health care costs, whereas in 1989 it was 26 percent and in 1990 45 percent (Barge & Carlson, 1993).

In addition to this, you have to consider the disability system in the United States. Workers' compensation costs have been spiraling out of control, also. From $34.8 billion in 1986, they increased 35 percent to $47.1 billion in 1988—just two years. In 1990, job-related injuries cost approximately $60 billion. Mental injuries that may be assessed for compensation are usually conceptualized in two forms. One is the single traumatic event, in which there is a job-related incident that causes the stress. This can be something major or an event as minor as a reprimand from a superior. The other form is the gradual job stress category, in which psychological injury is said to have developed over a period of time as a result of general employment conditions. These claims have increased dramatically over the past 15 years. California was one of the first states to pass enabling legislation for these types of claims. That state experienced a 700 percent increase in gradual stress claims between 1979 and 1988. California's laws were at one point so permissive that the fact that another person was not upset by the same event was irrelevant, the fact of a preexisting condition was irrelevant, and the existence of emotional stressors outside the job was also irrelevant. Not surprisingly, California has the second highest insurance rate in the nation; Montana is first because of high-risk industries, such as mining and timber.

Rising Costs and Fraud

One of the dynamics that increased support for managed care is insurance fraud. The existence and extent of insurance fraud are certainly disincentives to companies to provide any benefits. When the preexisting skepticism regarding MH/SA treatment is combined with an awareness of insurance fraud in that area, it is far easier to understand employers' reticence to provide these benefits.

Some examples are in order. In 1993, National Medical Enterprises, which owned 132 psychiatric facilities, agreed to pay Aetna, Metropolitan Life, and Cigna $125 million to settle charges that it had fraudulently filed over $700 million in bogus claims. The *Chicago Tribune* reported on a contest held by Charter Medical Corporation, which managed a number of psychiatric facilities. Charter Medical based the grand prize, a cruise for two in the Caribbean, on the number of admissions and referrals generated by employees.

Under the guidelines of the 1980s, some providers were even paying for a prospective patient's cross-country air flight after telephone screening by nonmedical personnel. Another example is Security Metal Corporation, which laid-off employees due to a slow down in the economy. Of the laid-off employees, 30 percent claimed mental stress caused by the lay-off and filed for claims of $25,000 each. The insurance company settled for $10,000 each. The insurance company later moved out of California because it could not afford the costs associated with locating there. There is also a case of a female employee who had been on disability for two years as a result of stress incurred by hearing a sexist remark while sitting on a planning committee for a company picnic.

There are also those who systematize fraudulent claims. These are called "stress claim mills," and, in one case, 40 of 90 employees, with nearly identical symptoms, from the same company filed stress claims on the same day through the same legal office. At the time, California law required only that 10 percent of an illness be work-related. The laws have since changed.

MANAGED CARE: A DEFINITION

Managed care has been said to be the only growth industry in mental health today (Baler, 1994). What is managed care and how does it work? Hoge et al. (1999) noted that managed care is hard to describe because "if you've seen one managed care program, you've seen one managed care program" (p. 51). Dorwart and Epstein (1993) wrote that managed care has become a "byword for cost containment rather than a description of a program that . . . determines the most appropriate and efficient treatment for the patient in question (pp. 49–50). Managed care has been described as any method or approach that regulates the utilization, site, or price of services to be managed (Austad & Hoyt, 1992). *Managed care* denotes "a range of financial mechanisms and organized delivery systems which attempt to balance access, costs, and quality" (Sharfstein, 1990, p. 137). It is an "evolving concept that refers to a variety of strategies in diverse settings (Stroup & Dorwart, 1997, p. 1).

Managed care has been described as an elastic term that describes a variety of health-care financing methods and delivery systems (Wernet, 1999). With regard to managed care in the public mental health arena, Minkoff (1997) wrote that public sector managed care (PSMC) does not necessarily mean managed care companies. With the growth of PSMC, CMHCs are having to compete more fiercely for government funds and to manage them in different ways. Minkoff noted that managed care is typically a mechanism to address numerous problems centered on funding with systems coordination, service integration and cost containment.

Because managed care is rooted in American business, it is not surprising that it mirrors other American business trends. One important characteristic of managed care is that smaller MCOs are quickly and constantly being merged into larger enterprises. One example is American Biodyne, which was purchased by Medco Containment Services Inc. and renamed Medco Behavioral Care Corp. In 1999, it was sold to Merck, Medco's parent company, and was slated to be renamed again (Hymowitz & Pollock, 1999). Several of the larger enterprises are owned by insurance companies, and the 10 largest MCOs providing mental health and substance abuse treatment generate an estimated 90 percent of the profits made by the industry (Iglehart, 1996). A private company that monitors MCO trends (Open Minds *http://www.open-minds.com/omnews.htm*) surveyed 40 of the larger for-profit companies providing managed behavioral health care. In 1995, these companies had estimated annual revenues of $2.1 billion. Over half of the companies used contracts that placed the financial risk on the provider (Oss, 1995). Placing the financial risk on the service provider and decreasing provider fees are becoming more common. One reason is that most larger MCOs are heavily burdened with debt stemming from mergers and acquisitions (Klein, 1999).

For some, managed care is an unreasonable intrusion (Zuckerman, 1989), whereas, for others, managed care is a prudent way to control health costs while maintaining quality (Patterson, 1990). While there is a diversity of definitions of *managed care*, it is not the fee-for-service payment (indemnity insurance) that was the norm 20 years ago (Sharfstein, 1990). Corcoran (1994) listed practices that are characteristic of managed care approaches: requiring authorization prior to treatment, mandating second opinions prior to authorization, reviewing ongoing treatment before reimbursing or authorizing continuation, and reviewing completed treatment. Corcoran summarized the first two practices as cost-effective and the last two as standard-of-care assessments to be carried out before payment. Stroup and Dorwart (1997) described mechanisms used to carry out some of the last practices:

- Utilization management. This is a group of techniques used to manage health-care costs through case-by-case assessment of the extent of care needed and the appropriateness of the care while it is being delivered. This mechanism includes authorization for treatment practices and concurrent review of treatment.
- Case management. This is a mechanism used particularly for special populations who are expected to generate large expenditures. Two examples of such populations are people with severe and chronic mental illness (also referred to as people with severe persistent mental illness [SPMI]) and children with severe emotional disturbances (SED). A variation on case managers are case reviewers, who use clinical protocols to guide them in assigning the least expensive, appropriate treatment. Frequently, mental health case managers and case reviewers are therapeutic professionals, such as psychologists and counselors. In mental health, there are two models of case management:
  - Cost-containment case management. In this model, case managers can be empowered to develop treatment plans that take into account the client's medical and social needs. This may include authorizing services beyond the coverage of the plan, particularly if such treatment proves less costly. Stroup and Dorwart (1997) gave the example of a client being referred for acute residential rather than inpatient treatment. The residential treatment was not specifically part of the covered services but was thought to be equivalent in effectiveness and superior in terms of cost containment.
  - Clinical case management. These case managers typically do not authorize treatment for clients but act as "brokers who facilitate access to services" (Stroup & Dorwart, 1997, p. 5). In public sector mental health (PSMH), these case managers coordinate services among numerous agencies and advocate for the client to receive the optimum service.
- Capitation. This mechanism is a financial arrangement designed to improve efficiency and reinforce actions toward that end. In a capitated system, the purchaser (a private employer or the government) pays a prearranged (per capita) fee for a defined set of benefits in a specific period of time. The idea is that overtreatment is discouraged, since the fee is paid up front for a clearly defined benefits package over a clearly delineated course of time. The service provider or managed care company that will be providing the benefits aims to set fees through risk adjustment. This process uses actuarial data to arrive at appropriate

payment amounts, which allow for services rendered to be covered as well as a profit, if applicable. As you can imagine, arriving at a prospective payment is very difficult with populations expected to generate large expenditures, and current trends are designed to more frequently place the provider at financial risk in such cases (Frank, McGuire, & Newhouse, 1995).

• Gatekeeping. This mechanism is designed to improve services and control costs. The gatekeepers are the people who authorize evaluations and treatments. One model of gatekeeping is primary care case management (PCCM), in which a primary care physician or nurse practitioner acts as the gatekeeper by providing assessment and nonspecialty treatment, as well as authorizing referral to specialists when necessary. In many instances, gatekeepers are offered financial incentives to keep referrals low.

Following are other important managed care related terms:

• Health maintenance organization (HMO). These are the prototype MCOs. The basic characteristic of an HMO is that a defined, comprehensive benefit plan is financed on a prepaid, per capita basis. The payment is per member, per month. Most costs incurred outside the HMO are not covered, with a few exceptions. The level of deductibles and co-payments are built in to be incentives for the member to stay within the system. Initially, HMOs had limited MH/SA benefits but now are expanding coverage through a range of providers who are therapeutic professionals. Many of these professionals contract out and are housed as part of CMHCs. Others are housed within the HMO. Sometimes the HMO will ask the member to choose a primary care physician (PCP), who then becomes the gatekeeper to other services or has the case-management responsibilities within the HMO. This person may not share the costs of the HMO but, as noted under the description of gatekeepers, does have financial incentives to keep costs at a minimum.

• Preferred provider organization (PPO). Another route for CMHCs to participate in managed care is to join a PPO. This is a network of providers that collectively offer comprehensive services or specialty care. Payers can contract for discounted rates and, in return, can sometimes guarantee providers a certain volume of referrals. The providers' only link with one another may be that they are part of the same PPO. They contract with the PPO administrator to provide specialized care within the benefits package. A third-party administrator may monitor the relationship between payers and PPOs. Providers are invited to join the PPO for a variety of reasons: reputation for quality, geographical location, area of specialization, and ability to compete economically. One drawback is that, generally, PPO providers are paid on a discounted fee-for service *after* the service is rendered. If the claim processing is held up, the provider must wait to be paid. Another risk to the provider is that its discounted fee, based on expected number of new clients, may not compensate for the actual number of new clients referred to it. More and more providers are complaining about discounted fees. As Klein (1999) noted, "there are some 400,000 licensed behavioral health care providers in the U.S. MCOs can always find someone to accept whatever fee they choose to pay" (p. 6). This is certainly not a seller's market for therapeutic professionals.

- Third-party administrators. These are firms that focus on claims processing and related services, such as the investigation of claim fraud and abusive billing practices. This has been a new area of business as Medicare and Medicaid have expanded over the past 20 years.

- Employee assistance programs (EAPs). These are described as a type of MCO. Some firms also offer providers such as CMHCs the opportunity to share the rewards and risks of meeting defined goals set up by the purchaser. In the past decade, these have been the most widely used mechanism in business to provide mental health services to employees. According to the Bureau of Labor (1989), most U.S. businesses (83 percent) with more than 5,000 employees offered mental health services through an EAP. EAPs began as programs to treat alcoholism and tend to have more of a history of client advocacy than MCOs in general. Many companies have both an EAP and MCO-based mental health care (Barge & Carlson, 1993).

- Independent practice associations (IPAs). These are groups of practitioners who use an HMO model and agree to accept a prepaid, capitated rate for services provided to enrollees. The members have a wider range of provider choice in this model, and the professionals usually have other types of clients, so they retain more autonomy in their practices.

THE EVOLUTION OF MANAGED MENTAL HEALTH CARE: ADVANTAGES

Managed care is newer in the sector of public mental health but fairly established in both general medical coverage and mental health services offered in private practice. Many surveys of MCOs and clinicians working under MCO arrangements indicate that MH/SA benefits are usually harder to come by than general medical benefits (Foster Higgins & Company, 1992; Thompson, Smith, Berg, & Berg 1991). As previously noted, economic planners generally view benefits for mental health treatment with suspicion because they do not fit very well into the disease model, which offers clear etiology, course, and treatment. Baler (1994) noted that the mental health professions lack treatment guidelines, standards for certain diagnoses, and information relating client levels of functioning to treatment outcome. These realities only fuel the aforementioned suspicion. In addition, mental health providers often lack triage protocols, and MCOs leave these in the hands of gatekeepers and case managers, many of whom are primary care physicians with little understanding of mental and emotional disorders. These deficits are noted as reasons mental health providers need to be monitored through managed care mechanisms. As noted by Corcoran (1994), "any program that influences from whom a client may receive services, what those services ought to be, and at what cost is understandably controversial" (p. 242). Many believe that it was only a matter of time before managed care moved into private practice mental health and then public sector mental health. Feldman (1992) noted that one of the most powerful factors in bringing managed care to these arenas is the therapists themselves, for not paying enough attention to the cost of treatment or the length of treatment. Feldman concluded that it was the therapists who "killed or at least seriously wounded, the goose that laid the golden egg" (p. iv).

In chapter 7, we explored the development of the CMHC movement and noted some of the problems that developed along with it. Two omnipresent questions, from the days of the almshouses to the present, have been who is responsible for paying for the services and which services ought to be paid for. Managed care is the latest approach to answering those questions. Managed care itself is a type of privatization taking place throughout medical care. Privatization is a process of using market-oriented economic principles to bring about cost-effectiveness. Some of the features associated with privatization (which we discussed under Managed Care: A Definition) include contracting with service providers for mental health services; providing vouchers in the form of benefits to covered individuals, who may then pick a service provider from a predetermined list; and relying on private sector mechanisms to ensure efficiency, cost-containment, and quality of care (Dorwart & Epstein, 1993). These types of privatization mechanisms have been practiced by Medicare for several years and now are being used by Medicaid. Privatization and managed care mechanisms are increasingly being used in public sector mental health care.

As you may recall from chapter 7, the Community Mental Health Centers Act of 1963 facilitated the creation of a large number of nonprofit agencies charged with providing mental health services. These agencies, funded largely by government monies, had little in the way of productivity demands. As noted, the CMHC Act of 1963 and the subsequent mental health funding acts, assumed that the federal monies would be phased out as more agencies found other sources of funding. Direct funding from the federal government ended in 1981. The failure of most agencies to replace government funds and the changes in economic policy in the subsequent decades left many nonprofit agencies in need of a fiscal solution. As states shifted more and more costs to Medicaid (so that the federal government shared the fiscal burden) the nonprofit agencies became more dependent on payment based on services delivered (Hoge, Davidson, Griffith, Sledge, & Howenstein, 1994). At the end of the 1980s, nonprofits were in the impossible position of needing to increase funding, improve efficiency, and provide comprehensive mental health services to clients without regard for clients' financial means (Stroup & Dorwart, 1997). One course of action was to draw in more clients who had some form of insurance and increase revenues from third-party payors. Obviously, this contributed to a decreased emphasis on people with chronic mental and emotional disorders, many of whom are unemployed and unable to hold the type of job that comes with such benefits. At the same time, the number of third-party payors multiplied at an unprecedented rate, and all attempted to trim benefits to balance for the increasing cost of medical care. A prime target, as noted, were mental health benefits, which were then limited, eliminated, carved-out, or offered in place of another benefit.

> One of my friends is a psychologist in private practice. He provides psychological services to clients in nursing homes and contracts with private nursing homes, as well as those under the ownership of larger corporations, which contract out for psychological services. As a self-employed psychologist, he has to purchase health insurance for himself and his family. He and his wife recently had a baby girl, and they have a teenage daughter. With the birth of their second child, their budget has been a bit tight. My friend, who has always been committed to promoting mental health in organizations and mental health coverage in benefit packages, had to choose between dental coverage and mental health benefits (what he called the "dental or mental" dilemma). He chose the dental benefits.

Managed care became widespread in the public sector in the 1990s. The initial thrust was to find cost-effective alternatives to inpatient care (and to cut costs generally). Since then, state and local governments have moved to contract with MCOs for mental health and substance abuse treatments covered by Medicaid (Iglehart, 1996). Interestingly, this is one of the few domestic political issues that has enjoyed bipartisan support. When states began using managed care mechanisms for Medicaid recipients, publicly funded benefits were introduced to utilization review, capitated financing, and cost-containment case management. Introducing managed care mechanisms into Medicaid had the effect of introducing nonprofit agencies to competition for Medicaid funds. Massachusetts was the first state to introduce a statewide managed care program for mental health services. Beginning in 1992, Massachusetts enrolled approximately 375,000 beneficiaries in a managed care program and contracted with a private company to manage the mental health benefits. Callahan et al. (1995) assessed the impact of the Massachusetts program and found that mental health costs were reduced by 22 percent of predicted levels for a nonmanaged care year ($47 million), with no overall decrease in quality of care or access to services.

In order to run a trial managed care program for Medicaid recipients, states must request and secure a waiver from the Health Care Financing Administration (HCFA), which approves them to deviate from traditional Medicaid funding protocols. States must submit a plan for the provision of services with the request for a waiver. Several states have applied for and received such waivers, including Massachusetts, Tennessee, Oregon, and Iowa. As competition for shrinking Medicaid resources increases, unanswered questions remain: are people who suffer from severe, chronic mental and emotional disorders receiving appropriate treatment and how do the various payment provisions affect quality of care? We will address these questions in the next section, on the disadvantages of managed care in public sector mental health.

THE EVOLUTION OF MANAGED MENTAL HEALTH CARE: DISADVANTAGES

As you probably know, managed mental health care has many critics. It has been referred to as "a growing crisis," "a national nightmare" (Karon, 1995), and "mangled care not managed care" (Torrey, 1997). In many professional papers directed at therapists, managed care is presented as the antithesis of quality (Miller, 1996; Murphy, DeBernardo, & Shoemaker, 1998; Phelps, Eisman, & Kohut, 1998). It has been noted that, initially, managed care was "a reasoned response to real problems" (Karon, 1995, p. 5). Karon noted that early studies did indicate that managed care principles could save money while maintaining care. He made the point that, initially, managed care programs were in a position to sponsor prevention, which was never covered under the old fee-for-service plans. However, many claim that the present state of managed care is quite different. Critics claim that prevention efforts have by-and-large been aborted, consumer needs have been subjugated to profit motives, long-term interests have been sacrificed for short-term gains, and there are ethical problems with financial incentives to keep the number of services accessed low.

Panzetta (1996) set managed mental health care into a four-phase context. He noted that the inconsistent definitions of the term exist because it is more a movement with distinct phases than a predetermined set of practices. In the first phase, managed care was synonymous with utilization review (UR). HMOs had been around for quite a while, but it was not until the widespread implementation of UR that the fee-for-service industry was affected. Because UR was seen as intrusive and threatening, the client/provider response to this phase of managed care was one of suspicion and resentment. The second phase of managed care Panzetta describes as the development of selective contracting between payors and providers. This resulted in indirect competition between providers, as some were included in the networks and some were not (although many chose not to participate because of discounted fees resulting in less reimbursement for services). Herron and Adlerstein (1994) made the point that, at this stage, MCOs drew more providers in by being able to capture large portions of the market and offer a steady stream of clients. Thus, at this stage, there could be a financial risk to therapists who chose to stay out of the market. This stage also resulted in suspicion and hostility toward MCOs. [The third stage incorporated provider risk strategies.] Capitation (prepayment) strategies closely followed selective contracting and divided the provider community into managed care "players and nonplayers" (Panzetta, 1996, p. 71). Because this phase increased the incentives for providers to closely monitor their cases, it decreased the need for external utilization review. This stage was met with a continuum spanning hostile participants to consenting partners. The final stage is still crystallizing, according to Panzetta. What Panzetta calls technology transfer marks this stage. As providers increasingly assume the risk for losses, they import the technology of utilization management into their own organizations. This situation works in favor of the larger organizations, which, as we have noted, are increasing in the managed care climate. It is significant that, according to Panzetta, each phase in this evolution has been met with hostility and suspicion. We will now examine some of the reasons underlying that hostility.

Since its inception, managed care has deemphasized the need for mutual choice between consumers and providers (Herron & Adlerstein, 1994). This is a particular focus of criticism in mental heath services where the therapeutic relationship (including therapist variables) is seen as one of the primary components of successful therapy (Beutler, Crago, & Arizmendi, 1986). There are also instances in which practitioners are removed unjustly from provider lists, and their clients must find another provider—one that is approved. One therapist surveyed reported that she was removed from a PPO list because she "used too many of the visits her patients were allowed" (Thompson et al., 1991, p. 288).

Another criticism of managed care mechanisms is that these mechanisms erode the autonomy of providers to make treatment decisions while cutting their income. This has been a criticism of managed general health care as well. Bernstein (1994) stated that providers must increasingly report to third-party payors to meet requirements for insurance, Medicare, and Medicaid client treatments. "Under managed care, they are forced to report to a reviewer or case manager to justify what more than twenty years of education and training has taught them is necessary to provide indicated and appropriate treatment for their clients" (p. 247). Bernstein pointed out that such mechanisms erode the basis of care and unethically place financial considerations above the client's welfare. Some firms that use UR to assess the need for services use professionals trained in the services they are assessing. However, many firms do not. Many utilization reviewers and case managers are reportedly poorly trained and are charged with making decisions they do not possess the expertise to make (Thompson et al., 1991). In the Thompson et al. study, one MCO was said to have representatives sit in on treatment team meetings and overtly direct treatment decisions.

The issue of credentials is also a divisive one in the context of managed care. In 1978, when the U.S. Senate Finance Committee heard evidence for expanding the coverage of mental health under Medicare and Medicaid, legislators were amazed at the degree of disagreement among mental health professionals regarding who was adequately trained to treat which conditions (Roth & Fonagy, 1996). The Finance Committee had the Federal Office of Technology Assessment (OTA) evaluate 130 therapeutic approaches for their effectiveness. The OTA report, published in 1980 (Office of Technology Assessment, 1980), found that, although therapy is generally effective, it could not be specified which therapies should be used for particular problems. Despite the general effectiveness of therapy, the importance of psychological treatments in national health-care planning and clinical practice guidelines has been deemphasized (Barlow, 1994).

As noted in chapter 1, there are numerous therapeutic professionals in the United States. MCOs seem to hire the less expensive practitioners, who are typically the ones with less training. In some instances, psychiatry has felt the effects of this, since MCOs prefer to use primary care physicians or other therapeutic professionals, such as psychologists and master's-level therapists, because they are less expensive to use (Iglehart, 1996). In other instances, it seems that master's-level therapists are not being chosen over psychiatrists or psychologists when quality of care would be impacted (Sturm & Klap, 1999). There is little research in the area of how choosing less expensive therapeutic professionals has had an impact on quality of care. Currently, even many master's-level therapists are finding it more difficult to earn a substantial wage in many managed care settings. In a paper published clearly for its ironic value, the anonymous author (1995) wrote that, clearly, one of the hidden benefits of managed care was that it was bringing all of the mental health professions together to fight a common enemy.

Another important concern regarding mental health care is the theoretical orientation of the therapists and the techniques based in that orientation. Concerns about the cost and effectiveness of mental health services are universal (Miller & Magruder, 1996). Roth and Fonagy (1996) made the critical point that "where appropriate research has not yet been done, the absence of evidence for efficacy is not evidence of ineffectiveness, and valuable approaches that offer appropriate and clinically effective care should not perish for lack of funding" (p. 44). In chapter 6, we discussed research in counseling and the inherent problems in "proving" the effectiveness of a given treatment.

One of the misinterpretations of the dearth of research on the effectiveness of, for example, psychoanalysis, is that it is not effective when, in reality, it is just a very difficult area to conduct controlled studies on. Be that as it may, many therapists, particularly psychodynamically oriented therapists, are feeling squeezed out of the managed care market. Alperin (1994) noted that particularly psychoanalytic therapy, with its focus on the treatment of long-standing character problems, is incompatible with managed care mechanisms, which focus on short-term, behavioral symptoms. Alperin also noted that managed care review procedures could easily disrupt the therapeutic process.

Perhaps the most consistent criticism is that managed care has limited the access to services by people suffering severe, persistent mental and emotional disorders. Such people are also referred to as the chronically mentally ill and are deeply affected when managed care principles are applied to public programs such as Medicaid. Leading this criticism is the National Alliance for the Mentally Ill (NAMI). In 1997, the NAMI issued a report card evaluating how well managed care programs in public mental health served people suffering from chronic mental illness (Hall, Edgar, & Lee, 1997). The report card graded four leaders in the managed care industry whose market share accounted for about 50 percent of the behavioral health-care market. These MCOs were rated on a number of services to people with severe mental illness and failed on each point. Following are these key points and NAMI's criticisms of managed care regarding its treatment of people with severe mental illness:

- Treatment guidelines. The NAMI authors maintain that the treatment guidelines for schizophrenia are out of date. In particular, they restrict access to psychotherapeutic and counseling services and emphasize access to psychotropic medications that have long since been outdated by newer medications with far more favorable side effect profiles. In addition, few companies express support for new-generation antipsychotic medications as a first line of treatment, despite the fact that psychiatry is quickly moving in this direction (Lieberman, 1997).
- Limited hospital care. One of the initial goals of managed care was to decrease psychiatric hospitalizations, and the NAMI report criticizes the industry on this point. It reviewed many policies in which hospital care is denied patients who may be noncompliant and disruptive—features typical of people suffering from severe mental illness.
- Suicide policies. Few companies surveyed defined suicide attempts as medical emergencies. As such, they lacked policies that would ensure immediate care in a suicidal crisis.
- Family involvement. Although MCOs claim to be proactive in involving patients and their families in their care, all MCOs surveyed failed on this count. Very few had policies and practices regarding educating clients about their conditions and involving families in treatment decisions.

- Outcome measures. Although all MCOs profess outcomes measurement that informs standards of care, none in the NAMI study examined key outcomes for clients with serious brain disorders. Presently, it would not be possible to determine through outcome measures which MCO would offer the best standard of care for a person suffering from schizophrenia.
- Residential issues. Most of the companies surveyed did not adequately address residential issues for their clients with severe mental and emotional disorders.

The NAMI has suggested action at the federal, state, and local levels to correct these deficits in managed mental health care for people with severe mental illness. Docherty (1990) summarized the misconceptions regarding managed care's relationship to people with severe mental illness:

- MCOs miscalculate when they assume that the way a patient behaves in an inpatient setting will be unchanged in an outpatient setting. If behavior were to remain unchanged in less restrictive environments, there would be no need for clinical case management after inpatient discharge. Currently, MCOs do address clinical case management adequately.
- It is incorrect to assume that all episodes of psychiatric disorders requiring hospitalization can be treated in 3–21 days. Clearly, one of the obstacles to effective risk-management practices for people with severe mental illness is the unpredictable nature of the illness course.
- MCOs lack evidence to assert that psychiatric medication alone can be sufficient treatment for people with severe mental and emotional disorders. Although the client's level of cognitive functioning is a crucial factor in determining whether she or he can benefit from counseling or psychotherapy, many people with severe mental illness do function at that level when their symptoms are in remission. Further, many of the clients who may not benefit from therapy benefit from clinical case management.
- It is not true that there are always appropriate and less restrictive treatment environments. If an MCO makes this assumption regarding all psychiatric hospitalization, it puts a significant percentage of clients at risk who, from time to time, do require hospitalization.
- Finally, it is not clearly supported that managed care is cost-effective for people suffering from severe mental illness.

In considering these disadvantages of managed mental health care, it is important to note that there seem to be two schools of response. The first is to accept managed care as a presence that is not going away and learn to work within the system. Lawless, Ginter, and Kelly (1999) and Sturm and Klap (1999) typify this view. The second view is to react against managed care by forming provider unions (see Volz, 1999) and other working alliances. One such alliance is the American Mental Health Alliance (AMHA), a national alliance of more than 2,000 therapeutic professionals who have developed a mental health-care delivery system that does not disrupt the therapeutic relationship the way managed care systems do. You can learn more about the AMHA at its web site at *http://www.mental-health-coop.com/*.

AN ASSESSMENT OF MANAGED CARE PROGRAMS

Counselors and other therapeutic professionals considering working for a managed care provider need a format for assessing the quality of the potential provider and how good a match they would be. This is particularly important with public-sector managed care programs, which may differ dramatically from program to program. Bear in mind that, in many cases, there will be more than enough therapeutic professionals competing to be part of any given program. Be that as it may, you will still want to gather information about the program before accepting work within it. Hoge et al. (1999) offered the following dimensions with which to assess public-sector managed care programs.

Program Objectives

What are the objectives of the managed care program? Programs must have stated objectives to be offering mental health services. Hoge et al. (1999) noted that there may be manifest and latent objectives. The manifest objectives are clearly stated, but the latent objectives may follow expectedly or unexpectedly. Part of the skill in this dimension is sorting out the objectives from the "official hyperbole" by studying project documents, public statements, and the political context of the project.

The Scope of the Program

The scopes of managed care programs vary a great deal, from serving a narrowly defined population to serving a broader population encompassing many different groups. In addition, the types of services offered vary a great deal. Managed care projects range from single-city projects to those that are statewide.

Organizational Structure and Authority

There are at least three levels to public-sector managed care projects. Typically, the top level of the organizational structure is occupied by government agencies, which act as payors and regulators. These agencies set policies, determine procedures, and provide oversight. The second level of management pertains to direct management of the program. Government payors are the ones who make the decision to carve out mental health benefits and contract with outside providers. The final organizational level is that of service providers, where "responsibility for service provision is high but authority over any aspect of the project's policies is generally low" (Hoge et al, 1999, p. 52).

Enrollment

The enrollment process is what determines who is eligible to be enrolled for services in a managed care project. The key factors related to enrollment are voluntariness, the options available, and the enrollment process. Some managed care programs are mandatory for individuals meeting certain criteria. If, in fact, enrollment is voluntary or mandatory, each person may have several options of basically different programs. In some states conducting managed care demonstration projects, clients may enroll in participating HMOs or pick a primary care physician and then be assigned to mandatory participation in a managed care carve-out. Above all, you will want to know how well the options are explained to potential clients and whether or not recruiters have been used (a practice that may be unethical).

The Benefit Package

The benefit package specifies the covered services that enrollees are eligible to receive. It also details the excluded services, which are not reimbursable. The benefits package must also spell out any ceilings, or lifetime limits, on services. The content of the benefits package is obviously important to people suffering severe mental or emotional disorders. The treatment for this population is quite different than for people suffering acute episodes, and this needs to be taken into consideration when assessing the overall program.

The Management of Utilization

Managing utilization is about managing costs and access to providers. As Hoge et al. (1999) note, "the managed care organizations most aggressively controlling utilization and costs tend to be the most restrictive about both provider selection criteria and the number of providers admitted to the network" (p. 53). This has implications for the number of referrals you will eventually receive as part of the project network. In addition, programs that require prior approval and referral before members can access a provider slow the process and put one more step between you and the client. Last, participants in managed care projects are allowed access to covered services only if those services are deemed "medically necessary." Thus, before joining a project, you will want to understand how that project defines "medically necessary."

Best Practices

Related to quality of care are the interventions and strategies identified as optimal in any managed care program. These are referred to as "best practices" and usually meet criteria such as the best care and the lowest cost in real-world settings. Because there is a paucity of data on clinical interventions in real-world settings, these practices are identified through many sources, including controlled research trials, treatment guidelines, peer review, and utilization review. In public-sector managed mental health care, these practices are usually aimed toward those suffering severe mental or emotional disorders, although some managed care programs neglect this population.

Financing

Hoge et al. (1999) noted that financial arrangements are perhaps the most variable dimension of public-sector managed mental health care. Whereas some projects use one source of funding (such as Medicaid), others may use multiple sources, depending on the client profile. Understanding the flow of funding is essential for a potential provider in a managed care system. For example, under some conditions, the managed care organization participating in a given project may be at higher risk for costs beyond a certain amount and may pass on that risk to the various providers. Some projects use case rates, in which providers are paid a fixed sum to provide treatment for a person with a specific diagnosis, regardless of the length or cost of treatment. Some projects may use "withholds," in which an MCO contracted to work in a managed care project holds back a portion of payments to the providers for a certain length of time and then distributes the money based on the financial performance or efficiency of the providers.

Quality Management and Outcome Systems

Managed care programs vary to the degree that they implement systems for quality management and outcome measurement. Hoge et al. (1999) noted that some programs that have arisen through federal waivers are required to evaluate the project's impact, although the scope of such evaluations varies a great deal. Evaluation may play a key component in terms of the bonuses or financial penalties that are meted out in accordance with provider performance. If a managed care project you are considering working for has done evaluations, they are important materials to figure in when making your final decision.

PRACTICE IN A MANAGED CARE ENVIRONMENT

Clearly, the managed care environment has both pros and cons. You should take a somewhat scientific approach to forming your opinions about managed care. Try to gather objective evidence about managed care's performance on well-operationalized criteria. There is a great deal of emotion in therapist circles around the techniques of managed care, but the managed care movement does offer some new possibilities for counselors and other therapeutic professionals. The evidence is pretty clear that mental health and substance abuse services are not only needed and useful but also can help employers save money on mental health–related losses.

Substance Abuse Costs

Of Americans who, on surveys of licit and illicit substance use, confirm using a legal or an illegal intoxicant, most are employed. An estimated 15 percent of the working population is dependent on alcohol or other drugs, whereas an additional 10 percent use alcohol or other drugs regularly before work or at the workplace (National Institute on Drug Abuse, 1991). Numerous studies have confirmed that alcohol and other drug abuse in the United States cost employers billions of dollars in lost productivity, absences, mistakes on the job, disability claims, and turnover. In addition, substance abuse increases the odds that employees will get sick and stay sick longer. The same pattern applies to on-the-job accidents. Employees who tested positive for drugs in their places of employment also had significantly more on-the-job accidents (Barge & Carlson, 1993). In contrast to the costs of employee substance abuse to employers, an investment in treatment can bring great financial gains. Many substance abusing employees who are successfully treated have lower than projected health and disability costs in the future. As noted earlier in this chapter, employers worry about the return on their investment for benefits to treat substance abuse, since these costs continue to be high. Barge and Carlson (1993) studied several databases of results for substance abuse interventions at large U.S. companies and reached four conclusions:

1. The value of substance abuse treatment can be assessed only when figuring in the projected costs to the company of employee relapse. It is easy to monitor the up-front treatment costs but far more difficult to determine dollar amounts of positive treatment outcomes. Basically, you have to figure in the productivity, quality of work, employee health and disability costs, retraining costs, and replacement costs that would be incurred if the employee were to relapse. Barge and Carlson recommended keeping benefits flexible enough to tailor treatment as needed to decrease the probability of relapse.

2. Treatment that prevents relapse results in reduced costs for the treated employee or dependent, as well as improved health. In one case example, aircraft manufacturer McDonnell Douglas Company found that treatment costs were actually reduced when the company EAP had the flexibility to tailor substance abuse treatment to the individual client. This may include inpatient treatment, which many large companies refuse to fund due to the expense. The point is, though, that some clients will have a higher probability of relapse without the inpatient treatment, so the company actually saves money by allowing the flexibility in treatment modalities. This obviously requires clinicians skilled in differential diagnosis to make accurate assessments.

3. Along similar lines, some patients will need more treatment than others to ensure a reasonable probability of remaining drug free. Again, flexibility is the key. If rigid limits are adhered to, there is evidence that it may actually cost the company more money. As with item #2, clinicians skilled in differential diagnosis are necessary to achieve a productive flexibility in tailoring treatment length to client needs.

4. Finally, the client's motivation is as important as the treatment approach used. If companies want to save money, this is an area in which careful screening can accomplish that goal. Sources for motivation include keeping one's job; retaining a professional credential, such as a license or certificate; and, often, keeping one's family and friends. Barge and Carlson also noted that significant co-pays can be worked into the treatment. These co-pays are then reimbursed over a period of time, as the client remains drug free as tested on an objective measure, such as drug screening.

Barge and Carlson's overall point is that employers profit from substance abuse treatment. As long as this is the case, there will be jobs for therapists who can work within the ever-changing framework of managed care.

Employee Mental Health Issues

A familiar theme recurring throughout this chapter has been the suspicion with which benefits providers have viewed mental health services. Whether this suspicion is deserved or not, all therapeutic professionals can address this by familiarizing themselves with the diagnostic nosologies and treatment guidelines that exist. As noted in chapter 1, it is important to understand and use universal constructs when conceptualizing client treatment. If all professionals speak the same language, at least the benefits providers will know that they have reviewed the treatment literature and are familiar with the latest approaches to mental health service delivery. With that in mind, we will now consider important skills for counselors and other therapists in the managed care climate and then some opportunities for employment for agency counselors.

Hersch (1995) made the excellent point that the managed care movement might just move in the direction of wellness, as long as those providing and purchasing benefits see that wellness strategies such as prevention, education, and health maintenance result in increased profits. Wiggins (1994) noted that lifestyle, behavior, and stress are significant factors in five of seven of the leading causes of death in the United States. In addition, most of the leading diseases treated by primary care physicians have significant stress-related elements. Some researchers have estimated that 60 percent of all visits to primary care physicians have stress-related elements (VandenBos & DeLeon, 1988). If trained professionals, such as counselors and psychologists, can show that their interventions decrease the stress-related health risks (and health-care costs), companies will hire them to do so. Currently, mental health services are given less priority than they were 10 years ago (Herron & Adlerstein, 1994). This is likely due to the suspicion with which these services are still viewed. Hersch recommends three broad strategies to correcting this situation that we believe are applicable to all therapeutic professionals. First, at the national level, health care reform and legislation need consistent monitoring and lobbying regarding mental health services. In conjunction with this, all therapeutic professionals need to work to lessen the stigma that many in our society still attach to mental health issues. Third, Hersch says we must work to import our "technologies" into mainstream health care. To this we add that, particularly at the academic level, we must conduct ongoing research that illustrates treatment outcomes for interventions as well as wellness and prevention efforts.

Skills for Working in the Managed Care Environment

The first skill in working in a managed care environment is what is called attitude management. As Hersch (1995) so aptly put it, "we cannot engage in appropriate and positive problem solving regarding managed care if we simply view it as an 'evil' monolith that exists only to destroy our profession" (p. 17). Although Hersch was speaking specifically to psychologists, this is good advice for all therapeutic professionals. In addition, Lawless, Ginter, and Kelly (1999) advocated the following skills as important in working in a managed care environment:

- Business savvy. This is not presently emphasized in any training of therapeutic professionals but will become an increasingly important skill for professionals to be able to profit from their hard-earned degrees.
- Ability to use the *DSM-IV*. Although the *DSM-IV* is not the ideal tool for all therapeutic situations, managed care environments rely heavily on its nomenclature, and students who are unfamiliar with it are at a disadvantage.

- Treatment plan writing. Working in a managed care environment requires the ability to write a treatment plan that is consistent with the practice guidelines or best practices recognized by the MCO.
- Record keeping and billing. Clinicians will need to understand the record-keeping procedures that the MCO expects and whether they meet the professional ethical guidelines. Also, providers to MCOs are increasingly being asked to used electronic billing processes.
- Training in brief therapy. Professionals are expected to know (and sometimes document training in) brief-focused and solution-focused therapies.
- Research skills. Now, more than ever, clinicians need to know how to collect data that evaluate the effectiveness of their interventions.
- Treatment philosophy. Clinicians need to be able to articulate a clear description of their treatment philosophy to clients and MCOs.
- Teamwork abilities. In the managed care environment, clinicians need to be able to work cooperatively as a team member. The team may include other services providers and utilization reviewers.
- Familiarity with the standards of practice for certain diagnostic entities.

Opportunities for Agency Counselors

In organizational psychology, there is a growing market in which psychologists can help companies determine the mental health risks and advise them on appropriate benefits packages. Many companies use stress measurement to focus company mental health benefits. Stress measurement has the advantage of being scientific, with at least a decade of research behind it, with its focus on health and wellness, and with its scope broad enough to include workplace and personal life stress. Despite these complexities, companies still look for ways to offer their employees mental health benefits. Employee assistance programs are one potential source of employment for therapeutic professionals and seem to work well for many companies.

SUMMARY

We covered a lot of ground in this chapter. As is true in most of life, there are many sides to the managed care issues, each with its own presentation of the truth. You are encouraged to do some of your own research on managed care organizations and to seek out experiences through which you can developed well-informed opinions about managed care practices. You can work with the following discussion items to begin this process.

Discussion Items

1. How comfortable are you thinking of yourself as a "businessperson"? If this label does not fit your image of yourself, why not? How do you think you would accommodate to the managed care environment described in this chapter?
2. What was your image of counseling work when you decided to pursue your degree? How is it similar to and different from the picture of counseling painted in this chapter?
3. Of all the aspects of managed care discussed in this chapter, which are of most concern to you as you contemplate the changing field and why?
4. Have you been a client in a managed care system? If so, how has your experience been with that system? In what ways do your managed care experiences color your perceptions of doing counseling in a managed care setting?
5. Do you think it is possible to do high-quality counseling in the managed care environment described? Why or why not?

References

Alperin, R. M. (1994). Managed care versus psychoanalytic psychotherapy: Conflicting ideologies. *Clinical Social Work Journal, 22,* 137–148.

Anonymous. (1995). Hidden benefits of managed care. *Professional Psychology: Research and Practice, 26,* 235–237.

Austad, M. F., & Hoyt, C. S. (1992). The managed care movement and the future of psychotherapy. *Psychotherapy, 29,* 109–113.

Baler, S. G. (1994). Community mental health in the year 2001: Is there a place for CMHCs? *Administration and Policy in Mental Health, 21*(4), 325–333.

Barge, B. N., & Carlson, J. G. (1993). *The executive's guide to controlling health care and disability costs.* New York: John Wiley & Sons.

Barlow, D. (1994). Psychological interventions in the era of managed competition. *Clinical Psychology—Science and Practice, 1,* 109–122.

Battaglia, M. (1994, June). Breaking with tradition. *Business and Health,* 53–56.

Bernstein, C. A. (1994). Is managed care good for clients? No. In S. A. Kirk & S. D. Einbinder (Eds.), *Controversial issues in mental health.* Boston: Allyn & Bacon.

Beutler, L. E., Crago, M., & Arizmendi, T. G. (1986). Therapist variables in psychotherapy process and outcome. In S. L. Garfield & A. E. Bergin (Eds.), *Handbook of psychotherapy and behavior change.* New York: John Wiley & Sons.

Callahan, J. J., Shepard, D. S., Beinecke, R. H., Larson, M. J., & Cavanaugh, M. D. (1995). Mental health/substance abuse treatment in managed care: The Massachusetts Medicaid experience. *Health Affairs (Millwood), 14,* 173–184.

Corcoran, K. (1994). Is managed care good for mental health clients? In S. A. Kirk & S. D. Einbinder (Eds.), *Controversial issues in mental health.* Boston: Allyn & Bacon.

Cummings, N. A., Budman, S. H., & Thomas, J. L. (1998). Efficient psychotherapy as a viable response to scarce resources and rationing of treatment. *Professional Psychology: Research and Practice, 29,* 460–469.

Docherty, J. P. (1990). Myths and mystifications of managed care. *The Journal of Mental Health Administration, 17*(2), 138–143.

Dorwart, R. S. & Epstein, S. S. (1993). *Privatization and mental health care: A fragile balance.* Westport, CT: Auburn House.

Dugger, D. E., McCarthy, P. R., & Burroughs, J. C. (1996). Do employers want mental health and substance abuse benefits for their employees? In A. Lazarus (Ed.), *Controversies in managed mental health care.* Washington DC: American Psychiatric Press.

England, M. J. (1993). Health reform and organized systems of care. In M. J. England & V. V. Goff (Eds.), *New directions for mental health services.* San Francisco: Jossey-Bass.

Feldman, S. (1992). *Managed mental health services.* Springfield, IL: Charles C Thomas.

Foos, J. A., Otters, A. J. & Hill, L. K. (1991). Managed mental health; A primer for counselors. *Journal of Counseling and Development, 69,* 332–336.

Foster Higgins & Company. (1992). *Health care benefits survey.* Princeton, NJ: Author.

Frank, R. F., Salkever, D. S., & Sharfstein, S. S. (1991). A new look at rising mental health insurance costs. *Health Affairs (Millwood), 10,* 116–123.

Frank, R. G., McGuire, T. G, & Newhouse, J. P. (1995). Risk contracts in managed mental health care. *Health Affairs (Millwood), 14* 50–64.

Gelman, D. (1986). Treating teens in trouble. *Newsweek, 20,* 52–54.

Hall, L. L., Edgar, E. R., & Lee, L. M. (1997). *Stand and deliver: Action call to a failing industry. The NAMI managed care report card.* Washington, DC: Authors.

Herron, W. G., & Adlerstein, L. K. (1994). The dynamics of managed mental health care. *Psychological Reports, 75,* 723–741.

Hersch, L. (1995). Adapting to health care reform and managed care: Three strategies for survival and growth. *Professional Psychology: Research and Practice, 26,* 16–26.

Hewlett, S. A. (1994). *When the bough breaks: The cost of neglecting our children.* New York: Basic Books.

Hoge, M. A., Davidson, L., Griffith, E. E., Sledge, W. H., & Howenstein, R. A. (1994). Defining managed care in public sector psychiatry. *Hospital and Community Psychiatry, 45,* 945–950.

Hoge, M. A., Jacobs, S., Thakur, N. M., & Griffith, E. E. (1999). Ten dimensions of public-sector managed care. *Psychiatric Services, 50,* 51–55.

Holtz, G. T. (1995). *Welcome to the jungle: The why behind generation X.* New York: St. Martin's Griffin.

Hymowitz, C., & Pollock, E. J. (1999, April 24). Cost-cutting firms monitor couch time as therapists fret. *Wall Street Journal,*

Iglehart, J. K. (1996). Managed care and mental health. *New England Journal of Medicine, 334,* 131–135.

Karon, B. P. (1995). Provision of psychotherapy under managed health care: A growing crisis and national nightmare. *Professional Psychology: Research and Practice, 26,* 5–9.

Klein, H. E. (1999). Why MCO rates can't rise. *Psychotherapy Finances, 25,* 6.

Lawless, L. L, Ginter, E. J., & Kelly, K. R. (1999). Managed care: What mental health counselors need to know. *Journal of Mental Health Counseling, 21,* 50–65.

Lieberman, J. (1997). Atypical antipsychotic drugs: The next generation of therapy. *NAMI Decade of the Brain Newsletter, 1,* 1–3.

Miller, I. J. (1996). Managed care is harmful to outpatient mental health services: A call for accountability. *Professional Psychology: Research and Practice, 27,* 349–363.

Miller, N. E., & Magruder, K. M. (Eds.). (1996). *The cost-effectiveness of psychotherapy: A guide for practitioners, researchers, and policy-makers.* New York: John Wiley & Sons.

Minkoff, K. (1997). Public sector managed care and community mental health ideology. In K. Minkoff & D. Pollack (Eds.). (1997). *Managed mental health care in the public sector: A survival manual.* Amsterdam: Harwood Academic Publishers.

Murphy, M. J., DeBernardo, C. R., & Shoemaker, W. E. (1998). Impact of managed care on independent private practice and professional ethics. A survey of independent practitioners. *Professional Psychology: Research and Practice, 29,* 43–51.

National Council on Compensation Insurance (1985). *Emotional stress in the workplace: New legal rights in the eighties.* New York: NCCI.

National Institute on Drug Abuse. (1991). *National household survey on drug abuse.* Washington, DC: Author.

Office of Technology Assessment. (1980). *The efficacy and cost effectiveness of psychotherapy.* Washington, DC: U.S. Government Printing Office.

Oss, M. (1995). More Americans enrolled in managed behavioral care. *Open Minds, 9,* 12.

Panzetta, A. F. (1996). Is public behavioral health care manageable? In A. Lazarus (Ed.), *Controversies in managed mental health care.* Washington, DC: American Psychiatric Press.

Patterson, D. Y. (1990). Managed care: An approach to rational psychiatric treatment. *Hospital and Community Psychiatry, 41,* 1092–1094.

Phelps, R., Eisman, E. J., & Kohut, J. (1998). Psychological practice and managed care: Results of the CAPP practitioner study. *Professional Psychology: Research and Practice, 29,* 31–36.

Roth, A., & Fonagy, P. (Eds.). (1996). *What works for whom? A critical review of psychotherapy research.* New York: Guilford Press.

Schreiber, G. J., Poullier, J. P., & Greenwald, L. M. (1991, fall). Health care systems in twenty four countries. *Health Affairs,* 23–37.

Sharfstein, S. S. (1990). Impact of managed care on the private hospital: An introduction. *The Journal of Mental Health Administration, 17*(2) 137.

Stroup, T. S. & Dorwart, R. (1997) Overview of public sector managed mental health care. In K. Minkoff and D. Pollack (Eds.) *Managed Mental Health Care in the Public Sector. A survival manual,* pp. 1–12. Amsterdam: Harwood Academic Publishers.

Strumwasser, I., Paranjpe, N. V., & Udow, M. (1991). Appropriateness of psychiatric and substance abuse hospitalization. *MedCare, 29* (supplement), AS77–AS89.

Sturm, R., & Klap, R. (1999). Use of psychiatrists, psychologists, and master's-level therapists in managed behavioral health care carve-out plans. *Psychiatric Services, 50,* 504–508.

Thompson, J. W., Smith, J., Burns, B. J., & Berg, R. (1991). How mental health providers see managed care. *The Journal of Mental Health Administration, 18*(3), 284–291.

Torrey, E. F. (1997). *Out of the shadows: Confronting America's mental illness crisis.* New York: John Wiley & Sons.

U.S. Dept. of Labor (1989). *Survey of employer antidrug programs.* Washington, DC: U.S. Government Printing Office.

VandenBos, G. R., & DeLeon, P. H. (1988). The use of psychotherapy to improve physical health. *Psychotherapy, 25,* 335–343.

Volz, J. (1999). Angered by managed care, practitioners look to unions. *APA Monitor, 30,* 1.

Wernet, S. P. (Ed.). (1999). *Managed care in human services.* Chicago: Lyceum.

Wiggins, J. (1994). Would you want your child to be a psychologist? (American Psychological Association Address). *American Psychologist, 49,* 485–492.

Zuckerman, R. L. (1989). Iatrogenic factors in "managed" psychotherapy. *American Journal of Psychotherapy, 43,* 118–131.

Author Index

Adams, H.E., 10
Adelman, H.S., 94
Adlerstein, L.K., 106, 257, 266
Agresti, A.A., 48
Alle-Corliss, L., 86
Alle-Corliss, R., 86
Allen, V.B., 77
Allers, C.T., 100
Alper, S., 184
Alperin, R.M., 259
Altekruse, M.K., 13
Altman, H.A., 71
Altucher, N., 63
American Association
    for World Health, 97
American Civil Liberties Union, 98
American Counseling Association, 29, 88
American Psychiatric Association, 90, 196
American Psychological Association, 144
Anastasi, A., 90
Anonymous, 258
Arizmendi, T.G., 208, 257
Armstrong, K., 78, 79
Ash, M., 10
Austad, C.S., 106
Austad, M.F., 250
Ayala, P., 52

Baker, M.J., 203
Baker, R.W., 152
Balcazar, F.E., 188
Baler, S.G., 237, 238, 249, 254
Bandura, A., 66
Banikiotes, P., 63
Bankart, P.C., 2

Barbera, S.S., 236
Barge, B.N., 247, 248, 253, 264, 265
Barlow, D., 258
Barlow, D.H., 3, 165, 172, 222
Barstow, S., 29
Baruth, N.E., 146
Basch, M.F., 177
Bass, R.D., 37
Bastien, R.T., 94
Battaglia, M., 246
Baucomb, D.H., 203
Baumgold, J., 66
Bayer, R., 196
Beers, C., 8
Beinecke, R.H., 255
Beis, E., 148
Beisner, E.N., 76
Bell, J.E., 26
Bell, L.V., 221, 226
Belz, P., 185
Bender, W., 9
Bennett Johnson, S., 203
Bennett, V.L., 52
Benshoff, J.M., 29
Berg, R., 102, 253, 257, 258
Bergin, A.E., 66, 192, 193
Berman, A.L., 166, 172
Berman, J.S., 5, 207
Bernard, L.D., 12
Bernstein, C.A., 257
Bertram, J.F., 188
Beutler, L.E., 203, 208, 257
Bilynsky, N.S., 104, 106
Black, F.W., 152, 156
Blanchard, C.A., 92

Subject Index

TO THE OWNER OF THIS BOOK:

I hope that you have found *Becoming a 21st Century Agency Counselor: Personal and Professional Explorations* useful. So that this book can be improved in a future edition, would you take the time to complete this sheet and return it? Thank you.

School and address: _____

_____

Department: _____

Instructor's name:_____

1. What I like most about this book is: _____

_____

_____

2. What I like least about this book is: _____

_____

_____

3. My general reaction to this book is: _____

_____

_____

4. The name of the course in which I used this book is:_____

_____

5. Were all of the chapters of the book assigned for you to read? _____

    If not, which ones weren't?_____

6. In the space below, or on a separate sheet of paper, please write specific suggestions for improving this book and anything else you'd care to share about your experience in using this book.

_____

_____

_____

_____

OPTIONAL:

Your name: _____ Date: _____

May we quote you, either in promotion for *Becoming a 21st Century Agency Counselor: Personal and Professional Explorations* or in future publishing ventures?

Yes: _____ No: _____

Sincerely yours,

Kathryn C. MacCluskie

R. Elliott Ingersoll

FOLD HERE

ATTN: Julie Martinez, Counseling Editor

BROOKS/COLE/THOMSON LEARNING
511 FOREST LODGE ROAD
PACIFIC GROVE, CA   93950-9968

FOLD HERE